Adventure Vacations

Adventure Vacations

A 50 State Guide to Rock Climbing, Horseback Riding, Spelunking, Whitewater Rafting, Snorkeling, Hang Gliding, and Ballooning

by Stephanie Ocko

A CITADEL PRESS BOOK
Published by Carol Publishing Group

A CITADEL PRESS BOOK
Published by Carol Publishing Group
Citadel Press is a registered trademark of Carol Communications,
  Inc.
Editorial Offices: 600 Madison Avenue, New York, N.Y. 10022
Sales and Distribution Offices: 120 Enterprise Avenue, Secaucus,
  N.J. 07094
In Canada: Canadian Manda Group, P.O. Box 920, Station U, Toronto,
  Ontario M8Z 5P9
Queries regarding rights and permissions should be addressed to
Carol Publishing Group, 600 Madison Avenue, New York, N.Y. 10022

Carol Publishing Group books are available at special discounts for
bulk purchases, sales promotion, fund-raising, or educational
purposes. Special editions can be created to specifications. For
details, contact: Special Sales Department, Carol Publishing
Group, 120 Enterprise Avenue, Secaucus, N.J. 07094

MANUFACTURED IN THE UNITED STATES OF AMERICA
10 9 8 7 6 5 4 3 2 1

Book Design by Robert Freese

Unless otherwise noted, all photographs courtesy of the author.

Library of Congress Cataloging-in-Publication Data
Ocko, Stephanie
    Adventure vacations : a 50-state guide to rock climbing, horseback
  riding, spelunking, whitewater rafting, snorkeling, hang gliding,
  and ballooning / by Stephanie Ocko.
      p.   cm.
    "A Citadel Press book."
    Includes index.
    ISBN 0-8065-1632-1 (pbk.)
    1. Outdoor recreation—United States—Guidebooks. 2. Vacations—
  United States. 3. United States—Guidebooks. I. Title.
  GV191.4.O35   1995
  796.5—dc20   94-45489
                                                       CIP

Contents

Preface

A good book on adventure opens the mind to new ideas. That's what this book intends to do.

Adventure in the United States these days is a combination of pioneering, escape, and discovery. The country is blessed with magnificent geography, good roads and rivers, two oceans, wilderness and wildlife, and a lot of interesting people. For these reasons, the adventures in this book span the distance between skydiving and snorkeling with manatees, climbing the 20,000-foot Mount McKinley and cooking with professional chefs.

It's all out there and it's never been so accessible. High-risk adventures, such as hang gliding and river rafting, are safer because of new equipment technology. Instruction is better, because more and more guides have been around for 20 years or so and know their business. And competition is so keen, outfitters strive to produce excellent travel products. Some offer specialty trips, such as river rafting and classical music; most will help you design the trip you want, whether it's a guide and gear for a big family get-together, or a combination rock-climb-and-dinosaur-dig. Ask.

In many activities, such as orienteering or archaeology, you will not need any prior experience; in others, such as caving and sailing, take instruction if you've never done it before. It pays to be honest about your physical limitations: A trick knee might give you some trouble if you skydive. If you are really tired, don't even think about hiking down and up the Grand Canyon.

You will be asked to sign a disclaimer form in high-risk adventures. These forms look terrifying because they cover possibilities you would rather not think about. But they let you know that the outfitter's primary concern is safety, and they force you to take responsibility for your own actions. The risk is shared.

If you are a beginner, read a lot before you go, and ask questions of the guide or outfitter. They will help you take the risk. On the second or third trip, however, you might have difficulty assessing your own ability: Where do you fit relative to the others who will be with you? Talk to the guide and tell him what you're confident about, and where you feel unsure. If you are reticent to do something because your confidence level or your mood is low, say so. *Never be goaded into doing something you don't want to do.*

Only price ranges are quoted in this book, because prices change. Costs range from free (being a volunteer on a dinosaur dig) to very expensive (staying in first-class lodges on a fishing trip in Alaska), with most falling in the middle range, designed to attract the widest possible public. Most deliver true value for your dollar. Remember, you're buying a whole experience.

Before you go, gather as many catalogs as you can. Then call the outfitter or organization and find out more. Some provide lodging or will advise you where to stay; most do *not* provide air transportation.

The adventures described here are a sampling of what outfitters offer. This book does not pretend to be a complete list. The material is presented in good faith, without intended bias or preference. Neither the publisher nor the author takes responsibility for outfitters' incompetence or for any accident or injury to any participant incurred on an adventure. All adventure is a risk.

The author wishes to thank Adam Barr for his guide to Las Vegas, Roger Archibald, an award-winning photographer, for his excellent photographs, and the many kind and generous people who took the time to share their experiences and ideas about adventure.

Enjoy.

Introduction

Adventure, the word, has been around at least since the Romans. It took on its present meaning during the Middle Ages when bankers sat at tables and brokered money for venture capitalists. The capitalists put their money on merchant seamen who had the moxie to take a ship across the unknown ocean to find new trading ports. What was involved in their adventure was what is involved in ours: going someplace else and risking something—money, security, a relationship, self-image, the usual way of doing things.

The medieval seamen's goal was profit; so is ours. Adventure involves challenge, and most adventurers go home feeling good about themselves, having mastered their fear or uncertainty and traded it for new skills or talents or ways of looking at themselves or the world. Adventure is the first step in a love affair.

Adventurers discovered this country, and adventurers opened it up. In the early 1900s, Teddy Roosevelt, an American president for whom the wilderness was to be conquered and explored, celebrated a birthday with his buddy John Muir, America's first environmentalist, in a California forest. Together they set ablaze a pine tree as their birthday candle. To them it was a sacred act: It symbolized their absolute love of the wilderness.

Today we express that love differently. By *preserving* what we have left of the wilderness, we can still experience the remnants of our own wildness. John Muir once threw himself onto a glacier and tumbled down and spent hours alone in the wilds, communing with nature spirits. Today most people only wonder at the force of nature, because, as one outfitter said, "We live in a restricted world with seat belts and locks."

That's why adventure is a good way to explain your need to seek the wild rapids of Montana's Flathead River or the bike paths of a volcanic rim in Hawaii: You want to feel the wind in your ears and celebrate an environment unlike your daily one. As one rock climber said, "I can hang on or I can fall off. I can do my best or my worst. I'm in control."

Adventure Vacations

Airplane and Airship Adventures

FIGHTER PLANE PILOTING

You're in the cockpit of a Marchetti SF 260 NATO air combat trainer, tearing along at 270 miles an hour upside down. Your hand on the stick, you hear a voice in your headphones that warns you of an approaching enemy fighter, coming up on your right. You do a flip, lock on to the enemy, track him up in your scope, and press the button that shoots directly at his engine. A trail of smoke rises up from his cockpit as his wing dips and he drops out of sight.

You've scored a victory in one of the six dogfights that you will encounter in the hour or so that you are a fighter pilot. This is not a simulated flight or virtual reality. Except for the computerized sound and smoke, the plane is real. You are *there*.

Clearly, this is not an adventure for everybody. Forty percent of the people who pay a hefty sum for an hour's worth of Top Gun are either pilots or those with some flight experience. But if you feel you can take the 6 positive G's ("Tighten your legs, your stomach, and grunt to bring the blood to your head," said a spokesman) and maybe 3 negative G's ("We try to avoid those"), you will be outfitted in the proper gear and have an hour's briefing that will include how to use a parachute, what you can expect, and where you'll go. Then you take off in formation with another Marchetti which will act as your antagonist. With you in the cockpit is a real pilot who will help you out if you can't take it, or who will take over if you go gonzo. A video camera will record you during your six dogfights.

After you land, you will need some time to come back.

"Even if they come out dog tired," said a spokesperson, "they are jumping in the air, screaming, and yelling. It's the ultimate experience. The adrenaline flow is insane!"

If you get hooked, you can go back for the other of the four phases, which increase in difficulty each time. Instruction in the first phase, for example, covers basic air combat maneuvers, such as high yo-yos, low yo-yos, lead and lag pursuits, pure pursuit, gunsight tracking, military rules of engagement, physiological effects of G forces, and a safety brief.

Will you have to use your parachute? Probably not, because the aircraft are propeller-driven and have a backup system that will allow the pilot to land safely. ($695: 1 hour in the air, 2 hours on the ground.)

Air Combat U.S.A. is the oldest fighter plane outfitter in the country and has a perfect safety record. It offers flights at more than twenty locations across the country.

Air Combat U.S.A, Inc., Fullerton Municipal Airport, P.O. Box 2726, Fullerton, CA 92633. (800) 522-7590

Several companies sell fighter-pilot trips. How do you tell a reputable one? The Federal Aviation Administration checks out all organizations, and this information is available from the organization. Ask for the pilots' qualifications (Years of experience flying this or a similar type of aircraft safely are what counts.) Is the company insured? How long has it been in business? What is its safety record? Ask for details.

CRUISING IN BLIMPS

In the entire world, there are no more than ten full-sized helium blimps, or airships. In summer most of them are emblazoned with product or company names and hover over baseball parks and

Motoring slowly above the earth, blimps take passengers on adventures unlike any other air trips. *Photograph courtesy Airship International, Ltd.*

beaches. But they spend winters in Florida with not a lot to do. That's the time they take passengers—six to a cabin, for about a 45-minute ride over Orlando, Disney World, and Sea World. You can see a lot because cruising speed is about 35 miles per hour, and the altitude is between 1,000 and 3,000 feet. Airship International accepts only same-day reservations, however, because weather, which determines if a blimp can go up, is a last-minute thing. ($95 for 45 minutes.)

Contact: (In Orlando) Airship International, (407) 351-0011 or (407) 870-7433.

SIMULATED RIDES

For an as-close-to-the-real-thing experience as you can get, without having to buy extra insurance, try The Right Stuff Mach 1 Adventure at the Six Flags Great Adventure in Jackson, New Jersey. This is a flight simulator in which you can sit in the cockpit of a T-38, a military supersonic training jet, strapped into a seat that will move, with sounds and lights duplicating the real thing.

Six Flags Great Adventure, P.O. Box 120, Jackson, NJ 08527.
(908) 928-2000 (ask for Information Center)

NAVAL AVIATION HISTORY

Spend four days in September immersed in the history and future of U.S. naval aviation on an adventure that features a tour of the San Diego Aerospace Museum, front seats at the Miramar Air Show, home of Top Gun pilots, with a demonstration by the Blue Angels, plus lectures about dive-bomber pilots and interrogation techniques used during World War II, and a tour of the U.S. Navy Fighter Weapons School.

Smithsonian Institution, Study Tours and Seminars, 1100 Jefferson Dr.,
SW, MRC 702, Washington, DC 20560. (202) 357-4700

Archaeology

In search of artifacts, diggers slowly take away layers of dirt at a site at Crow Canyon Archaeological Center, Cortez, Colorado.

The "discovery" of America is a conglomeration of myth, legend, theories, and the unknown. Assuming that Native Americans "discovered" America, archaeologists argue over *when*: a few thousand years ago? Tens of thousands of years ago? Hundreds of thousands of years ago?

The race is on underground. Yearly, new sites are uncovered that push back the date of the first migrants across the Bering Land Bridge from Asia. Because of the Ice Age, the traditional belief for a long time was that hunters did not come earlier than 12,000 years ago, when receding ice allowed an open route, and did not migrate to the East Coast until a couple of thousand years after that.

But recently archaeologists have found:

- a site in Pennsylvania with a piece of basket dated to 19,000 years ago.
- mastodon bones near Tallahassee, Florida, dated to 12,200 years ago, with clear evidence of having been butchered by humans.
- a cave site in New Mexico with a handprint in hardened clay dated to 27,900 years ago.

Many professional archaeologists welcome amateur diggers: They need all the help they can get. Archaeology is a labor-intensive adventure—laying out grids, digging, and hauling buckets of dirt. The discipline also requires skills, which you will be taught: how to uncover something without disturbing it, by brushing away the dirt with a toothbrush, and how to pick out the important things—a tooth, a seed, a tiny claw—from the pile of gravel and dirt in the sifter. And it requires endurance: Most digs take place in the summer; many are under the hot sun in dry places; some are in remote locales which require camping at the site.

But the rewards are terrific. It's thrilling to reveal a skull or a pot or a bone after you've stuck with the dirt, the heat, and the cramped positions.

Some private organizations offer sessions of 2 weeks or longer with food and lodging, lectures, and immersion in archaeology. (Free to $400 per week. Lodging may be extra.)

The Four Corners School of Outdoor Education organization sponsors 5- to 10-day digs in the Southwest, including Chaco Canyon, one of the largest Anasazi sites, dating no later than A.D. 1300. Some digs are combined with rafting and camping.

> Four Corners School of Outdoor Education, P.O. Box 1029,
> Monticello, UT 84535. (801) 587-2859

Crow Canyon offers a variety of archaeological programs for adults and children: laboratory and digging programs; cultural workshops with Native American artists and musicians, including Carlos Nakai, well-known Navajo flutist; hikes among Anasazi ruins; special programs for teachers and groups of school kids; and weeklong lecture tours.

> Crow Canyon Archaeological Center, 23390 County Rd. K,
> Cortez, CO 81321. (800) 422-8975; (303) 759-9212

Archaeologists, students, teachers, and interested amateur diggers have been part of the 30-year-old Center for American Archaeology, with digs in a vast area of the Illinois River Valley, where Native Americans lived from 8,000 years ago. Amateur archaeologists looking for a solid week of instruction, excavation, and lectures can join high school students and teachers any week throughout the summer, or can register for the 1-week adult field school program.

> *Center for American Archaeology, Box 366, Kampsville, IL 62053.*
> *(618) 653-4316*

Joining a dig with the Andover Foundation for Archaeological Research in a cave in southwest New Mexico might put you at the leading edge of American archaeology. A handprint found in clay and dated to 27,900 years ago has created a lot of controversy in the archaeological community. Working with lab specialists, AFAR has also uncovered bones of several extinct species of horses and sloths, dated to about 30,000 years ago, some of which show what might be signs of humans having worked them. Lodging is provided in a ranch on these two-week digs. The expedition includes side trips to nearby interesting places, such as Gila Ruins in Mexico.

> *Andover Foundation for Archaeological Research (AFAR), Box 83,*
> *Andover, MA 01810. (508) 470-0840*

Amateur archaeologists are invited to join the Lost World Trading Company in a dig in August in southern California, where archaeologists will investigate an extensive group of temporary hunting camps occupied from 9,000 years ago to the time of the first European contact. Extinct camel bones, rock art, and lots of stone tools are on-site. Instruction will be provided. Lodging is in a tented base camp with field showers and a good cook.

> *Lost World Trading Company, P.O. Box 365, Oakdale, CA 95361.*
> *(209) 847-5393*

The following organizations offer many American archaeological expeditions that change from year to year. A typical expedition lasts 2 weeks and includes food and lodging. Contact:

> *University Research Expeditions Program, University of California,*
> *Berkeley, CA 94720. (510) 642-6586*
> *Earthwatch, Box 403, Watertown, MA 02272. (800) 338-4797;*
> *(617) 926-8200*
> *Elderhostel, 80 Boylston St., Suite 400, Boston, MA 02116.*
> *(617) 426-7788*

For a comprehensive list of digs and other low- or no-cost activities in the field, lasting from a weekend to 1 month and listed by state, ask for a *Passport in Time Newsletter*, a twice-a-year publication of the Forest Service, the Department of Agriculture, and CEHP, a private organization, from:

> *CEHP Inc., P.O. Box 18364, Washington, DC 20036. (202) 293-0922*

For a list of hands-on archaeological programs in the Southwest, ask for the free booklet *Public Archaeology on the Colorado Plateau,* from:

> The Grand Canyon Trust, Route 4, Box 718, Flagstaff, AZ 86001.
> (602) 774-7488

Many states offer opportunities for amateur archaeologists to join temporary digs. For a list of state archaeologists, contact:

> Archaeological Institute of America (AIA), 675 Commonwealth Ave.
> Boston, MA 02215. (617) 353-9361

The AIA compiles *The Archaeological Fieldwork Opportunities Bulletin,* an annual guide to archaeological sites. The price is $10.50, plus $3 shipping, from:

> Kendall/Hunt Publishing Co., P.O. Box 1840, Dubuque, IA 52004-1840.
> (800) 228-0810

For an annual list of North American sites to visit or digs to join, read *Archaeology Magazine,* the annual May/June issue.

ANASAZI SITES

Whoever the Anasazi were—and they left no word—they built, between A.D. 1000 and 1300 in the American Southwest, some of the most beautiful cities in the world. Spanish explorers had heard there were cities of gold, but by then, about 1550, the Anasazi and the gold had disappeared, possibly because of drought, disease, or political or economic collapse. Sometime around 1300 they left, and their road network that connected them with trade in Mexico became overgrown, their cities decayed.

Anasazi is a Navajo word meaning "not our people," and refers to those who preceded them. You can view Anasazi remnants at two World Heritage sites:

> Mesa Verde National Park (in southwestern Colorado),
> ARA Mesa Verde Co., P.O. Box 277, Mancos CO 81328.
> (camping reservations), (303) 529-4461
> Chaco Canyon (in central New Mexico), Chaco Culture Historic Park,
> Star Route 4, Box 6500, Bloomfield, NM 87413.
> (camping reservations), (505) 786-7014

Part of the Chaco culture network is Chimney Rock, an unusual formation of two sandstone pillars, around which a Great House with two giant kivas was built in A.D. 1076. For those interested in archeo-astronomy, Chimney Rock is one of two sites known to have been linked to the heavens: the moon stands still every 18 years between the two pillars. The other site at Chaco Canyon is the Sun Dagger, a spiral which the sun pierces with a dagger light on the solstice.

Pagosa Ranger District, San Juan National Forest, P.O. Box 310, Pagosa Springs, CO 81147. (303) 264-2268

Many other sites are located in the Four Corners area (where Colorado, Utah, Arizona, and New Mexico meet), and numerous isolated cliff dwellings exist wherever there are canyons in the Southwest, including the Grand Canyon.

ACOMA

The oldest continuously inhabited city in the United States is at Acoma Pueblo, about 50 miles west of Albuquerque. Built on a mesa, Acoma has been home to a small group of families since around A.D. 1150. You can visit it with a guided tour that leaves regularly from the Tourist Center nearby. For more information, contact:

Acoma Tourist Visitor Center, P.O. Box 309, Acoma, NM 87034. (800) 747-0181; (505) 252-1139

NEW ENGLAND

On the East Coast, rumors persist that several early explorers visited or settled. Among them:

- Irish monks around A.D. 600
- Chinese explorers around A.D. 800
- Vikings around A.D. 1000
- Portuguese explorers in the 1500s

The so-called Mystery Tower in Newport, Rhode Island, located in the center of town, is an eight-columned round stone tower, unlike any other structure found in the world. Recently excavated by Danish archaeologists, the tower remains a mystery and is thought to have been built by Vikings, Irish monks, or a colonial governor. For information, contact the Newport Chamber of Commerce, (800) 326-6030.

America's Stonehenge, a privately owned farm with a collection of large stone rooms, with underground tunnels and site stones marking the solstices and other solar and lunar events, might have been built by early Native Americans or Europeans. Investigation continues.

> *America's Stonehenge, Mystery Hill, Haverhill Rd., North Salem, NH 03073. (603) 893-8300*

MIDWEST

In the center of the country, the famous Mound Builders, a collection of different cultures that spanned the period from 1000 B.C. to A.D. 1500, have left hundreds of complex earthwork structures, many of them burials or ceremonial platforms. Sites are scattered all across the United States, west from the Appalachians to the Great Plains, and south from the Great Lakes to the Gulf of Mexico.

An interesting group of sixteen mounds, the largest of which is 45 feet high, is *Bottle Creek Mounds* in the Mobile-Tensaw Delta in Alabama. Contact:

> *Alabama Historical Commission, (205) 242-3184*

A major site is *Cahokia Mounds*, located directly across the river from St. Louis, Missouri, in Illinois. This is on the United Nations' World Heritage List because of its importance and size—the largest prehistoric site in the United States, with a hundred mounds. Contact:

> *George Holly, Contract Archaeology Program, SIUE. (618) 692-2059*

Effigy Mounds National Monument is a fascinating collection of mounds in the shapes of animals and birds. Contact:

> *Effigy Mounds National Monument, RR 1, Box 25A, Harpers Ferry, IA 52146. (319) 873-3491*

Astronomy

Building telescopes is a craft; using them is an art. Here, astronomers prepare for a solar eclipse. *Photograph by Roger Archibald.*

A treeless mountaintop, a clear moonless night, and a good telescope constitute adventure for stargazers. A lot goes on in the heavens—satellites, wandering asteroids, comets, planets, distant nebulae, quasars, and zillions of stars.

SEARCH FOR EXTRATERRESTRIAL INTELLIGENCE

If you want to look or listen seriously for life in other parts of the universe, get involved in the SETI (Search for Extraterrestrial Intelligence). No longer funded by NASA, SETI is supported by private organizations and overseen by the SETI Institute, which

11

also sponsors FOSTER, Flight Opportunities for Science Teacher EnRichment. SETI publishes *SETI News*. For information, contact:

> SETI Institute, 2035 Landings Dr., Mountain View, CA 94043.
> (415) 961-7099

The Planetary Society is a membership organization led by Carl Sagan, who serves as president. Among other things, the Society funds the SETI Project and operates detection systems in Cambridge, Massachusetts, and near Buenos Aires, Argentina, continuously scanning 8.4 million radio channels. ($20 per year.)

> The Planetary Society, 65 N. Catalina Ave., Pasadena, CA 91106.
> (818) 793-5100

Ohio State University runs Big Ear, a constantly tuned radio telescope, in operation since 1973. Publishes monthly newsletter, *Signals*.

> NAAPO, Otterbein College, Dept. of Physics/Astronomy,
> Westerville, OH 43081. (614) 823-1516

SETIQuest is a summary publication of events, places, people, and techniques involved in listening. ($39 per year.)

> SETIQuest, Helmers Publishing Inc., 174 Concord St.,
> Peterborough, NH 03458-0874. (603) 924-9631

VARIABLE STARS

This is an area where amateurs can make a major contribution to astronomy: Hook onto a variable star, keep good data, and send it into a main computer bank where professional astronomers can use it in their research. The American Association of Variable Star Observers (AAVSO) has a list of 50,000 variable stars, or stars that vary in brightness over short periods of time. Volunteers around the world observe them regularly with the naked eye, binoculars, or telescopes. To be a part of the project, send a letter stating your star-watching experience, your interest, and the location from which you watch, and they will send you a packet of information to guide you to which stars to observe, and when; plus how to keep the data and send it in. Membership ($50 per year) includes newsletters, bulletins, and a journal of information on variable stars and other astronomical phenomena.

> American Association of Variable Star Observers, 25 Birch St.,
> Cambridge, MA 02138-1205. (617) 354-0484
> e-mail: BITNET aavso@cfa8

STAR PARTIES

Like birdwatchers, star watchers travel to the best spots for observing their quarry. Over the years, "star parties"—5- or 6-day gatherings that are annual or occur during times of celestial events—have grown up around places guaranteed to be light-free. Star parties usually feature lectures by guest astronomers, sometimes a visit to a nearby observatory, and lots of networking and information trading. Plus, they are fun. Stargazers stay up all night and keep watch. Then they camp out or stay in local hotels.

Dark skies over the Davis Mountains and the McDonald Observatory make this one of the biggest star parties:

> *Texas Star Party, Southwest Region of the Astronomical League,*
> *1604 Boundbrook Lane, Irving, TX 75060*

Skies in late December are clear in southern Florida, and the Winter Star Party in Key West has become a major event.

> *Southern Cross Astronomical Society, Inc., Bob or Sharon Grant,*
> *5401 SW 110 Ave., Miami, FL 33165. (305) 595-8778*

Most of the Southwest is smog-free and clear as a bell.

> *Enchanted Skies Star Party, P.O. Box 743A, Socorro, NM 87801.*
> *(505) 835-0424*

TELESCOPE MAKERS

Galileo set the standards for those in love with stars: Make you own telescope, polish the lenses, perfect optical performance, and enter it in a competition. For star watchers who are interested in getting together with other amateur telescope makers to watch stars, try Stellafane. Members of this organization meet annually in the summer in Springfield, Vermont, where they camp out, hold a competition, swap parts, and watch the heavens. ($12 per year for membership.)

> *Stellafane, P.O. Box 50, Belmont, MA 02178*

STAR WATCHERS ($9–$200 per day. Includes lodging.)

The Grand Canyon sky viewing is superb. The Grand Canyon Field Institute sponsors a late-spring weekend with an astronomer which includes classroom lectures and telescopes. Viewing takes place on the South Rim.

Grand Canyon Field Institute, P.O. Box 399,
Grand Canyon, AZ 86023. (602) 638-2485

For four days in July, interested stargazers can visit the largest optical, infrared instrument in the world, the Keck Telescope on the 13,600-foot peak of Mauna Kea in Hawaii. The visit is preceded by lectures on the latest advances in astronomy and looking through smaller telescopes at the 9,200-foot base camp, in preparation for the ascent to the peak.

Smithsonian Study Tours and Seminars, P.O. Box 98074,
Washington, DC 20077-7607. (202) 357-4700

Twice a year the Custer Institute Astronomy Group, located in the wine country on Long Island, offers get-togethers for beginners and anyone interested in stars. Their summer Family Astronomy Day invites kids for a weekend of star adventures. At the new moon in October, their Astronomy Jamboree is a celebration of stars with lectures, slide presentations, sci-fi films, telescope talk, star watching, as well as tips on how to spot the Space Shuttle and other satellites, as part of NASA's SPARK program; $9.

Custer Institute Astronomy Group, Main Bayview Rd.,
Southold, NY 11971. (516) 765-2626

CELESTIAL NAVIGATION

At sea, the only way to know exactly where you are is to peg your position relative to the sun or a couple of stars. Learn how to use a sextant and a reduction table. On the coasts (oceans and lakes), call your local U.S. Coast Guard to find out if they offer a course in celestial navigation.

On this 2-day course, off St. Petersburg, Florida, you can cruise and learn at the same time. ($75 to $250 per course.) Contact:

Annapolis Sailing School, P.O. Box 3334, Annapolis MD 21403.
(800) 237-0795

OTHER SOURCES

For a monthly listing of star parties, read *Astronomy* magazine. *Sky and Telescope* magazine regularly lists clubs and events, and publishes a complete list of clubs, observatories, organizations, etc., in their September issue.

For a computer linkage between pros and amateurs, try *CompuServe* 76620,1721.

Celestial navigation teaches sailors how to triangulate the sun and fix their location in the open ocean. *Photograph by Roger Archibald.*

Ballooning

Hundreds of balloons fill the sky above thousands of people at the International Balloon Fiesta in Albuquerque. *Photograph courtesy Kodak Albuquerque International Balloon Fiesta, Inc.*

Check any local tourist guidebook, and you will probably find a ballooning company that will take you up at dawn or at sunset and give you some gustatory delight along with it. It looks simple: You get into the goldola, go up, drift, come down, and get in the van that has been following you. But ballooning is deceptive; those who've done it report a tremendous adrenaline rush. "You *float!*" said one. Each year a lot of people get married in balloons.

Riders of balloons remark on the apparent motionlessness in the air: As you drift with the wind, it appears that you are stationary. But if you hit a cold wave of air and begin to drop and put your hand outside the gondola, you'll feel the rush of air and realize that you are very much in motion and very dependent on the elements.

Before boarding the wicker basket, passengers are invited to watch as the huge uninflated balloon is spread out on the ground while blowers fill it with air. In the gondola, which usually holds three to eight passengers within a chest-high railing, a propane flame heats the air in the envelope, and the balloon slowly rises. Although balloons have gone as high as 50,000 feet, most commercial ascents reach 1,000 to 2,000 feet. At that altitude the air is colder, so the propane is used occasionally during the flight to warm up the air inside the balloon and keep it afloat. The propane flame shoots out in a rush, but except for that noise, balloon flights are the quietest way to travel. The balloon descends when an opening in the top is triggered and hot air escapes.

Trouble is, balloons can't be steered, and navigation depends on a clever reading of the weather, the drift and speed of the wind, and understanding the wind directions at different temperature levels. Ballooning can have its tricky moments. A first-time balloonist remembered the trip when the wind completely died while the balloon was hovering over a swamp, and the guide announced that the propane fuel was "in an emergency management state." The balloonist wasn't worried about not wearing a life jacket—"I was trying to figure out how you get out of *quicksand*," he said. Luckily, an errant gust of wind put the balloon back in business just long enough to float over the road and be rescued by the support vehicle.

Winds and weather determine the best places to balloon. In the United States the best are in the Napa and Sonoma valleys, over the coastal ocean in Florida and southern California, and at the fantastic annual Kodak International Balloon Fiesta in Albuquerque, New Mexico, in October, when more than 600 propane-fired and gas balloons gather to race and to participate in mass ascensions at dawn and dusk. (Average cost is $125 to $195 per flight.)

Remember: All flights depend on weather. Winds above 10 mph might cause cancellation. Book flights early and allow time for possible cancellation. Dress warmly in layers. Trips aloft last between one and one and a half hours; from start to finish, they last three hours.

FLORIDA

One of the advantages of ballooning is that you can be an unobtrusive observer of wildlife, even track a herd of grazing deer. For photography, there is no better mode of travel. In northern Florida, balloon rides carry you from the Gulf to the ocean and over miles of wilderness area and silver rivers. Orange juice and champagne served aboard.

Balloon Adventures, Inc., 6110-7 Powers Ave., Jacksonville, FL 32217
(904) 739-1960

SOUTH DAKOTA

Balloon past Mount Rushmore and see the four famous faces up close. These balloon rides also seek out herds of antelope, elk, and bison, fly over Crazy Horse Monument, and Devil's Tower in Wyoming. Champagne is served after the flight. Custom photography or wedding flights can be arranged. Offers package tours with log cabin lodging.

> Black Hills Balloons, Inc., P.O. Box 210, Custer, SD 57730.
> (605) 673-2520

COLORADO

You can balloon anytime, including the middle of winter, over the Colorado Rockies above Aspen, to 3,000 to 4,000 feet. Dawn trips include hotel pickup and champagne. Special custom trips can accommodate as many as 200 passengers in the large Unicorn balloon fleet.

> Unicorn Balloon Company of Colorado, Inc., 300 B AABC,
> Aspen, CO 81611, (800) 468-2478; (303) 925-5752

NEW MEXICO

In Albuquerque during the first week in October, hundreds of balloons in the Kodak International Balloon Fiesta crowd the skies from dawn to sunset. At night, tethered balloons are lit. For one whole day the Special Shape Rodeo fills the air with an array of balloons that outdoes Disney—balloons in the shape of a peanut, a sneaker, a cow jumping over the moon, Noah's Ark with twenty-eight animals and a rainbow, and a motorcycle with wheels 52.5 feet in diameter. You can join them on a 45-minute "hop" with World Balloon Corporation, the only concessionaire of the fiesta. Flights leave at dawn; celebrate with a champagne toast.

> World Balloon Corporation, 4800 Eubank N.E.,
> Albuquerque, NM 87111. (505) 293-6800

For information on the Fiesta:

> Albuquerque Convention and Visitors Bureau, P.O. Box 26866,
> Albuquerque, NM 87125. (800) 284-2282

ARIZONA

Ballooning over the Sonoran Desert is a photographic delight, filled with such wildlife as gila monsters and roadrunners. There are also breathtaking mountain views, and lots of stories, which the guide recounts. Dawn rides, or, in winter, late afternoon.

> A Balloon Experience, 7119 E. Shea Blvd. #363, Scottsdale, AZ 85261.
> (800) 866-3866; (602) 820-3866

CALIFORNIA

Several balloon companies service the Napa and Sonoma valleys. Most flights start shortly after dawn; most last approximately one hour and are accompanied or followed by Napa champagne. For a list of FAA-approved balloon companies, contact the Napa Valley Conference and Visitors Bureau, (707) 226-7459, and the Sonoma Valley Visitors Bureau, (707) 996-1090.

The following is a random sampling of companies:

The Above the West company provides a pickup in San Francisco (as early as 4 A.M.), a full after-flight breakfast in a restaurant in the valley, and a return to San Francisco. They guarantee small groups.

Above the West Hot Air Ballooning, P.O. Box 2290,
Yountville, CA 94599. (800) 627-2759; (707) 944-8638

For a balloon company that offers wedding flights, photography/ nature flights, wine-tasting flights, and a balloon flight with a picnic lunch in the country, try Bonaventura. Balloons take off at dawn from a vineyard, the "drift like a butterfly" across the brightening landscape.

Bonaventura Balloon Company, 133 Wall Rd., Napa, CA 94558.
(800) FLY NAPA; (707) 944-2822

Float over the Sonoma Valley on a "nature walk in the sky." Flights are followed by champagne brunch. Some are part of a package that includes lodging.

Air Flambuoyant, 250 Pleasant Ave., Santa Rosa, CA 95403.
(707) 838-8500

Biking

Moab's tough backcountry paths attract mountain bikers from all over the world. *Photograph by Roger Archibald.*

Skinny-tire bicycles are fast and maneuverable and are used in most serious races as well as for pleasure touring. But they don't allow riders to venture comfortably off the beaten path. Mountain, or fat-tire, bikes go where only hikers used to go. In addition to being able to tolerate rough backcountry, on or off a path, they can zip up steep mountain trails and bump down flights of stairs. The empowerment of mountain bikes has produced enough controversy between hikers and bikers that several organizations currently are in the process of creating new trails exclusively for mountain bikes.

Legend is divided over where mountain biking was born: Crested Butte, Colorado, takes credit, but so does Mount Tamalpais, near San Francisco. Wherever it was born, Moab, Utah, is where most mountain bikers eventually bike.

Whether you ride a touring bike or a mountain bike, always wear a helmet. Also, carry water and all the appropriate tools for fixing any mechanical problems. On off-road biking, it pays to carry a first-aid kit, along with a compass and a map. ($65–$150 per day; Rentals: $15–25 per day.)

The National Bicycle Trail Network

During the U.S. bicentennial celebration in 1976, an organization called Bikecentennial developed the National Bicycle Trail Network, a series of bicycle routes stretching across the country. Bikecentennial's philosophy was that serious bicyclists want to explore America's back roads and they aren't afraid of putting on the miles. Now called the Adventure Cycling Association, the group has mapped more than 19,000 miles for bike touring and is currently developing mountain bike trails in conjunction with the National Forest Service.

You can become a member, buy maps and related books from Adventure Cycling, or join one of their organized bike tours, which last from 10 to 93 days and cover states, national parks, specific trails, such as the Lewis and Clark Trail (for mountain bikes), or the whole country from Virginia to Oregon. Some are camping treks, others are vehicle-supported tours, and some are combos, such as biking-and-fly-fishing in Montana.

Adventure Cycling Association, 150 E. Pine St., P.O. Box 8308, Missoula, MT 59807-8308. (406) 721-1776

BICYCLE TOURING

The Whole Country

Each year in early summer, the League of American Wheelmen sponsors a tour from Los Angeles to Boston in 48 days—sightseeing and one river-rafting trip are included, as well as motels and a support van.

Pedal for Power, P.O. Box 898, Atkinson, NH 03811. (800) 762-BIKE

The West

Timberline offers nine-day Adventure Cycling road bike tours of the Rocky Mountains and national parks. Support van; inns & lodges at night, included.

Timberline, 7975 E. Harvard, #J, Denver, CO 80231. (303) 759-3804

New England

MASSACHUSETTS

The famous island of Martha's Vineyard is 45 minutes by ferry from the mainland, hard to hike, easy to bike. There are 3-day tours in the summer, beginner to moderate, 15 to 35 miles a day, with gourmet meals, nights at an inn in a canopied bed, and a visit to a vineyard.

Bike Riders, Inc., P.O. Box 254, Boston, MA 02113. (800) 473-7040

Mid-Atlantic

NEW YORK STATE

New York State is forested and filled with vineyards and mansions. Spend 5 days biking from the Pennsylvania border to Lake Placid at an easy to moderate pace, between 30 and 60 miles a day.

Cycle America, P.O. Box 485, Cannon Falls, MN 55009.
(800) 245-3263

NEW YORK CITY

Take Back the Night Ride is a midnight bike tour of New York City, which, despite all you might have heard about the city, is described not only as safe but as an excellent way to see and understand the different ethnic neighborhoods. According to Steve of Transportation Alternatives, a group of cyclists in the early hours of the morning is such a novelty that in even the worst neighborhoods, they can make friendly connections. TA also sponsors regular Sunday evening rides in Central Park and a Bike to Work Week in May, and publishes *City Cyclist*.

Transportation Alternatives, 92 St. Marks Pl., New York, NY 10009.
(212) 275-4600

NORTH CAROLINA

Cape Hatteras is windswept and romantic. Bike through small villages and the Cedar Island National Wildlife Refuge, then take a ferry to Ocracoke Island. Six-day tours, easy to moderate, 30 to 45 miles a day.

Vermont Bicycle Touring, P.O. Box 711, Bristol, VT 05443.
(802) 453-4811

South

FLORIDA

Bicycling on the back roads of Florida can mean long, straight paths with canopies of trees, or coastal beach roads with palm

trees. Off-the-beaten-path tours stop at bed-and-breakfasts along the way.

Outdoor Adventures, 6110-7 Powers Ave., Jacksonville, FL 32217.
(904) 739-1960

MISSISSIPPI

The pace in Mississippi is luxuriously slow, but you can cycle as fast as you want on this guided inn-to-inn that goes past Civil War sites and stops for you to take a horse-and-carriage tour of old Natchez. Six days.

All Adventure Travel, 5589 Arapahoe, Suite 208, Boulder, CO 80303.
(800) 537-4025; (303) 440-7924

Midwest

MICHIGAN

The coast of Lake Michigan in northern Michigan has been compared to the Mediterranean: rugged shores, pine woods, peaceful towns. Two-day leisurely tours; hotel lodging.

Lookfar Adventures, P.O. Box 3005, Hilton Head, SC 29928.
(800) 882-4424

West

OREGON

You set your own pace as you bicycle around southern Oregon's Crater Lake, the remnant of an ancient volcano, and the deepest lake in the country. Small groups will travel about 140 miles in 4 days, stay in country inns, and have a support van.

Bicycle Adventures, P.O. Box 7875, Olympia, WA 98507.
(800) 443-6060; (206) 786-0989

WASHINGTON

This 6-day coastal adventure in the San Juan Islands includes bicycling and watching whales from a sea kayak. Nights are spent in hotels. Average distances 25 to 30 miles a day, for energetic beginners to advanced cyclists.

CycleWest, 75 Bush St., Ashland, OR 97520. (800) 831-5016

Alaska

The Gold Rush produced a trail that became the Richardson Highway, from Valdez to Fairbanks to Anchorage. This 8-day ride is for intermediate cyclists, because it averages 75 miles a day. Lodging is in hotels. Support van.

Saga Alaskan Bicycle Adventures, 2734 Iliamna Ave.,
Anchorage, AK 99517. (800) 770-SAGA; (907) 243-2329

MOUNTAIN BIKING

New England

VERMONT

The Green Mountains offer deep valleys and steep slopes and perfect autumn colors, with both tough and gentle mountain bike trails. For 4-hour day trips in the Mad River Valley, with rentals, advice, and maps:

Clearwater, Route 100, Waitsfield, VT 05673. (802) 496-2708

Great Plains

SOUTH DAKOTA

The Custer Area Mountain Bike Trail System was developed from 1870s gold-mining trails and railroads. As a result, it travels past ghost mines and ghost towns. The Custer Bicycle Club has developed an excellent map of the trail that descends from a fire lookout along logging roads to Mount Rushmore National Monument.

Custer Bicycle Club, Route 2, Box 201 G, Custer, SD 57730.
(605) 673-4764

For guided bike tours of the Black Hills of South Dakota:

Southern Hills Adventures, Inc., Route 2, Box 201 G, Custer, SD 57730.
(800) 531-5923

Rocky Mountains

MONTANA

Backcountry in Big Sky Country means canyons, lodgepole pine forests, mountain lakes, alpine meadows, hot springs, and country inns. No van support means that only experienced cyclists who are in good shape should attempt this trek. Hilly and steep single-track roads; 10 to 22 miles a day.

Backcountry, P.O. Box 4029, Bozeman, MT 59772. (406) 586-3556

COLORADO

Durango and Crested Butte are the sites of world-class biking events in the summer. The triangle connecting Ouray, Crested

Butte, and Silverton is a famous trail, and Winter Park's 660 miles of bicycle trails has been called the state's best. Fat Tires Tours in Winter Park, (303) 726-8452, has a Jeep-up/bike-down arrangement for bikers.

Hut-to-hut mountain biking on the 10th Mountain Division Hut System between Aspen and Vail in Colorado is about 110 miles and can be challenging. Four-day trips are for advanced riders, 5-day trips are for strong intermediate riders, and 6-day trips include side rides and a layover day to hike. July through September; *book early.*

> Aspen Alpine Guides, Inc., P.O. Box 659, Aspen, CO 81612.
> (800) 643-8621; (303) 925-6618

Beginner mountain bikers in good shape can take the 205 miles of dirt roads from Telluride, Colorado, to Moab, Utah, via the San Juan Hut System. These are wooden huts, stocked with food, with padded bunks for sleeping. Bathing is in streams and lakes. Riders must have first-aid skills, carry pump and patches, and be able to repair a bike. Riders must also be able to read a map and find a route.

> San Juan Hut Systems, Box 1663, 117 North Willow St.,
> Telluride, CO 81435. (303) 728-6935

UTAH

Biking in the high desert of the Colorado Plateau requires some special precautions on soil known as 'microbiotic, or cryptogamic, soil crust.' This fragile topsoil is the only thing keeping the Plateau from turning into sand dunes. Composed of soil particles with blue-green algae, the crust is vulnerable to damage from footsteps or bicycle tires, and takes 50 to 100 years to be restored. Stay off it if you can, or if you have no choice, follow in previous paths.

Moab is the unofficial center of mountain biking, and Utah offers what mountain cyclists need: backcountry paths, hills, crests, and beautiful scenery. The Kokopelli Trail starts in Grand Junction, Colorado, runs through red rock canyons to mountains, then ends in Moab with a dramatic 4,000-foot descent to Slickrock Trail. Five days for intermediate and advanced cyclists; lodging in inns and camping.

> Road Less Traveled, P.O. Box 8187, Longmont, CO 80501.
> (303) 678-8750

Four days, 90 miles: This is for the biker whose motto is "Life is short . . . play hard," says the Holiday River and Bike catalog. The White Rim Trail in Canyonlands National Park in Utah is filled with spires, arches, basins, mesas, and the confluence of the Green and Colorado rivers. This is for experienced and in-shape bikers. You can rent a bike or bring your own; they provide meals, a guide, and vehicle support in case you lose a lug nut.

> Holiday River & Bike Expeditions, Inc., 544 East 3900 South,
> Salt Lake City, UT 84107. (800) 624-6323; (801) 266-2087

The Maze in Canyonlands National Park is a labyrinth of canyons and monoliths and requires technical expertise to negotiate loose rock descents, stair-step climbs, and slickrock. Six days, with guides, April and September. Start in Hite, Utah.

> Nichols Expeditions, 497 N. Main St., Moab, UT 84532.
> (800) 635-1792; (801) 259-7882

For a list of outfitters in Utah, request the latest Bicycle Utah Vacation Guide:

> Bicycle Utah, P.O. Box 738, Park City, UT 84060. (801) 649-5806

For trail and road maps for each of the nine sections of Utah, with details about elevation, length, best season, and special things to see, contact:

> Bicycle Vacations Guides, Inc., P.O. Box 738, Park City, UT 84060.
> (801) 649-5806

[Each booklet costs about $5.00.]

West

CALIFORNIA

Technical rides mean heavy-duty terrain, high up, with some mean creeks and hair-raising downhills. A 2-day High Sierra Slickrock and Singletrack Tour starts at 7,000 feet and goes up to 8,361 feet. An afternoon swim in a glacial pool provides the juice to get back to your chalet at a mere 4,000 feet. Eat, sleep, and do it all again the next day.

> Southern Yosemite Mountain Guides, P.O. Box 301,
> Bass Lake, CA 93604. (415) 309-3153

Mammoth Mountain is 11,053 feet high. You take a gondola up and you mountain bike down. This is the site of a race called the Kamikaze Downhill. Mammoth also has a Dual Slalom race course and an Obstacle Area for improving your mountain-biking technique. Two- and 3-night packages include everything, including a bike and lodging at the Mammoth Mountain Hotel.

> Mammoth Adventure Connection, Box 353, Mammoth Lakes, CA 93546.
> (619) 934-0606

Alaska

Mountain bike in Wrangell–St. Elias National Park, then raft on its four wilderness rivers. On the fifth day of this weeklong guided trip, sail out to Growler Island, where you can kayak, and hike in Prince William Sound. All of this and gourmet meals too.

Alaska River Journeys, P.O. Box 220204, Anchorage, AK 99522.
(800) 349-0064; (907) 349-2964

Hawaii

On Maui the Haleakala Volcano crater, at 6,500 feet, puts nothing between you and the gods at sunrise. Then biking down the 38 miles of spiral, well-paved roads puts a spin on an experience you will never forget. Bob Kiger, known as Cruiser Bob, has biked around the world with 150 pounds of gear, including a video camera, a still camera, and a computer. Today he encourages everyone to leave the car behind and use a bike. Cruiser Bob's in Maui offers guides and bikes for sunrise and gourmet-picnic-lunch trips. Ride up in a van with bikes, then cruise Haleakal downhill. All ages welcome, but you must be a competent biker.

Cruiser Bob's, 99 Hana Hwy—Box B, Paia, HI 96779.
(800) 654-7717; (808) 579-8444

Spend a week biking the Big Island, including Volcanoes National Park, where you spend the night. Snorkle and swim; first-class meals and hotels along the way. Guides and equipment provided.

Worldwide Rocky Mountain Cycle Tours, P.O. Box 1978,
Canmore, Alberta, Canada TOL 0M0. (800) 661-2453

OTHER SOURCES

Organizations

Contact the American Bicycle Association for information on off-road bicycle races.

American Bicycle Association, P.O. Box 718, Chandler, AZ 85244.
(602) 961-1903

The National Off-Road Bicycle Association is a membership organization that sanctions mountain bike races. Working with several other organizations, NORBA is trying to establish a National Mountain Bike Patrol, a group of volunteers who monitor backcountry trails for hikers, bikers, horseback riders, or anyone in need of assistance.

> National Off-Road Bicycle Association, U.S. Cycling Federation,
> 1 Olympic Plaza, Colorado Springs, CO 80909. (719) 578-4581

The International Mountain Bicycling Association oversees access to routes and works closely with NORBA, above.

> International Mountain Bicycling Association, P.O. Box 7578,
> Boulder, CO 80306. (303) 545-9011

The League of American Wheelmen, which began in 1880, is a membership organization composed of enthusiastic cyclists who work to keep access to paths in cities and rural areas. Membership entitles you to discounts from major airlines for shipping bikes.

> League of American Wheelmen, 190 West Ostend St., Suite 120,
> Baltimore, MD 21230. (800) 288-2453

Tread Lightly! is a private nonprofit membership educational organization that works in league with the Forest Service to make the public aware of the potentially damaging effects of recreational use on public lands. Works to keep open trail access.

> Tread Lightly! Inc., 298 24th St., Suite 325-C, Ogden, UT 84401.
> (801) 627-0077

The Rails to Trails Conservancy is an organization devoted to salvaging unused railroad routes and turning them into trails for biking, hiking, cross-country skiing, and horseback riding. Membership includes a list of trails and a pocket guide, Sampler of America's Rail-Trails.

> Rails to Trails Conservancy, 1400 16th St., NW, Washington, DC 20077.
> (202) 797-5400

Magazines

Bicycle magazine and Mountain Bike magazine are two of several speciality magazines devoted to cycling and mountain biking.

Birdwatching

Birdwatchers listen and search for birds shortly after dawn in the Corkscrew Swamp, Florida. *Photograph by Roger Archibald.*

Birdwatchers start out casually noticing a robin or two and then find themselves "getting up at five in the morning to go hide in the woods," said a spokesperson at the Cornell Laboratory of Ornithology. It's an adventure easy to get hooked on, and once hooked, birdwatchers do things like sit for hours on a frozen lake behind a telescope or raft a river to find an eagle's nest. "I guess you could say we're a dedicated bunch," explained one watcher.

The U.S. is fantastic birdwatcher's territory, home to numerous species of city birds, shorebirds, songbirds, raptors, and some rare birds; it is also a temporary stopping place for birds en route from northern Canada to the tropics of Central and South America. It has some dramatic birds, like bald eagles and whooping cranes, whose numbers always hover close to endangered; and places where hundreds gather at one time, such as Utah's Great Salt Lake, temporary home to Wilson's phalaropes.

Some committed birdwatchers follow certain species; others create must-see lists and go to bird hot spots. Gear is minimal: a good pair of field binoculars and hiking shoes, plus one or two bird-watching bibles—mentioned below—are all you really need. ($80–$200 per day.)

Mid-Atlantic

New Jersey

The World Series of Birdwatching began here in 1983 when a couple of teams competed to count the highest number of species in a 24-hour period. Today more than fifty teams from all over the world gather to spend one midnight-to-midnight in mid-May during the peak overlap period when migratory and resident birds are at their greatest numbers. A recent winning team counted 218 species. Winning cups are bestowed in three divisions, and the money from corporate and nonprofit team sponsors goes to bird conservation. To be a part of the World Series, get a team, get a sponsor, and be ready to "bird till you drop," said director Peter Dunne.

> Peter Dunne, Cape May Bird Observatory, 707 East Lake Dr.,
> P.O. Box 3, Cape May Point, NJ 08212. (609) 884-2736

South

North Carolina

North Carolina is only one of the bird destinations for trips with field guides. A birding tour and travel service, they will help you design and realize your trip. Professional birder Peter Harrison understands the difficulties involved in birdwatching and will help plan the best strategies for viewing.

> Field Guides, Inc., P.O. Box 160723, Austin, TX 78716.
> (800) 728-4953; (512) 327-4953

Florida

The Dry Tortugas is a subtropical group of uninhabited islands 70 miles southwest of Key West and is one of the best places in the world to see migrating birds in the spring and fall, and nesting birds in the summer. Some, like the black noddy, are rare; others, like frigatebirds and sooty terns, congregate in huge numbers. The place is remote—only an abandoned Civil War fort remains—and there is no water. Ten camping sites have toilets, but you must bring your own water.

For camping information:

> Fort Jefferson National Monument, P.O. Box 6208, Key West, FL 33040

For information on the islands:

> Fort Jefferson National Monument, c/o The Everglades National Park,
> P.O. Box 279, Homestead, FL 33030. (305) 247-6211

To get to the Tortugas, you must take a boat or fly. Key West Seaplane Services is the only seaplane flying from the Keys to the islands. They transport birders for a half day, a full day, or overnight for camping.

> Key West Seaplane Services, Inc., 5603 Junior College Rd.,
> Key West, FL 83040. (305) 294-6978

Guided spring birdwatching weekends (April to May) in the Dry Tortugas are offered by:

> WINGS, Inc., P.O. Box 31930, Tucson, AZ 85751.
> (602) 749-1967

WINGS also offers a 6-day trip to the Florida Keys and the Dry Tortugas on a boat that takes watchers to most of the Tortugas islands. Lots of birds. Sleep aboard.

Midwest

INDIANA

The Jasper-Pulaski wildlife area in northern Indiana is an excellent site from which to watch some of the tens of thousands of sandhill cranes that migrate north in the spring and south in the fall. These close relatives of whooping cranes are part of a 1 day guided trip from Chicago in March and November, which also includes an ecological look at wetlands. Limited to 12.

> Wilderness Institute, Box 4085, Naperville, IL 60567.
> (708) 369-0438

WISCONSIN

The combination of wild places and diverse habitats south of Green Bay in northeastern Wisconsin make this area rich in ospreys, snow geese, great blue herons, and scarlet tanagers—just some of the 280 species that live or visit here. Wild Fox Tours will facilitate your birdwatching expedition, from providing information and maps to organizing a guided tour.

> Wild Fox Tours, 2108 N. Ullman St., Appleton, WI 54911.
> (414) 830-2469; (414) 733-2097

Rocky Mountains

WYOMING

The Greater Yellowstone Ecosystem in Wyoming harbors an incredible number of bird species. Jackson Hole, for example, is home to ten species of owls, from the Great Gray Owl, with a 6-foot wingspan, to one that weighs less than 3 ounces. You can spend weekends in the spring and summer studying the evolution and ecology of owls, as well as eagles, hawks, and other local birds, with research professors and professional birders.

Teton Science School, Box 68, Kelly, WY 83011. (307) 733-4765

MONTANA

The remote wildlands of north-central Montana are beautiful even if you aren't looking for birds. Moose, elk, deer, and antelope are permanent residents in the Red Rocks Lakes National Wildlife Refuge; but in the spring sandhill cranes come to nest, and in late summer, thousands of ducks and geese stop on migration routes. The main resident, however, is the 4-foot-tall trumpeter swan, for which the refuge was established in 1935, when they numbered less than 100. Since then, 400 to 500 breeding trumpeter swans live on its 43,500 acres. Centennial Birding Tours offers weeklong tours, from June through October, with lodging, good Western food, and lots of exciting birding and wildlife.

Centennial Birding Tours, P.O. Box 741, Dillon, MT 59725

Southwest

TEXAS

In all seasons and in all its diverse regions, Texas is home to a huge variety of birds, including whooping cranes. Rockport, near Corpus Christi, is one point where migrating and resident shorebirds and landbirds come together.

Victor Emanuel Nature Tours runs a bird workshop here in December. For five days, expert Ken Kaufman gives lectures, in the field and at night, to beginners and advanced birders on watching birds and really seeing them, in addition to identifying them.

Big Bend National Park—the bend is in the Rio Grande River, which cuts through the 8,000-foot Chisos Mountains here—is a Texas desert that is home to two species, the Colima warbler and the Lucifer hummingbird, that don't visit any other states. These are just two of the dozens of species that spend the summer here or fly over from Mexico in late summer; among them, hawks, thrashers, tanagers, and orioles. Victor Emanuel offers a 7-day guided tour of Big Bend in late July.

> *Victor Emanuel Nature Tours, P.O. Box 33008, Austin, TX 78764.*
> *(800) 328-VENT*

Big Bend National Park has many year-round campgrounds, including backcountry sites. For information and reservations:

> *Big Bend National Park*
> *Big Bend National Park, TX 79834*

The Aransas National Wildlife Refuge, on the Gulf Coast of Texas, is a wintering ground for whooping cranes, as well as other northern species, such as ducks and geese. One of the best ways to get a good view is to take a boat, available at the Rockport Yacht Basin or Sandollar Marina. To contact the refuge: (512) 286-3559.

ARIZONA

August in southeastern Arizona is the time when more than 190 species of hummingbirds and songbirds gather to compete for nectar on the agave flowers. Spend 7 days tracking hundreds of hummingbirds, including the possibility of sighting a plain-capped starthroat, called "the unicorn of Mexican hummers." Hiking and stops at historic sites and other wildlife viewing are included in this excursion, guided by two naturalists.

> *Borderland Productions, 2550 W. Calle Padilla, Tucson, AZ 85745.*
> *(800) 525-7753; (602) 882-7650*

West

WASHINGTON

Bald eagles flock to the Skagit River in the North Cascades National Park in winter to catch the salmon. Serious birders can camp in the year-round backcountry sites and raft down the Skagit to see the eagles. Breathtaking scenery, lots of waterfalls and glaciers.

The Nature Conservancy has more information on the eagles: (206) 343-4344.

Orion River Expeditions runs 1- to 6-day raft and kayak trips of the Skagit, December to February, Class II–III rapids. Other wildlife are elk and bighorn sheep.

> *Orion River Expeditions, Inc., 2366 Eastlake Ave. E., #305,*
> *Seattle, WA 98072. (800) 553-7466; (206) 322-9130*

For camping reservations, write:

> *North Cascades National Park Service Complex, 2105 Hwy 20,*
> *Sedro Woolley, WA 98284.*

Alaska

The Alaska Chilkat Bald Eagle Preserve in Haines, Alaska, attracts eagles that come to mate in the spring in dramatic courtship displays, after which they nest. At the same time, migrating trumpeter swans and other shorebirds gather by the dozens along edges of the estuaries in the preserve.

But in the late fall and winter—from November to January, when birders are the only tourists in Alaska—bald eagles gather by the thousands to catch late-spawning salmon.

Alaska Nature Tours provides a natural history guide and an expedition bus that "functions as a warming hut, bird blind, and diner" in the winter, and as a blind for photographers at other seasons. Tours are daily.

> *Alaska Nature Tours, Box 491, Haines, AK 99827. (907) 766-2876*

For information on the preserve:

> *Alaska Department of Natural Resources, Juneau, AK 99811.*
> *(907) 465-4563*

WINGS, Inc. offers a 14-day tour with two professional birders to Alaska in June, looking for breeding birds. Nome, the Pribilofs, and Denali National Park attract such birds as loons, red-faced cormorants, tufted puffins, bar-tailed godwits, and numerous other species.

> *WINGS, Inc., P.O. Box 31930, Tucson, AZ 85751. (602) 749-1967*

For a custom-designed birding trip in Alaska with an excellent guide, try Wilderness Birding Adventures.

> *Wilderness Birding Adventures, P.O. Box 103747-B,*
> *Anchorage, AK 99510-3747, (907) 694-7442*

BIRD COUNTS
AND SCIENTIFIC PROJECTS

The only way to know if birds are happy and healthy is to count their numbers. Because they are so mobile, it helps to have counters spread out over the country. Cornell University's Project FeederWatch invites anyone who feeds birds in the winter to watch the birds once every two weeks, count the numbers and kinds of birds, and record the information on forms they provide. (Cost: $14 a year. In return for your work, you get a copy of their newsletter, *Birdscope*, which contains count results.)

If you want to get more deeply involved, you can take part in the National Science Experiment Seed Preference Test, in which you identify exactly what kinds of seeds the birds at your feeder prefer.

To know more about birds, try the Cornell Lab's Home Study course.

Cornell Lab of Ornithology, P.O. Box 11, Ithaca, NY 14851-0011.
(800) 843-BIRD; (607) 254-2421

The National Audubon Society is the founding organization of birding and is dedicated to protecting all forms of wildlife and habitats. Annually, from December 17 to January 2, you can join their Christmas Bird Count in your area and count migrating birds. Call the National Audubon Society for information.

Many states have their own Audubon Society which disseminates information and organizes tours to spots frequented by particular birds during particular seasons throughout the year.

National Audubon Society, 700 Broadway, New York, NY 10003.
(212) 979-3000; (212) 979-3083 (Christmas Bird Count)

Hawk Watch International follows and counts all migrating diurnal birds of prey. You can offer your help at any of nine migrating sites in five states.

This is serious birdwatching. At the Goshute site, for example, between Utah and Nevada, an hour's hike off-road, you must carry your sleeping shelter and cooking gear, plus all the water you'll need while there. The working elevation is 9,000 feet; you can expect winds of up to 40 mph. And you must wear dark or neutral clothes so as not to distract the birds.

But the rewards are great. Between 11 A.M. and 5 P.M., you might count as many as 800 raptors.

Hawk Watch International, P.O. Box 660,
Salt Lake City, UT 84110-0660. (800) 726-4295; (801) 524-8511

OTHER SOURCES

Organizations

The American Birding Association, a membership organization, publishes *Birding* magazine and *Winging It*, a newsletter. It also publishes *Birdfinding Guide Series*, including *Birdfinding in 40 National Forests and Grasslands*, and *Hot Spots Guide*, a list of twenty of the best birding places in the U.S. Their *Directory of Volunteer Opportunities for Birders* ($2.00) lists 300 ways to get involved. Ask for a catalog of titles that they publish and distribute.

American Birding Association, P.O. Box 6599,
Colorado Springs, CO 80934. (719) 578-9703

The Massachusetts Audubon Society publishes *Natural History Travel News*, a roundup of bird trips around the world.

The Massachusetts Audubon Society, Lincoln, MA 01773.
(800) 289-9504; (617) 259-9500

Books

Books of interest to birdwatchers include *The Audubon Society Field Guide to North American Birds* (by region) (Knopf, 1990); *National Geographical Society Field Guide to the Birds of North America* (1987); and *Where the Birds Are* (W. Morrow/Quill, 1990), by John Oliver Jones. Check your local bookstores for other regional guides.

Magazines

Wildbird, Birder's World, Bird Watcher's Digest, Audubon, and *Living Bird* are some of the other magazines of interest to birders.

Body and Soul

Dawn and the ocean. These fitness seekers begin each day
with yoga and deep breathing. *Photograph courtesy
Global Fitness Adventures, Aspen, Colorado.*

Groups offering courses and workshops in stress management,
consciousness raising, and an enhanced lifestyle are offered
at an increasing number of centers around the country. They
are in response to a growing need to make sense out of a life
that seems to stall out occasionally on the information super-
highway.

The search for authenticity and meaning, for some kind of res-
onance between inner experience and outer lifestyle, begins in the
body, with exercise or diet, and in the soul, with meditation,
retreats, or studying with a shaman; and it ends with conceptual-
izing a lifestyle more in tune with the environment. (Fitness:
$100–$300 per day; Meditation: $40–$80 per day.)

FITNESS CENTERS

For more centers, please see *Other Sources*, on next page.

VERMONT

The Institute for the Study of Human Knowledge sponsors weekend sessions, in the summer or in the fall, that include relaxation techniques, a personalized lifestyle assessment, recommended exercises, healthy food, and canoeing, hiking, sculling, and other activities at a camp in the Northeast Kingdom.

> *Institute for the Study of Human Knowledge, Craftsbury Sports Center,*
> *P.O. Box 31, Craftsbury, VT 05827. (800) 729-7751;*
> *(802) 586-7767*

NEW YORK

Climb the 50-foot alpine tower, do Zen meditation, take a Step-Plus class, have a seaweed wrap—these are only some of the ways to get yourself back into shape when you visit the New Age Health Spa. Take as many days as you want; they will fix you up with a roommate to trim costs.

> *New Age Health Spa, Neversink, NY 12765. (800) 682-4348*

TEXAS

Run by the Father of Aerobics, Dr. Kenneth Cooper, the Cooper Wellness Program provides long experience and a serious fitness assessment at the 30-acre Cooper Aerobics Center. Tracks, Cybex strength and cardiovascular equipment, two lap pools, tennis and racquetball courts, and steam and sauna rooms are world-class. One- to 13-day programs include medical evaluation, physical fitness assessment, and a program of exercise, stress management, nutrition (including cooking classes), and teambuilding, plus a 30-day follow-up.

> *Cooper Wellness Program, 12230 Preston Rd., Dallas, TX 75230.*
> *(800) 444-5192; (214) 386-4777*

ARIZONA

The red sandstone rocks of Sedona are beautiful and steep, and best enjoyed if you diversify your adventure. The Sedona Challenge, offered two times a month from October to June, except January, combines challenging group hikes and respites with toning and stretching at a luxury resort. Seven days of good health surrounded by beauty.

> *The Sedona Challenge, Deborah Sturgess, P.O. Box 5489,*
> *Glendale, AZ 85312. (800) 448-9816*

"What is stress, other than being out of harmony with the universe?" is the philosophy of Global Fitness Adventures. Their program includes empowering you to achieve your physical fitness goals in a daily ritual of sunrise yoga and meditation, stretch class, hikes, tai ch'i, horseback riding, windsurfing, or kayaking, massage, gourmet organic meals, and after-dinner lectures or discussions. An international company, their three U.S. centers are Aspen, Colorado, Sedona, Arizona, and Santa Barbara, California.

Global Fitness Adventures, P.O. Box 1390, Aspen, CO 81612.
(800) 488-TRIP; (303) 927-9593

Other Sources

To find a spa, try Spa-Finders Travel Arrangements, Ltd., (800) 255-7727, or read the book *Fodor's Healthy Escapes*, (Fodor, 1993) by Bernard Burt.

MEDITATION AND VISION QUESTS

John P. Milton has been doing personal vision quests and rites of passage for almost 40 years, and taking others on quests for 16 years. An experience called the Sacred Passage begins with 3 days of mental and spiritual preparation in a group, with instruction in camping and safety. Then for 7 days, the vision quester goes solo into the wilderness with nothing to read or distract him from nature. A buddy system with daily check-ins makes sure the quester is okay, but otherwise, he is alone. The final 2 days are spent back with the group. Sacred Passage "usually results in a profound rebirth of love and compassion." Many report it is an excellent way to come back from divorce, death of a loved one, or job change. Sites in Arizona, Colorado, Hawaii, West Virginia, and around the world.

John P. Milton, Sacred Passage, Drawer CZ, Bisbee, AZ 85603.
(602) 432-7353

Dedicated to the study of the integration of body, mind, and spirit, the Institute of Noetic Sciences, begun by former astronaut Edgar Mitchell, sponsors scientific studies in the physiological aspects of mental and spiritual states, does research on altruism, and offers sensitive travel programs around the world. In a California desert, alone for 3 days and 3 nights in April, participants can undergo a vision quest.

Institute of Noetic Sciences, Box 909, Sausalito, CA 94966-0909,
(800) 383-1586

Taoism, Zen, and the Maine Woods in August is an 8-day moderately difficult backpacking experience in backcountry Maine. Mornings begin with meditation, and there are discussions and silence throughout the day.

Myths and Mountains, Inc., 976 Tee Court, Incline Village, NV 89451.
(800) 670-6984; (702) 832-5454

The Zen Mountain Monastery provides weekend and weeklong retreats for beginners and advanced students of Zen Buddhism. Working from the belief that meditation promotes an integrated body/mind experience, the monastery offers weeklong retreats that include meditation coupled with an activity such as rock climbing or canoeing in the wilderness.

Zen Mountain Monastery, P.O. Box 197PC, South Plank Rd.,
Mt. Tremper, NY 12457. (914) 688-2228

The Nyingma Institute offers weekend retreats featuring courses and workshops on Tibetan Buddhist texts and prayer wheels. The institute also offers intensive monthlong Human Development Training Programs.

Nyinga Institute, 1815 Highland Pl., Berkeley, CA 94709.
(510) 843-6812

Canoeing and Kayaking

A kayaker maneuvers the rapids through the Feather River Canyon, California. *Photograph by Roger Archibald.*

C anoeists go where few others can. Slipping quietly through clear waters and weaving among islands, they can get to the best places to fish, the richest sanctuaries for wildlife, and the prime spots for photographs. Usually packing two people, canoes these days are light enough not to pose a problem if you have to portage around heavy rapids or waterfalls, or if one lake ends, and you must walk to the next lake. Canoes offer travel flexibility; they allow you to camp in the wilderness; their single-blade paddles provide moderate physical exercise, as do hikes, if you portage; and there is no better way to get away from it all.

Kayaks and duckies (inflatable kayaks) are propelled by double-bladed paddles. The lower body, with legs straight out in the front, provides balance (once you get over the sense of confinement), while the upper body gets a royal workout with the paddles, which require a rotating-elbow-and-waist motion.

While experienced canoeists are able to negotiate moderate whitewater, kayakers welcome a greater challenge and are usually found on the same rivers that offer whitewater rafting. Whitewater kayaks are maneuverable in rough water, and kayakers and duckie paddlers learn what to do if rapids tip them over. Most whitewater rafting outfitters also outfit kayak trips (*see the chapter on river rafting*). In general, on rivers, canoeing is for couples, families, and groups who want to explore quietly and camp. Kayaking is more recreational, aimed at surfing and negotiating whitewater.

Most states have rivers with flatwater ideal for canoeing; some, like Minnesota, Montana, Utah, and Maine, have rivers flowing through unusual wilderness. If you are canoeing, it pays to ask ahead what you can expect to encounter in terms of whitewater, and to take a guide if offered. (Excursions: 2 days with lodging: $300–$350, 11 days in Alaska: $2,000; Clinics: 1 day $75–$100; Outfitting (canoe and all gear): about $135–$220 per person for 2 days)

The Lewis and Clark National Historic Trail, part of the National Trails System (on land) administered by the National Park Service, follows 4,500 miles of water and land routes, some of them planned, from the Mississippi River in St. Louis to the mouth of the Columbia River in Astoria, Oregon. It took Lewis and Clark two years to accomplish this journey, and they were outfitted with presidential privilege. Some few brave souls periodically re-create that trip, or part of it, by kayak.

Professional paddler Joe Glickman recently kayaked a part of the Lewis and Clark Trail from Montana, along the Beaverhead River to the Missouri River, across North and South Dakota, and through Nebraska to St. Charles, Missouri, and the Mississippi, where he linked up with the Illinois River and kayaked to Chicago. Glickman had biked the Lewis and Clark Trail a couple of years earlier, but doing it by water gave the trip much more "historical verisimilitude," he said. In all, Glickman traveled 2,500 miles in 70 days.

For information on the trail:

> Lewis and Clark National Historic Trail, NPS, 700 Rayovac Dr., Suite 10, Madison, WI 53711

In Chicago, Glickman changed from his cozy 36-inch-wide kayak, carrying 300 pounds of gear, to an 18-inch-wide surf-ski to participate in the annual Finlandia Vodka Clean Water Challenge, from Chicago to New York. With proceeds donated to the Finlandia Clean Water Fund to preserve American waterways, the Challenge enlists competitors who race in surf-skis, or ride-on-top kayaks, 1,000 miles across three of the Great Lakes and through the Erie

Canal to the Hudson River. Warning: This is a physically demand-ing race. For more information on this and other canoe events, contact the American Canoe Association, (703) 451-0141.

New England

MAINE

Maine has moose, wilderness, and lots of water, and numerous rivers run that through dense forests and wind up at the Atlantic Ocean. The Allagash Wilderness Waterway, a collection of 100 miles of rivers and lakes that run through the wild backcountry, is a beautiful summer canoe trip. Some whitewater might require portaging.

> *Allagash Wilderness Outfitters, Box 620-L HCR 76,*
> *Greenville, ME 04441. (207) 723-6622*

Offers complete or partial outfitting and guides, and organizes 3- to 8-day trips.

This outfit offers 3- to 8-day trips on the St. Croix, Machias, and St. John rivers; will custom-design your trip.

> *Sunrise County Canoe Expeditions, Inc., Cathance Lake,*
> *Grove Post Office, ME 04638. (207) 454-7708*

Gilpatrick's offers one-week unguided trips for those with white-water experience on the Allagash, St. John and Penobscot rivers; and guided trips with on-hands learning for beginners.

> *Gilpatrick's Guide Service, P.O. Box 461, Skowhegan, ME 04976.*
> *(207) 453-6959*

VERMONT

Vermont has high peaks, warm valleys with fields of flowers, waterfalls with hidden swimming holes, covered bridges, and lots of flatwater rivers. Canoeing is calmer here, on the Winooski, White, and Lamoille. The Vermont Institute of Natural Science (VINS) provides natural history guides, with information on ecosystems, plants, and local wildlife on some trips.

Organized trips with the VINS, inn-based unguided trips, inn-to-inn 6-day trips, and custom trips.

> *Battenkill Canoe Vacations, P.O. Box 65, Historic Route 7A,*
> *Arlington, VT 05250. (800) 421-5268; (802) 362-2800*

Rents canoes, provides instruction and guides, and 1- to 2-day fishing trips.

> *Umiak Outfitters, 1880 Mountain Rd., Stowe, VT 05672.*
> *(800) 479-3380; (802) 253-2317*

An established school that offers group and private paddling instruction at all levels throughout New England.

> *Outdoor Center of New England, 10 Pleasant St.,*
> *Millers Falls, MA 01349. (413) 659-3926*

Mid-Atlantic

NEW YORK

The romantic Hudson River winds past beautiful mansions, Ichabod Crane and Rip Van Winkle country, and ends up in the Atlantic Ocean at New York City.

This center offers instruction in canoeing and kayaking, plus their own bed-and-breakfast.

> *W.I.L.D./W.A.T.E.R.S. Outdoor Center, HCR-01, Box 197-A,*
> *Warrensburg, NY 12885. (518) 494-7478*

PENNSYLVANIA

The Youghiogheny (called the Yok) is one of the premier rivers in the East for all types of watercraft. The Lower Yok has Class III and IV rapids, and is challenging for kayakers. The Middle Yok is a quiet Class I–II.

Many guided and unguided trips, including group kayak trips.

> *Laurel Highlands River Tours, P.O. Box 107, Ohiopyle, PA 15470.*
> *(800) 4-RAFTIN; (412) 329-8531*

Solid basic instruction in all phases of kayaking.

> *Whitewater Challengers Kayak School, P.O. Box 8,*
> *White Haven, PA 18661. (717) 443-9532*

South

NORTH CAROLINA

The Nahantahala River is beloved by canoeists, rafters, and kayakers. Class II and III rapids with a waterfall run through a beautiful gorge near the Great Smoky Mountains National Park.

Instruction is offered at all levels as well as guided and unguided trips on the Nahantahala.

> *Nahantahala Outdoor Center, 13077 Highway 19W,*
> *Bryson City, NC 28713-9114. (800) 232-7238 (rafting reservations);*
> *(704) 488-6737 (instruction)*

Guided canoe and kayak trips are offered at:

> *Rolling Thunder River Co., P.O. Box 88, Almond, NC 28702.*
> *(800) 344-5838; (704) 488-2030*

KENTUCKY

Among the most interesting of Kentucky's rivers is the Green River, which runs at a gentle Class II rapids through Mammoth Cave National Park, which is loaded with wildlife and caves.

> *Canoe Kentucky, 7265 Peaks Mill Rd., Frankfort, KY 40601.*
> *(800) K-CANOE-1; (507) 227-4492*

FLORIDA

For a completely different canoeing experience, try the Everglades River, or River of Grass, in Florida's southwestern corner. Here, both fresh and salt water run through tall sawgrass prairies and dense mangrove forests, filled with exotic tropical birds as well as the bald eagle; it is also home to alligators and crocodiles and the threatened Florida panther. Heat and mosquitoes prevent enjoyable summer excursions, but December and January are perfect months for exploring in a canoe. Wildlife is more easily seen in the winter.

Currently the site of the world's largest ecosystem restoration project, the Everglades, officially listed as a World Heritage Site in Danger, is in the process of recuperating from decades of dam building and agricultural and industrial pollution.

For information on camping in the park:

> *Everglades National Park, P.O. Box 279, Homestead, FL 33030.*
> *(305) 242-7700*

Maintains a limited number of boat-in campsites on wooden platforms, called *chickees.*

For guided tours:

> *North American Canoe Tours, P.O. Box 5038,*
> *Everglades City, FL 33929. (813) 695-4666*

Offers guided 1- to 7-day canoe tours; custom trips; and rents canoes for unguided trips.

Wilderness Southeast offers guided natural history tours of the entire southeastern U.S., including the Everglades. Seven-day trips include hiking in the sawgrass prairies and mangrove swamps, canoeing, exploring backcountry waterpaths, ecosystems, and wildlife, and camping.

> *Wilderness Southeast, 711 Sandtown Rd., Savannah, GA 31410-1019.*
> *(912) 897-5108*

This outfit offers 1- to several-day canoe trips, some by the light of the full moon.

> *Canoe Safari, 3020 N.W. ER 661, Arcadia, FL 33821.*
> *(813) 494-7865*

LOUISIANA

This is the Deep South—sleepy rivers overhung with Spanish moss, alligators spying on the surface of the water, armadillos scuttling away in the underbrush. Louisiana has both the largest coastal marshland refuge on the Gulf of Mexico and lots of bayous, or swamps. The Rockefeller Wildlife Refuge, 142,000 acres on the coast in southwestern Louisiana, is an excellent haven for birds and is good for fishing as well as photography.

> *Atchafalaya Basin Backwater Tours, P.O. Box 128, Gibson, LA 70356.*
> *(504) 575-2371*

Offers guided paddle tours and rents dugout canoes.
For the Rockefeller Refuge:

> *Sabine Refuge, Hwy 27 South, 3000 Main St., Hackberry, LA 70645.*
> *(318) 762-3816*

The Jean Lafitte National Park is a wildlife preserve filled with still waters and alligators. Expect to see nutria, egrets, bald eagles, deer, raccoons, and a snake or two.

> *Bayou Barn, Hwy 45, #313H, Crown Point, LA 70072.*
> *(800) TO-BAYOU; (504) 689-2663*

Owner Tony Ting runs 2-hour guided canoe tours: The guide talks, you paddle. Also rents canoes.

Midwest

NORTHERN MINNESOTA

The premier canoeing country—and the largest in the world—is in northern Minnesota. Thousands of lakes dominate forested land bridges in the Boundary Waters Canoe Area. The place where Indians encountered French fur trappers, or *voyageurs*, as the early explorers were known, is true canoe country, filled with wildlife from huge moose to tiny mink; fish, among them record-breaking walleyes, bass, and northern pike; and birds, including bald eagles and great blue herons.

Voyageurs National Park maintains a system of lakeside campsites, reachable by canoe. Because numbers are limited, reserve a place in the park well in advance of your trip.

> *Voyageurs National Park, HCR 9, Box 600,*
> *International Falls, MN 56649*

For more information on the wilderness area, contact:

> *Superior National Forest, Box 338, Duluth, MN 55801. (218) 720-5324*
> *Friends of the Boundary Waters Wilderness, 1313 Fifth St., Suite 329,*
> *Minneapolis, MN 55414. (612) 379-3835*

Numerous outfitters provide lodges, instruction, fishing licenses, and guides, as well as canoes, food, and beds. Many outfitters design custom trips, some from lodge to lodge, or in preerected tents; all encourage families and children.

For a list of Gunflint Trail Canoe Outfitters:

> Gunflint Trail Association, Gunflint Trail, Grand Marais, MN 55604

Two from that list are:

> Piragis Northwoods Co., 105 North Central Ave., Ely, MN 55731.
> (800) 223-6565
> Hungry Jack Outfitters, 434 Gunflint Trail, Grand Marais, MN 55604.
> (218) 388-2275

The Kayak and Canoe Institute is a paddling school that offers courses in whitewater and flatwater, plus guided trips.

> Kayak and Canoe Institute, University of Minnesota—Duluth,
> 121 Sports and Health Center, 10 University Dr., Duluth, MN 55812.
> (218) 726-6533

IOWA

Dubuque, Iowa, is the site of the largest annual dragon boat race, with more than 40 teams from around the world gathering to compete. Dragon-boat racing is becoming increasingly popular throughout the country, having been introduced a few years ago from the Orient. Originally part of a ceremony in memory of a leader who died in 400 B.C., and considered training for military officers, today it is a recognized recreational and competitive sport and meets are held in the spring and summer throughout the country. Winners in the New York Dragon Boat Race go to the world competition in Hong Kong.

Most dragon boats are made out of teakwood and are brightly colored, with a dragon head on the prow and a dragon tail on the stern. Each dragon boat holds twenty paddlers, a steersperson, and a drummer who sets the rhythm for the strokes. The paddles are like canoe paddles, but the stroke is different, and each paddler must catch the cadence of the lead paddler in the pattern transmitted by the drummer.

To receive information on becoming part of a dragon boat team and a list of races and events, contact:

> Deb Sawvel, American Dragon Boat Association, P.O. Box 477,
> Dubuque, IA 52001. (319) 582-5406

OKLAHOMA

Canoeing in the Oklahoma Ozark Mountains on the Illinois River can make you feel as if you were a first explorer. Part of the jurisdiction of Oklahoma Scenic Rivers Commission, the Illinois flows

70 miles with mostly flatwater, with some challenging whitewaver interruptions, through sloping hills of oak and hickory forest. Fishing is good. For a list of outfitters, ask for the *Floater's Guide* from:

> State of Oklahoma Scenic Rivers Commission, P.O. Box 292, Tahlequah, OK 74465, (800) 299-3251; (918) 456-3251

Rocky Mountains

COLORADO

> Dvorak's Kayak and Rafting Expeditions, Inc., 17921-B U.S. Hwy 285, Nathrop, CO 81236. (800) 824-3795; (719) 539-6851

A large outfit in Colorado that runs a whitewater duckie paddling school, 3 to 7 days, lectures and hands-on. Also outfits numerous trips throughout the West.

Southwest

TEXAS

Texas has a lot of quiet rivers, but one of the most scenic is the Guadalupe. Texans are big on tubing, and many outfitters will provide you with an inner tube and pick-up transportation at your landing point on a river. You can also paddle.

Guided 1-day trips; canoes or tubes.

> Rio Raft Co., P.O. Box 2036, Canyon Lake, TX 78130. (210) 964-3613

Guided canoe trips, with time for smelling Texas roses.

> Piney Woods Canoe Co., P.O. Box 1994, Kountze, TX 77625. (409) 274-5892

ARIZONA

The Grand Canyon is the largest and deepest canyon in Arizona, but several smaller canyons have quiet rivers running through them which are perfect for canoe trips. Fishing, wildlife, colorful scenery, and overwhelming cliffs (some with ancient petroglyphs) characterize Southwest canoeing.

Expeditions, Inc. runs guided kayak and canoe trips through the Grand Canyon and smaller canyons. Includes hikes and swims where possible.

> Expeditions, Inc., Route 4, Box 755, Flagstaff, AZ 86001. (602) 744-8176

For kayakers with prior experience, this organization runs a group tour in duckies through the Grand Canyon.

> Orange Torpedo Trips, Inc., P.O. Box 1111, Grants Pass, OR 97526. (503) 479-5061

Runs 1- to 6-day canoe trips through flatwater in smaller canyons. Welcomes families.

> Jerkwater Canoe Co., Inc., Box 800, Topock, AZ 86436.
> (800) 421-7803; (602) 768-7753

ARIZONA

This group outfits guided 3- to 5-day canoe trips on the Green River through Stillwater and Labyrinth Canyons.

> Moki Mac River Expeditions, Inc., P.O. Box 21242,
> Salt Lake City, Utah 84121. (800) 284-7280; (801) 268-6667

West

CALIFORNIA

California is full of rivers, especially in the north. Most of them are best for whitewater rafting, but many lakes are ideal for canoes.

All levels of instruction, plus a place to stay in northwest California.

> Otter Bar Kayak School, Box 210, Forks of Salmon, CA 96031.
> (916) 462-4772

Whitewater and flatwater courses are offered at:

> California Canoe and Kayak Schools, 8631 Folsom Blvd.,
> Sacramento, CA 95826. (800) 366-9804

Guided canoe trips on many rivers.

> Laughing Heart Adventures, P.O. Box 669, Rove Creek, CA 95573.
> (800) 541-1256; (916) 629-3516

Trowbridge Recreation offers 1- to 4-day canoe trips on the Russian River.

> Trowbridge Recreation, Inc., 20 Healdsburg Ave., Healdsburg, CA 95448.
> (707) 433-7247

OREGON

Orange Torpedo Trips runs the Rogue River in Oregon, the Klamath in northern California, and the Salmon in Idaho for groups of kayakers in (orange) duckies. Completely outfitted, with guides. Wide variety of trips.

> Orange Torpedo Trips, P.O. Box 1111, Grants Pass, OR 97526.
> (503) 479-5061

Sundance runs a 9-day basic kayak school for complete beginners, as well as programs for intermediate and advanced kayakers. Outfits trips on the Rogue and Illinois rivers in Oregon.

> Sundance Expeditions, Inc., 14894 Galice Rd, Merlin, OR 97532.
> (503) 479-8508

Alaska

CanoeAlaska provides instructors and offers guided canoe trips on the Alaska River through wilderness in the interior part of the state.

CanoeAlaska, Box 81750, Fairbanks, AK 99708. (907) 479-5183

For kayakers with experience, Nova offers weeklong trips on various Alaskan rivers.

Nova, P.O. Box 1129, Chickaloon, AK 99674. (907) 745-5753

Sourdough Outfitters outfits canoe trips for all levels of ability and desire to rough it in the wilderness. Some rivers with rapids, some that are flatwater.

Sourdough Outfitters, P.O. Box 90, Bettles, AK 99726. (907) 692-5252

Alaska Kayak outfits wilderness kayak expeditions, 1 day or longer. Also offers instruction.

Alaska Kayak, 3732 Encore Circle, Anchorage, AK 99507. (907) 349-4588

Please note: For Alaska water trips, ask your outfitter or guide about mudflats. Stay off them. They look harmless, but they have pockets of quickmud, and rescue is very difficult.

Hawaii

Paddling in Hawaii is like paddling in a jungle movie: Waterfalls careen into green pools strewn with orchids and long red-tailed birds flutter out of grottoes. There are small jungle rivers on the island of Kauai, where the waters are calm, the rapids never more than Class I, and the nature spectacular.

Kayak Kauai outfits canoe trips with or without a guide. Good for beginners and families.

Kayak Kauai, P.O. Box 508, Hanalei, HI 96714.
(800) 437-3507; (808) 826-9844

DRAGON BOATS

American Dragon Boat Racing has about fifty teams that compete in scheduled meets around the country. (*For information, see Iowa, above.*)

SWAN BOATS

Swan boats differ from dragon boats: They have a round bottom which adds to their racing speed, the rhythm is set by a whistler, and the teak bow ends in a swan's head. Glen Green, the president of the Swan Boat Racing Association, creates a team of the best paddlers from the U.S. Nationals, and that team competes in the world's only international race in Thailand.

Glen Green, 312 Duff Ave., Wenonah, NJ 08090. (609) 468-4646; (215) 595-0505, x132

OTHER SOURCES

For information on kayaking:

The American Whitewater Affiliation, P.O. Box 85, Phoenicia, NY 12464. (914) 688-5569

For more information on kayaking and canoeing, and Olympic canoeing and kayaking events:

American Canoe Association, 7432 Alban Station Blvd., Suite B-226, Springfield, VA 22150-2311. (703) 451-0141

For more information on canoeing, networking with canoe clubs, and marathon canoe racing:

U.S. Canoe Association, c/o Jim Mack, 606 Ross St., Middletown, OH 45044. (513) 422-3739

For information on noncompetitive, relaxed, recreational paddling on lakes throughout the U.S., request *Lakeside Recreation* brochures on the section of the country that is of interest to you from:

U.S. Army Corps of Engineers, Regional Brochures, CEWES-IM-MV-N, 3909 Halls Ferry Rd., Vicksburg, MS 39180-6199.

For help with booking canoeing trips nationally, contact the following nonprofit group:

Wilderness Inquiry, 1313 5th St. SE, Box 84, Minneapolis, MN 55414-1546. (612) 379-3858

For a guide to outfitters in each state, see *Paddle America* by Nick Shears (Starfish Press, Washington, D.C.; published annually).

Outdoors outfitting stores usually carry regional guides to rivers in the U.S.

Paddler and *Canoe & Kayak* magazines are full of information on outfitters and areas, plus equipment and races. *Canoe & Kayak* magazine publishes *The Complete Guide to Kayak Touring* each January.

Caving

Caving is not for the claustrophobic. Hard hats barely clear the rocky roof. *Photograph by Roger Archibald.*

The earth is full of caves—interior rock rooms connected by tunnels and corridors, where limestone drips into stalagtite sculpture, where primitive hunters painted pictures of wild game, and where Hollywood writers have dreamed up the offices of secret organizations with walls that squeeze closed.

The world's largest caves are in the United States: Mammoth Cave in Kentucky is 340 miles long, and the second longest cave system in the world rings the Black Hills of South Dakota. Cumberland Caverns in Tennessee—the part that is explored—is 28 miles long. Many large caves, such as Mammoth Cave and Carlsbad Caverns in New Mexico, are lit and open to visitors, but countless others are meant for spelunkers, or cave explorers, who enjoy rummaging around in the dark belly of the earth.

If you have never caved before, first take a tour of a commercial cave. Then join the National Speleological Society. Their 11,000 members are distributed in local chapters throughout the United States, and they can put you in touch with a responsible group so that you can learn the art and learn the area. Most of the caves in the U.S. are in the eastern and central parts of the country, and many of them are on private land. Others are on federal property, but all require permission before you enter them.

This dangerous sport emphasizes safety big-time simply because rescue is so difficult. The bottom-line rules:

- Know what you are doing before you go.
- Always go in a group of at least three people.
- Wear a headlamp and carry two backup lighting systems.

The experience of caving is unique; don't try it if you are claustrophobic. Caves are dark, cold, damp, and slippery. Voices echo or sound strangely flat. Corridors can be large or so narrow that you must crawl on your stomach. Sudden drops occur, and you must know how to rappel using a rope. Hypothermia is a real problem, as the temperature can be 30 or 40 degrees colder below ground. Flash floods are not uncommon. You can hit your head on unseen rocks; you might be breathing air polluted with the dead bodies of small animals that became trapped; you might alarm sleeping bats.

But the rewards are great. Crawling through a tiny tunnel and suddenly coming upon a great hall filled with crystals that sparkle in your lamplight, or huge limestone columns or curtains of needles, or walls filled with fossils are what make addicts of spelunkers. Some cavers map new caves or photograph what's there; advanced cavers take on caves that require rock climbing or scuba diving. Some enjoy camping in caves.

The National Speleological Society publishes a newsletter and a list of state caving clubs, sells books on caving and specific areas, and distributes safety and conservation literature. ($20 per year.)

National Speleological Society, Cave Ave., Huntsville, AL 35810.
(205) 852-1300

To make reservations to visit Mammoth Cave, write:

Mammoth Cave National Park, Mammoth Cave, KY 42259.
(502) 758-2328 or call MISTIX (800) 365-2267

CAVE CONSERVATION

Because so many caves have been abused and disfigured by vandals, many are now gated. While a federal law is pending, state laws vary in their punishment of cave vandalism. In Kentucky, it is a felony to remove anything from a cave. In some areas, caves are polluted by sewage or insecticides which run off from nearby towns and farms.

The American Cave Conservation Association is a national membership organization that works to gate caves that need protection. Located between Louisville, Kentucky, and Nashville, Tennessee, they will take you on a tour down 300 feet into the Hidden River Cave, an example of a cave that has been environmentally restored. For 50 years this cave was closed because of sewage pollution, until members of the American Cave Conservation Association worked to stem the source of pollution and returned the cave groundwater to its original purity.

American Cave Conservation Association, 131 Main and Cave Streets, P.O. Box 409, Horse Cave, KY 42749. (502) 786-1466

CAVE MAPPING

The Cave Research Foundation is a private, nonprofit organization that maps and promotes scientific research in many caves, including Mammoth Cave, which they discovered was more than 340 miles long. Advanced cavers who believe they have enough experience to map caves are encouraged to join the Cave Research Foundation on a 1- to 9-day mapping expedition at one of six sites in the U.S.

The foundation is currently engaged in mapping caves on the Buffalo National River in Arkansas; the Lava Beds in King's Canyon Karst, both in California; Carlsbad Caverns in New Mexico; Mammoth Cave Region in Kentucky; and a site in Missouri. Many veterans of cave-mapping expeditions start university careers in caving, according to foundation president Melbourne Park.

If you are an experienced caver and would like to lend a hand mapping caves, write a letter outlining your cave experience to:

Cave Research Foundation, 1541 Peabody Ave., Memphis, TN 38104. (502) 786-1466; (901) 448-5984

CAVE ARCHAEOLOGY

In the Ozarks in Missouri, 200 caves along the riverbanks of the Current and Jacks Fork hold secrets of human occupation. In a 5-year study, archaeologists hope to harvest evidence of former inhabitants, in addition to the Civil War soldiers known to have used one cave as a hospital. Contact:

> Mark J. Lynott, Midwest Regional Archaeologist, National Park Service.
> (402) 437-5392

COMMERCIAL CAVES

The National Caves Association publishes an annually updated full-color list of more than eighty-five commercial caves in the U.S. Request the free *Caves and Caverns Directory*.

> National Caves Association, 4138 Dark Hollow Rd.,
> McMinnville, TN 37110. (615) 668-3925

CAVE DIVING: *Please see SCUBA.*

OTHER SOURCES

Books: To start, the NSS recommends *Caving Basics* (Tom Rea, editor), available from the National Speleological Society (above) for $10 (members), $11 (nonmembers). Ask for a publications list.

For a guide to 200 caves open to visitors in the U.S., try *Gurnee Guide to American Caves* (softbound: $9.95), from National Caves Association Books (above).

Cooking and Food Adventures

Being guided through the chemistry of cooking with a chef is like working out with a physician: You really know what's happening. Here, students experience the delights of American Southwest cooking. *Photograph courtesy Jane Butel Cooking School, Albuquerque, New Mexico.*

Ask any chef: Cooks are among the most adventurous people around, probably because cooking is a highly competitive activity, fired by an increasingly refined palette. If fungi are any indicator of cooking's popular appeal, you have only to check out the extensive mushroom section of your local chain supermarket. Even if you're not a cook, but appreciate food that smells, looks, and tastes delicious, you can take to the kitchen for a Lucullan vacation and risk your rational self in the sensuous delights of food. (Single class: $25–$40; weekend: $180–$500.)

New England

The New England Culinary Institute offers three or four weekends a year for anyone who would like to focus on food. Each weekend has a theme—for example, seafood, organic gardening products, or Italian cooking for a third; and offers cooking classes and special meals. Because there are no age limits, this is open to interested teenagers, their parents, and even grandparents.

> New England Culinary Institute, 250 Main St.,
> Montpelier, VT 05602-9720. (802) 223-6324

The magic of what you learn to cook at a Culinary Magic 2-day seminar is in dishes that are both low-fat and sumptuously delicious. Chefs Deedie and Charlie Marble, trained in France, have produced Vermont's Best Apple Pie, according to *Yankee* magazine, and will teach you things like New England Lobster Chowder, Flaky Date Scones, and Pretty Potato Prune Pudding. The weekend package includes a 6-course dinner, a full day of cooking, and lodging in the inn, which has been the winner for three years running of Ben & Jerry's Best Inn of the Year award. Offered four times a year.

> Culinary Magic Cooking Seminars, The Governor's Inn, 86 Main St.,
> Ludlow, VT 05149. (800) 468-3766; (802) 228-8830

Vermont Offbeat offers autumn in New England and a weekend at a former dairy farm with chef Terry Blonder. You'll learn how to make low-fat, high carbohydrate dishes such as curried squash soup, chicken and artichoke heart salad, rhubarb sauce and frozen yogurt. Lots of rolling hills on the farm, autumn foliage, and hot cider.

> Vermont Offbeat, P.O. Box 4366, South Burlington, VT 05406-4366.
> (802) 863-3227

Throughout the year, this school, which trains international chefs, offers a variety of weekend cooking courses. Creating With a Chef weekends provide 2 nights of intensive cooking and eating with chefs who teach you how to prepare a variety of ethnic and American dishes.

> The College of Culinary Arts, Johnson and Wales University,
> 8 Abbott Park Place, Providence, RI 02903. (800) 343-2565, ext. 1145

Great Lakes

Near the Boundary Waters country around Lake Superior, you can hike, fish, take nature walks, *and* learn how to cook the kind of food that smells terrific when you come in from the outdoors. Chef Sally Bresnahan of the Bearskin Lodge shares her skills for a 2-day course in such things as pies, breads, and soups.

> Bearskin Lodge, 275 Gunflint Trail, Grand Marais, MN 55604-9701.
> (218) 388-2292

Southwest

People come here from all over the world to spend a week learning New Mexican Pueblo cuisine, which Butel says is based on "three C's: chilis, corn, and cumin." The course includes lacy tamales, sopaipillas, and salsas that are unique to New Mexico. Also offers weekend courses.

> Jane Butel's Southwestern Cooking School, 800 Rio Grande Blvd., Suite 14,
> Albuquerque, NM 87104. (800) 473-8226; (505) 243-2622

The Sante Fe School of Cooking offers unusual two-hour cooking classes featuring local cuisine. Cooks prepare and eat the meal, and take home the recipes. Reservations required.

> Santa Fe School of Cooking, 116 West San Francisco St.,
> Santa Fe, NM 87501. (505) 983-4511

Rocky Mountains

The chef at the Crow Canyon Archaeological Center is also an anthropologist, and his course in chili peppers stems from his interest in history as well as cuisine. His weeklong course includes other culinary items from the pueblos, which participants cook and enjoy.

> Crow Canyon Archaeological Center, 23390 County Rd. K,
> Cortez, CO 81321. (800) 422-8975

West

Take 1- to 3-day classes two times a year (November's is holiday cooking). The cuisine is French; dinners are all six-course. Cooks can stay at their French chateau bed-and-breakfast, and visit Yosemite National Park, 20 minutes north.

> Erna's Elderberry House Cooking School, P.O. Box 2413,
> Oakhurst, CA 93644. (209) 683-6800

Enjoy classes in Italian, Indian, Vietnamese, Thai, Mexican, and French cuisine, plus Cooking With Your Coat On. If you are in Bellevue with friends or family, the Everyday Gourmet staff will do the shopping, provide the linens and the place, and you and your friends can do the cooking for a dinner out.

Everyday Gourmet, 677-120th Ave. NE, #155,
Bellevue, WA 98005-3002. (206) 451-2080

FESTIVALS

Crabs

Eating crabs on Maryland's Eastern Shore is one of life's more sensuous experiences, maybe because of the mountainous residue of crabshells and legs spread out on your newspaper-tablecloth, or maybe because you get wet up to your elbows. The National Hard Crab Derby weekend inspires crab eaters to other delights, with a series of events from parades to feasts to crab races. Every Labor Day.

The National Hard Crab Derby, P.O. Box 215, Crisfield, MD 21817.
(800) 782-3913 (Chamber of Commerce)

Garlic

If you want to consume garlic, be consumed by garlic, and be surrounded by others who are fanatical about garlic, go to Gilroy, California (south of San Francisco), during the annual Gilroy Garlic Festival, the last full weekend in July. Garlic grows well there, as your nose will tell you. During the festival, you can taste garlic cooked into just about everything from shrimp scampi to ice cream and chocolate bonbons, learn how to braid garlic, watch field hands in a garlic-topping contest, and schmooze with other members of the garlic brother- and sisterhood. About 1,000 people each year enter a recipe contest from which eight finalists are chosen to cook their specialty before a jury of experts. The winner gets $1,000 and their winning recipe included in the *Gilroy Garlic Cookbook.*

Gilroy Garlic Festival Association, P.O. Box 2311, Gilroy, CA 95021.
(408) 842-1625

Aspen Food and Wine Classic

Famous chefs, such as Julia Child, give seminars and demonstrations at the Aspen Food and Wine Classic, held annually in June in Colorado. Considered to be the biggest food festival in terms of the names it attracts and the numbers of culinary people who exhibit there, this is the festival for all who want to be au courant about what they serve and are served.

Aspen Food and Wine Classic. (800) 494-6394

SPECIAL TOURS

Rocky Mountains

IDAHO

If being outdoors makes you voraciously hungry, paddle-raft the Salmon River through beautiful wooded hills with chef Phillip Costas from Kathleen's Restaurant in Stamford, Connecticut. Six days of rafting workout and six nights of such things as herb-smoked salmon, wood-grilled reggiano pizza with prosciutto and wild mushrooms, and corn/pecan rum bread. Come a week early and take Salmon River Outfitters' Wilderness Wine Tasting rafting trip, with selections from California and Pacific Northwest wineries.

> Salmon River Outfitters, P.O. Box 32, Arnold, CA 95223.
> (209) 795-4041 (for reservations)
> or
> P.O. Box 1751, McCall, ID 83638. (208) 634-4426

West

CALIFORNIA

Even France recognizes the Napa and Sonoma Valley wines. You can tour and taste by balloon, train, boat, bike, or wagon.
(*See listings under Balloons.*)

Train   The plush 1915 Pullman coaches of the Napa Valley Wine Train, with mahogany and polished-brass trim, will carry you past the St. Helena vineyards (Beaulieu, Mondavi, and others) while you dine on a four-course dinner. The 3-hour trip covers 36 miles, and serves brunch, lunch, or dinner.

> Napa Valley Wine Train, 1275 McKinstry St., Napa, CA 94559.
> (800) 522-4142

Boat   The Napa River waters the valley and empties into San Pablo Bay above San Francisco. From Napa, you can take an historic sternwheeler on an excursion through wine country that can include dinner or a champagne lunch.

> Napa Riverboat Co., 1200 Milton Rd., Napa, CA 94559.
> (707) 226-2628

Wagon   Closer to the Pacific coast and irrigated by the Russian River, the Sonoma Valley is home to numerous wineries, vineyards, and orchards. Horse-drawn wagon tours leave regularly for tours with tastings. Gourmet lunch included.

> Wine Country Wagons, P.O. Box 1069, Kenwood, CA 95452.
> (707) 833-2724

Bicycle Bicycle for 5 days past the wineries, with stops for tasting, gourmet meals, and massages at some of the country's premier
spas. Lodging is in luxurious old hotels. A support van carries
whatever bottles you buy.

> *Backroads, 1516 5th St., Suite L101, Berkeley, CA 94710-1740.*
> *(800) 462-2848; (510) 527-1555*

Request a Calendar of Events in the Napa and Sonoma valleys
from:

> *The Redwood Empire Association. (415) 543-8334*

OREGON

Oregon is famous for its pinot noirs. You can take a half-day, full-
day, or longer tour of Oregon vineyards, with gourmet picnic
lunch. You can also take an evening tour of Portland's microbreweries, which includes some sumptuous munching.

> *EcoTours of Oregon, 1906 SW Iowa St., Portland, OR 97201.*
> *(503) 245-1428*

New England

RHODE ISLAND

The East Coast has its share of wineries, as well. One of the oldest is Sakonnet Vineyards in Rhode Island, where the grapes are
nourished by fogs from the Atlantic Ocean. Once a month,
famous Rhode Island chefs give a daylong course for ten interested
amateur cooks who create a meal and enjoy it at the end of the
day.

> *Sakonnet Vineyards, 162 West Main Rd., P.O. Box 572,*
> *Little Compton, RI 02837. (401) 635-4356*

For a list of New England wineries:

> *The New England Wine Council, c/o George Mathiesen, Chairman,*
> *Chicama Vineyard, Stony Hill Rd., West Tisbury, MA 02575*

Great Lakes

MICHIGAN

Southwestern Michigan calls itself the Napa of the Midwest.
Sandy soil and the gentle Lake Michigan climate promote the
growth of European hydrids as well as American grapes. Numerous
vineyards exist. Tabor Hill Winery, the oldest to grow award-winning European-style wines, has free tastings and tours, and offers
sleigh rides and cross-country skiing.

> *Tabor Hill Winery, 185 Mt. Tabor Rd., Buchanan, MI 49107.*
> *(616) 422-1161*

Breweries

Beer is brewed throughout the United States, and state guides mention where and when you can visit local breweries.

For maps of brewery locations in California, the Pacific North-west, and the Rocky Mountains, get the catalog from:

MapLink, 25 East Mason St., Santa Barbara, CA 93101.
(805) 965-4402

Books on the subject include Steve Johnson's *On Tap: The Guide to U.S. Brewpubs* (Clemson, S.C., 1994), and Stuart A. Kallen's *Beer Here: A Traveler's Guide to American Brewpubs and Microbreweries* (Citadel Press, 1995).

OTHER SOURCES

For a list of cooking schools that sponsor vacations, read *The Guide to Cooking Schools* (Shaw Guides, 1994).

For some food festivals: Alice M. Geffen and Carole Berglie's *Food Festival* (1994).

Covered Wagon Tours

Crossing a part of the Oregon Trail, a pair of outfitters in period costume spend a moment relaxing. *Photograph courtesy Oregon Trail Wagon Train, Bayard, Nebraska.*

During the 1800s, hundreds of thousands of families risked everything they had and moved West with the hope of finding land, prosperity, and a better life for their children. Many of these pioneers traveled on the 2,000-mile Oregon Trail that ran from Independence, Missouri, to the Oregon coast. Driving cattle and ponies, they spent 4 to 6 months crossing the dusty plains and the Rocky Mountains, with their families and their possessions loaded into horse-drawn covered wagons, called prairie schooners. They cooked over fires and slept under the stars, and probably never looked upon themselves as being romantic figures who would inspire vacationers to follow their routes in the 1990s. (One night: $130–$150; six nights: $580–$675.)

NEBRASKA

Spend 1 to 6 days riding in a wooden-wheel covered wagon on Nebraska's stretch of the Oregon Trail on a tour that re-creates history. Pony Express riders occasionally accompany the wagons, with a surprise ambush by Native Americans from time to time. Learn to muzzle-load a rifle and to square dance; take a hay ride through a 1910 farm. Dinner is a chuck-wagon cookout with stew, hoecakes, spoonbread, and vinegar pudding. Sleep under the stars, in the wagon, or in a tent. This trip goes through a pass in the Scotts Bluff National Monument, part of the Wildcat Hills, strewn with wind-torn rock formations. Ruts from the original prairie schooners are still visible on the trail.

> *Oregon Trail Wagon Train, Route 2, Box 502, Bayard, NE 69334.*
> *(308) 586-1850*
> *Nebraska Tourism and Travel, (800) 228-4307;*
> *(800) 742-7595 (in Nebraska)*

WYOMING

Ride in a prairie schooner (authentic, but modified for comfort with padded seats and rubber tires) in the foothills of the Rocky Mountains, near the Tetons, on 2- to 6-day tours that travel back roads and meadows. Cowboys sing around the campfires at night.

> *Wagons West, Afton, WY 83110. (800) 447-4711; (307) 886-9693*

The Oregon Trail Wagon Train Revisited tour crosses the Sweet-water River Valley, bumps through streams, and ascends the rough Rocky Ridge to a mountain pass on an authentic 6-day historical trip. Nightly living-history programs.

> *Great Divide Tours, 336 Focht Rd., Lander, WY 82520. (800) 458-1915;*
> *(307) 332-2686*

Ride the Oregon, California, Mormon, Bridger, or Bozeman trail in a comfortable covered wagon with springs. Start in historic Casper.

> *Historic Trails Expeditions, (800) 804-RIDE; (307) 266-4868*

COLORADO

Spend 3 or 6 days riding a wagon train or saddle horse through some of southeastern Colorado's spectacular canyons. Cowboys man a chuck wagon each night, sing, and tell tall tales.

> *Kirkwell Wagon Train, American Wilderness Experience, P.O. Box 1486,*
> *Boulder, CO 80306. (800) 444-0099; (303) 444-2622*

OTHER SOURCES

For the most part the Oregon Trail from Missouri to Oregon follows state or interstate highways, and is visible (ruts in the grass) only in certain places. Nevertheless, it was used not only by covered wagons transporting families to new lives in the West, but by the Pony Express, Mormons, gold miners, and others.

For a map of the whole Oregon Trail with a self-guided tour:

Wyoming Division of Tourism, Cheyenne, WY 82002. (307) 777-7777

In Nebraska, ask for a copy of The Oregon Trail map from:

Gage County Visitors Committee, Beatrice Chamber of Commerce, Beatrice, NE 68310. (800) 755-7745; (402) 223-2338

Croquet

Taking a bead on the wicket, an intent croquet player prepares to wonk her ball. *Photograph by Roger Archibald.*

L ike orienteering and rock climbing, croquet is a game of strategy. Good chess players, able to plot and read the variables, make the best croquet players. Despite its trimmed green lawns and players dressed in white linen, sports croquet, played with heavy wooden balls, a heavy, long-handled mallet, and six narrow iron wickets, can leave losers down for the count. Like all strategic games, it's the thinking ahead that wins, and losing, though bloodless, can be devastating.

Croquet went international a few years ago, and the U.S. Croquet Association sponsors several national events throughout the year, in places like Newport, Rhode Island, and Palm Beach, and sends its best players to international competitions. Hundreds of local clubs and university teams get together more informally, but sports croquet's zingy takeoff from the nine-wicket, long-grass backyard croquet many Americans grew up with is probably in direct proportion to the USCA's current membership, of which a whopping 25 percent are millionaires.

If sun, grass, white clothes, wonked balls, and grace under pressure are your game, try a croquet school. Beginners to advanced can take intensive 3-day classes from November to April with pros at the USCA in Palm Beach Gardens. (School, 2 days, under $500.)

United States Croquet Association, 500 Avenue of the Champions, Palm Beach Gardens, FL 33418. (407) 627-3999

For a vacation where you can taste the panache and polish your game, try these resorts:

Located in the Great Smoky Mountains, the Etowah Valley Country Club offers unlimited croquet and serious competitors.

Etowah Valley Country Club, P.O. Box 2150-C, Hendersonville, NC 28793. (800) 451-8174

Located on Lana'i, the more or less empty island across from Maui, The Manele Bay Hotel offers British croquet on two lawns.

Manele Bay Hotel, Lana'i, HI 96763. (800) 223-7637

Dinosaurs
and Fossils

Paleontologists dream of uncovering a whole dinosaur skeleton, like this one in the College of Eastern Utah Museum of Paleontology, Price, Utah. *Photograph by Roger Archibald.*

Dinosaurs lived for about 160 million years (from 205 million to 65 million years ago) and evolved into hundreds of different species, from the size of birds to the size of large buildings. Some were swift runners, others lumbered along; some ate leaves, others ate each other. Many of them lived in what is today the Rocky Mountain region of the U.S., in Utah, Colorado, Montana, and Wyoming, where herds of dinosaurs have left footprints, bones impressed into sandstone rocks, and huge nests. (From free–$1,000 per week, with lodging.)

VIEWING DINOSAUR REMAINS

Reconstructed dinosaurs or their bones are scattered around the country in various museums. Good introductions to dinosaurs on the East Coast are in New York City at the American Museum of Natural History (Central Park West at 79th St., New York, NY 10024, (212) 769-5100 for hours), and in Pittsburgh at the Carnegie Museum of Natural History (4400 Forbes Ave., Pittsburgh, PA 15213, (412) 622-3243).

In fact, it was a paleontologist from the Carnegie Museum who first found evidence of dinosaurs in Utah. In the wilderness of Utah in 1908, Earl Douglass spotted the skeleton of a brontosaurus more or less completely set into a sandstone cliff. This was the first of many found in what is today the Dinosaur National Monument on the border of Utah and Colorado, 211,000 acres with the largest known Jurassic-period quarry, in an area known as the Morrison Formation. The Quarry Visitor's Center has an excellent display of some of the 350 tons of bones that have been excavated and an ongoing dig in one of its walls. Camping is available about 5 miles from the visitors' center. The park abounds in wildlife and is good for hiking.

Dinosaur National Monument, Box 210, Dinosaur, CO 81610.
(303) 374-2216

The College of Eastern Utah Prehistoric Museum is the repository for many of the more than 17,000 bones found in nearby Cleveland-Lloyd Dinosaur Quarry, considered by many paleontologists to be the richest source of dinosaur species. This is near where Utahraptor, a fast dinosaur with a wicked single hook for skewering prey, was found shortly after director Steven Spielberg created the similarly hooked velociraptor for the film *Jurassic Park*. On display are the bones of a mammoth, a giant sloth, and Al the Allosaurus pretty much as he came out of the ground, complete and very big.

CEU Prehistoric Museum, 155 Main St., Price, UT 84501.
(801) 637-5060

RAFTING THROUGH DINOSAUR COUNTRY

You can scope the canyon walls for more dinosaur bones as you whitewater raft through the Dinosaur National Monument on the Green and Yampa rivers.

Dinosaur River Expeditions, P.O. Box 3387, Park City, UT 84060.
(800) 247-6197

Offers 2- to 5-day trips in beautiful wilderness of Utah and Colorado. Class III–IV rapids.

Adrift Adventures, P.O. Box 192, Jensen, UT 84035. (800) 824-0150

Offers a 4-day "Jurassic Journey" for families with kids 5 to 12 years old. Includes Class III river rafting on the Green River, with short hikes to dinosaur country, and a visit to the museum. Camping, cooking out, and children's activities help parents vacation too.

DIGGING FOR DINOSAURS

COLORADO AND WYOMING

Paleontologists invite interested dinosaur fans to help them track down and study evidence of dinosaurs in Colorado and Wyoming. Five-day field trips (with hotel accommodations) leave through the summer; minimum age is 13. People interested in more serious dinosaur study can accompany expert Dr. Robert Bakker at a site near Medicine Bow, Wyoming; minimum age is 18.

Children 6 to 12 are invited to join their families in 5-day excursions with the Family Dino Camp in Colorado, with total focus on dinosaurs.

All of the above and more are available from:

Dinosaur Discovery Expeditions, Dinamation International Society, P.O. Box 307, 325 E. Aspen, Fruita, CO 81521. (800) 344-3466

UTAH

Volunteer diggers can join paleontologists throughout the season digging at the Utahraptor Quarry, near Price, where more than 400 bones were excavated last summer. No experience needed; volunteers will be trained on-site. Weekends or longer. Contact:

Don Burge, Director, CEU Prehistoric Museum, 155 East Main, Price, UT 84501. (801) 637-5060

MONTANA

Introductory and advanced field paleontology instruction is offered at an unusual dinosaur nesting colony in Montana, on the eastern slope of the Rocky Mountains. Here, eggs, embryos, nests, and bones have been found. Programs include 1- and 2-week sessions; lodging is in tepees. All ages above 15 are welcome.

Museum of the Rockies, Montana State University, Bozeman, MT 59717-0272. (406) 994-2251

Baby dinosaurs also turn up in abundance in central Montana at the Judith River Formation, along with lots of other turtle, fish, and mammal fossils. Why dinosaurs preferred to nest in this area of the continent is one of the questions the lead paleontologist will try to answer. The 2-week program includes instruction, lectures, daily hikes; lodging is in a ranch.

> *University Research Expeditions Program*
> *University of California, Berkeley, CA 94720. (510) 642-6586*

OTHER DINOSAUR SITES

UTAH

Dinosaurland, in northern Utah, includes the Dinosaur Quarry with more than 2,000 dinosaur bones on display, and numerous opportunities for hiking, horseback riding, and camping. For information on the area in general:

> *Dinosaurland Travel Board, 25 East Main, Vernal, UT 84078.*
> *(800) 477-5558; (801) 789-6932*

TEXAS

Tyrannosaurus rex was only one of many dinosaurs that walked in Texas and left tracks. See them at:

> *Dinosaur Valley State Park, P.O. Box 396, Glen Rose, TX 76043.*
> *(817) 897-4588*

OTHER FOSSILS

Trilobites

UTAH

In a private quarry, interested fossil hunters are invited to dig out some of the thousands of trilobites embedded in the rock. Worm tracks, sponges, brachiopods, and other fossils from the former ocean that covered this part of the U.S. are also present. Instruction and assistance are given in half- and full-day digs. Minimum age is 8. (Approximately, $20 for 4 hours.)

> *U-Dig Fossils, P.O. Box 1113, Delta, UT 84624. (801) 864-3638*

Insects

COLORADO

Volcanic ash preserved Oligocene insects, seeds, leaves, and plants, as well as birds and mammals in Florissant, Colorado, the world's largest fossil-insect site. Paleoentomologists come from around the world to see some of the 80,000 specimens. Hiking and camping are available.

Florissant Fossil Beds National Monument, Box 185,
Florissant, CO 80816. (303) 748-3253

Rhinos and Camels

NEBRASKA

It's hard to believe rhinoceroses and camels once lived in Nebraska. Their 20-million-year-old bones are easy to view at the Agate Fossil Beds National Monument.

Agate Fossil Beds National Monument, c/o Scotts Bluff National Monument,
Box 27, Gering, NE 69341. (308) 668-2211

Woolly Mammoths

SOUTH DAKOTA

Later than dinosaurs, rhinos, and oceanic fossils, huge woolly mammoths roamed North America until a few thousand years ago, where they were hunted by small groups of early Americans. One mammoth was a good catch: It could provide a family of ten with more calories than a whole season's corn crop, according to archaeologist Richard MacNeish, who found the first evidence of farming in the Southwest.

Unlike later hunters on horseback with bows and arrows, who chased bison, early Americans hunted mammoths on foot, often wounding and tracking them until the game fell.

At a site in South Dakota, huge numbers of woolly mammoths appear to have fallen into a sink hole about 20,000 years ago. Today you can visit the dig and see what paleontologists have revealed, which to date is fifty whole mammoths, and close to 1,000 bones and tusks.

The Mammoth Site, Highway 18, Hot Springs, SD.
(800) 325-6991 (for hours); (605) 745-6017

You can join a paleontologist on a 2-week excavation. Lodging is in a dormitory. No experience is needed.

Earthwatch, P.O. Box 403, Watertown, MA 02272.
(800) 338-4797; (617) 926-8200

CALIFORNIA

Located more or less in the center of Los Angeles, the La Brea Tar Pits trapped mammoths that did not look where they were going, and some of the predators that followed them 40,000 years ago.

*George C. Page Museum of La Brea Discoveries, 5801 Wilshire Blvd.,
Los Angeles, CA 90036. (213) 936-2230*

OTHER SOURCES

Recommended books are *Dinosaur Safari Guide*, by Vincenzo Costa
(Voyageur Press, 1994), an excellent compendium of dinosaur
sites; *Digging Dinosaurs*, by John R. Horner and James Gorman
(Workman, 1988), which describes the dinosaur nesting site in
Montana; and *The Complete T. rex*, by John R. Horner and Don
Lessem (Simon & Schuster, 1993).

For a video aimed at kids (but also educative for adults) that
gives safety advice and proper instruction on fossil digging as well
as a sense of what a dig is like, you can order *I Dig Fossils* for
$23.90 (includes postage) from:

Mazon Productions, Box 2427, Northbrook, IL 60065-2427.
(800) 332-4344

Dogsledding

An eight-dog speed team seen galloping along a mountain trail.
Sprint-trained dogs, being similar to sprint-trained human
runners, gallop the entire length of the trail, which is usually
one mile per dog on the team. *Photograph by Michelle Cusick.*
Photograph and caption courtesy of the International Sled Dog Racing

Dogsledding is one of those sports, along with canoeing and horse-
packing, that once had the purely functional purpose of transporting goods and people over terrain not otherwise navigable.
"Mush," the command that moves huskies to run, is a corruption
of the French *marche*, or "walk," a remnant of French fur trappers
who carried their goods from the wilderness to trade centers.

Today dogsledding is a sport that depends on the breeding, training, and care of dogs, the refined design of sleds, and the physical fitness of the drivers (or mushers, formerly *marcheurs*). Billed as The Last Great Race on Earth, the Iditarod Trail Sled Dog Race is an annual event in March when sleds and dogs race more than a thousand miles from Anchorage to Nome in Alaska. Because the trip takes 2 to 3 weeks to complete, enthusiasts can follow it by flying to stops along the trail.

If you like dogs and snow, there is no better experience than taking part in a dogsledding expedition. Most take place in Alaska, where dogsledding is the state's official sport. Several-day trips take amateur mushers into the backcountry, where they camp out or sleep in lodges and participate in the care and feeding of the huskies. Since dogsledding is a winter sport and Alaska can be bitterly cold, many outfitters provide the extreme-cold-weather gear you will need. And since the dogs can pick up speed, you can expect to race across the snow at about 6–10 miles an hour. You should be in fairly good shape to accommodate the sudden turns your sled might take and to be able to give your dogs a hand and push the sled up a slippery hill. ($200–$250 per day.)

If you are really in for an adventure, try *skijoring*. This sport leaves the sled behind, and with a rope around the waist, the skier gets pulled by the dogs.

For partial lists of outfitters, ask for the booklet *Alaska, the Winter Destination*, from:

> *Alaska Tourism Marketing Council, Dept. 208, P.O. Box 110801, Juneau, AK 99811-0801. (907) 465-2010*

You may also want to request the *Anchorage Visitors Guide*, from:

> *Anchorage Convention and Visitors Bureau, 1600 A St., Suite 200, Anchorage, AK 99501-5162*

Some expeditions are based from a lodge, which allows you to go out for as little as a half-day if you choose, just to get the feeling for dogsledding.

> *Alaska Wildland Adventures, P.O. Box 389, Girdwood, AK 99587. (800) 334-8730; (907) 783-2928*

One- to 5-day tours are possible with:

> *Adventures and Delights, 414 "K" St., Anchorage, AK 99501. (800) 288-3134*

In Denali National Park, you can combine cross-country and downhill skiing with 3 days of dogsledding and a spot at the start of the Iditarod in Anchorage. Eight days. Organized by:

> *CampAlaska Tours, P.O. Box 872247, Wasilla, AK 99687. (800) 376-9438*

You can dogsled across a glacier and camp beneath northern lights. Expeditions offered by:

> *Ultima Thule Outfitters, 3815 Apollo Dr., Anchorage, AK 99504.*
> *(907) 333-2073; (907) 276-8282*

In March the following company offers a week of instruction and practice in dogsledding, a place at the start of the Iditarod in Anchorage, a chance to try skijoring, and bush flights to the interior of Alaska to view the progress of the race:

> *Nature Encounters, Ltd., 8438 Melrose Pl., Los Angeles, CA 90069.*
> *(213) 852-1100*

Dogsledding is not confined to Alaska. Forty of the fifty states have some kind of winter dogsledding activity, and those states without snow have wheeled rigs pulled by dogs.

MAINE

Several outfitters offer rides and instruction in driving.

> *Down East Sled Dog Club, Nooksack Kennel, RFD No. 1 Box 3261,*
> *Mechanic Falls, ME 04256. (207) 539-4324*
> *Mahoosuc Guide Service, Polly Mahoney and Kevin Slater, Bear River Rd.,*
> *Newry, ME 04261. (207) 824-2073*

MINNESOTA

In northern Minnesota, in the Boundary Waters Canoe Area, many summer lake outfitters turn to cross-country skiing and dogsledding when the snow falls.

Gunflint Northwoods outfits dogsled rides lasting from 1 hour to several days.

> *Gunflint Northwoods Outfitters, 750 Gunflint Trail,*
> *Grand Marais, MN 55604. (800) 362-5251; (218) 388-2296*

This college offers two days of instruction, plus lectures on the history and significance of the dogs. Lodging provided.

> *Vermilion Community College, Environmental Studies,*
> *1900 East Camp St., Ely, MN 55731. (800) ELY-WOLF*

The Wilderness Inquiry offers a 6-day yurt-to-yurt dogsled expedition in remote Superior National Forest. Yurts are heated circular tents.

> *Wilderness Inquiry, Inc., 13133 Fifth St., SE, Box 84,*
> *Minneapolis, MN 55414-1546. (800) 728-0819; (612) 379-3858*

OTHER SOURCES

For more information of the sport in general and on contacting local clubs, contact:

International Sled Dog Racing Association, Inc., P.O. Box 446, Nordman, ID 83848-0445. (208) 443-3153

Friends of Northern Dogs offers a nationwide placement service for retired former sled dogs. Also provides information to owners of northern dogs, such as huskies.

Friends of Northern Dogs Foundation, Headquarters, P.O. Box 767, Elkhorn, WI 53121-0767. (414) 642-7541

Farm Vacations

Farm Day at the New
Hampshire Farm Museum
allows families to experience
farm activities from the 1900s,
including dowsing with twigs.
*Photograph courtesy New
Hampshire Farm Museum,
Milton, New Hampshire.*

For anyone who has ever wanted to get up at dawn, haul hay to the horses, milk the cows, feed the chickens, and collect eggs for breakfast, a few farms open their doors to tourists for a modified down-on-the farm experience. Instead of being workers, guests are more likely to visit farm animals and the fields, be taken on hayrides, and encouraged to go horseback riding in the woods or canoeing on the local river. Stays usually include meals and lodging.

Some working fruit tree farms open their doors in season for harvest picking.

NEW HAMPSHIRE

The New Hampshire Farm Museum is a working 1890s farm, with a museum and special events designed to introduce people of all ages to sustainable agriculture. Demonstrations of dowsing, spinning angora wool straight from the rabbit, and feeding farm animals.

> *The New Hampshire Farm Museum, Inc., Rte. 125, Plummer's Ridge, P.O. Box 644, Milton, NH 03851. (603) 652-7840*

WISCONSIN

Goats, sheep, ducks, and chickens live at Our Little Country Place, a "mini-farm," where guests can stay in the main farmhouse. Cross-country ski, hike, or bike, or visit a bison farm nearby.

> *Our Little Country Place, W6219 Mulberry Lane, Medford, WI 54451. (715) 748-3343*

Trillium is an 85-acre diversified farm that grows organic crops, raises livestock, and maintains a hardwood forest. Horseback ride in the woods, canoe on the nearby Mississippi, or read a book in front of the stone fireplace.

> *Trillium, Route 2, Box 121, La Farge, WI 54639. (608) 625-2252*

For a good list of farm vacations in Wisconsin, request a *Recreation Guide* from the Wisconsin Division of Tourism, (800) 432-TRIP.

MICHIGAN

Southwestern Michigan grows fruits in abundance, and visitors are invited to pick their own strawberries, peaches, apples, plums, nectarines, and pears in season. Tree-Mendus Fruit, a 600-acre fruit farm, is open June to Labor Day, allows you to pick your own and, in July, to participate in the Cherry Pit Spit, with a prize to the one who spits a pit the farthest.

> *Tree-Mendus Fruit, 9351 East Eureka Rd., Eau Claire, MI 49111. (616) 782-7101*

For maps and information on harvest times in southwestern Michigan, contact:

> *Southwest Michigan Tourist Council, Dept. GG, 2300 Pipestone Rd., Benton Harbor, MI 49022. (616) 925-6301*

LOUISIANA

Louisiana raises fish, alligators and turtles, in addition to crops. Ask for information on the aquaculture farm visits. On working farms that raise sugarcane, pecans, hot peppers, and tobacco (to name a few), visitors can help in the harvest, stay nearby. Contact:

> *Louisiana Dept. of Agriculture and Forestry, Office of Marketing, P.O. Box 3334, Baton Rouge, LA 70821-3334. (504) 922-1277*

MONTANA

The Vacation Farm raises berries and vegetables, but it's less of a farm and more like visiting Grandma's, or going home, if you grew up in the country or wished you had. Located near Montana's beautiful Flathead Lake, this large house has a pool, croquet lawn, cross-country ski trails, and the use of a boat for the lake if you stay for a week or more.

Vacation Farm, Inc., 566 Creston Rd., Kalispell, MT 59901.
(800) 882-8217; (406) 756-8217

Father-and-Son Adventures

A father and son explore the islands off the coast of Maine in their sea kayak. *Photograph courtesy Indian Island Kayak Company, Camden, Maine.*

Fathers and sons often feel they "don't get no respect" from each other. Sometimes facing challenging wilderness experiences can open up new avenues of understanding and communication. For this reason, some outfitters provide expeditions exclusively for fathers and sons. Who brings whom is up to you. ($165–$250 per person; per day.)

The Green River, which runs through Colorado and Utah, has some of the best rapids in the West, but has also been called, by *Canoe* magazine, "some of the best flatwater on mother earth." Onshore/Offshore Explorations offers a 9-day trip in August for fathers and sons of all ages, guided by a father-and-son team. A mountain hike is followed by canoeing through canyons, with riverbank camping and hikes through little-visited side canyons.

Onshore/Offshore Explorations, P.O. Box 3032, Flagstaff, AZ 86003.
(800) 947-4673

Fathers and sons of any age can spend time together camping and hiking in the hills and backcountry around the Red Rocks in Sedona, Arizona. Several 4-day trips leave from June to September, led by Dr. Ken Byers, a social behaviorist who specializes in men's studies. The dynamics of male relationships in the wilderness allow participants to connect and grow.

Journeys Together, 172-A Langton St., San Francisco, CA 94103.
La Mesa, CA 91944. (415) 487-0217

Fathers and sons (or daughters) are welcome on this weekend kayak expedition around Father's Day in June. Owner Jennifer Hahn will take you to see seals, eagles, and otters (*elakah* means sea otter in Chinook), teach you some ocean navigation, and tell you which seaweeds are edible. No experience necessary. Minimum age is 12.

Elakah! Kayak Tours, P.O. Box 4092, Bellingham, WA 98227.
(206) 734-7270

Fishing

Waist deep in the Madison River in Yellowstone National Park,
an angler casts his fly across the calm water.
Photograph by Roger Archibald.

All fishing is an adventure. First there is the tug on the line, what naturalist and author Peter Mathiessen calls "the message from the center of the earth." Then there is the thrill of seeing what you caught, which is like unwrapping a present.

Bass, salmon, and trout abound in American lakes and rivers; halibut of mythical proportions live in the Alaskan ocean; tuna and king salmon haunt the California coast; marlin and sailfish play off Florida; and striped bass, bluefin tuna, and schools of bluefish ride the Northeast.

But several species are disappearing because of pollution and commercial overfishing. Many deep-sea anglers remember the day when you might see four or five blue marlin in one afternoon; now you have to search far and wide for one.

Much sport fishing these days is *catch-and-release*: You get the thrill of the fight, and the fish gets to live. After the fish is netted, the angler gingerly pulls out the hook, which has just enough of a barb to catch the fish, but not tear the flesh. If you catch one that takes your breath away, the guide will take a picture of you smiling with the fish against your chest. Then you put it back.

In most states you will need a license to fish. If you hire the services of a guide or an outfitter, your license is included in the price. Licenses are usually limited to a couple of days and can be renewed.

Most state tourism offices will provide information on fishing. Some have fishing hotlines. (Lessons: 3 days: $500–$650; With boat and guide: $125–$300 per day; 7 days, Alaska: $2,300–$4,500.)

FRESHWATER

The mystique of fly fishing was captured in the scenes of fishing on Montana's Blackfoot River in *A River Runs through It*: the sun, the rushing river, the whip of the rod and the floating of the yards and yards of the threadlike line, plus the continuous casting to make sure the fly is "presented" to the fish in the most seductive way. Fly anglers have one objective—to outsmart the fish. The fish, some of them big bulls, sit lazily on the bottom summer and winter, rising up occasionally to snap an insect from the surface of the water, which the angler hopes is his or hers. Experienced guides say it becomes almost spiritual the way you begin to sense where the fish are and how to make the perfect, effortless cast.

To do it right, take lessons from a friend, a guide, or a school.

New England

VERMONT

Orvis offers 2-1/2-day fly-fishing schools in Manchester, Vermont and Evergreen, Colorado. Also offers weekend salt water fly-fishing courses in New England. This is just a sampling of what they offer new and seasoned anglers: They've been around since 1856.

Orvis Services, Rte. 7A, Manchester, VT 05254. (800) 235-9763

MAINE

Known for its rugged ocean coastline, Maine has abundant rivers with smallmouth bass and brown trout. You choose where you want to go; a Maine fishing guide will supply the rest.

Maine Sport Outfitters, P.O. Box 956, Route One, Rockport, ME 04856. (800) 722-0826; (800) 244-8799 (in Maine); (207) 236-8797

For a list of Maine guides:

> *Maine Professional Guides Association, P.O. Box 159, Orono, ME 04473.
> (207) 785-2061*

Mid-Atlantic

NEW YORK

Lake Ontario and the Niagara River are full of trout and chinook salmon. For information on fishing there, get a free *Oswego County Fishing Kit* from:

> *Oswego County Dept. of Promotion and Tourism, 46 East Bridge St.,
> Oswego, NY 13126*

WEST VIRGINIA

New River Scenic Whitewater Tours is one of many whitewater rafting outfitters on the New River to offer combo rafting-fishing trips. Two days Upper and Lower New, fishing for redeye and smallmouth bass, and camping out. Anglers "are expected to paddle when necessary" on some muscle-making rapids. Cookouts on the banks include pig roast or vegetarian stir-fry, for which they are famous.

> *New River Scenic Whitewater Tours, Inc., P.O. Box 637, Hinton Bypass,
> Hinton, WV 25951. (800) 292-0880; (304) 466-2288*

Great Lakes

WISCONSIN

Wisconsin has more than 450 miles of shoreline on Lake Michigan and Lake Superior, where the fish are big and the fight is like deep-sea fishing. For a list of charter boat guides, get a copy of *Recreation Guide* from the Wisconsin Division of Tourism, (800) 432-TRIP.

Note: Fishermen in the Great Lakes as well as in some of their tributaries are warned that they will encounter zebra mussels, tiny creatures that cling to boat bottoms and motors and multiply faster than space aliens. Rinse your boat and engine cooling system with hot water, and check your lures too. For information on how to deal with boats and mussels, ask for Publication FS-054 from:

> *Ohio Sea Grant College Program, The Ohio State University,
> 1314 Kinnear Rd., Columbus, OH 43212-1194. (614) 292-8949*

MINNESOTA

In the Boundary Waters Wilderness, the largest collection of lakes in the world, fish from a boat or from the dock for lake trout, guaranteed to be at least 3 pounds. The Gunflint Lodge provides boats, gear and lodging, and invites the whole family to fish.

> Gunflint Lodge, 750 Gunflint Trail, Grand Marais, MN 55604.
> (800) 328-3325; (218) 388-9429

Rocky Mountains

In any river in the Rocky Mountain West, Off the Beaten Path will design and execute every detail for your personal itinerary. If you would like to combine fly fishing with another activity, simply tell them, give them the dates of your travel, what level of comfort you like, what kind of rivers you like and the fish you like to catch: they do the rest.

> Off the Beaten Path, 109 East Main Street, Bozeman, MT 59715.
> (406) 586-1311

MONTANA

When Montana suffers from summer drought, it asks anglers to lay off for a while. But when the rivers are high, Montana rivals Alaska as a premier place to fish for brown, cutthroat, brook, rainbow, bull, and lake trout.

Near Yellowstone National Park, this longtime school and gear shop gives instruction, gear, and both wading and float trips.

> George Anderson's Yellowstone Angler, 14 Bighorn Dr.,
> Livingston, MT 59047. (406) 222-7130

Fish and raft on the North and Middle Forks of the Flathead River through Glacier National Park with experienced guides who know the territory. Custom trips arranged around your needs.

> Montana Raft Company and Glacier Wilderness Guides,
> Box 535, West Glacier, MT 59936. (800) 521-RAFT;
> (406) 888-5466

In Montana many anglers come from around the world to fish the Bighole River, as close to Eden's river as you can get. For instruction, gear, plus lodging and good food. Near Butte.

> The Complete Fly Fisher, P.O. Box 127, Wise River, MT 59762.
> (406) 832-3175

On the Blackfoot, Bighole, Clark Fork, and other rivers. Offers guides and gear in float, wade, and float tube fishing expeditions from a half day to 5 days.

> Streamside Anglers, 317 South Orange, Missoula, MT 59801.
> (800) XL CATCH; (406) 728-1085

WYOMING

Jack Dennis Fishing Trips provides guides, instruction, and gear for a day or longer on the Snake River. Also gives a 2-hour how-to flycast seminar on a pond on a private golf course.

Jack Dennis Fishing Trips, Jackson WY. (307) 733-3270

West

CALIFORNIA

The Fly Shop offers a free whole-day seminar on fly fishing, with lectures and practice casting on a lawn. Then move on to fishing with a guide on a river or a stream in a drift boat or in waders. This major mail order company runs an excellent school that includes fly knot tying in its basic course. Also offers special clinics throughout the year in such subjects as bass fishing, and a 6-week course in fly-tying. The Fly Shop's travel service will set you up with a fishing expedition anywhere in the world.

The Fly Shop, 4140 Churn Creek Rd., Redding, CA 96002.
(800) 669-3474; (916) 222-3555

OREGON

Rogue Wilderness, Inc., will introduce you to challenging white-water and steelhead salmon from a drift boat on the Rogue River. All-year 3- or 4-day trips, camp or lodge based.

Rogue Wilderness, Inc., P.O. Box 1647, Grants Pass, OR 97526.
(800) 336-1647; (503) 479-9554

Alaska

It's hard to know what fishermen did before Alaska. Now outfitters abound. Some offer heli-fishing and luxury lodges where your catch is frozen; others will drive you in the pickup to the best secret spot in the state.

King salmon run May, June, and July; coho salmon, August, September, and October; red salmon, June to August; halibut, May through September; grayling, char, and rainbow, all year.

Anglers have a daily allowance of what, how many, and what size fish they can keep.

Float trips on remote rivers with a wildlife biologist will take you to king salmon, sockeye, red, coho salmon, rainbow trout, grayling, and northern pike at the best seasons. Guided 5- to 7-day trips, or custom trips.

Eruk's Wilderness Float Tours, 12720 Lupine Rd., Anchorage, AK 99516.
(907) 345-7678

Katmai National Park is one of the premier spots for king salmon. Sportfishing tours provides guides, floats, gear, and base at one of several lodges.

> *Angler's Paradise Lodges, Katmailand, Inc., 4700 Aircraft Dr.,*
> *Anchorage, AK 99502. (800) 544-0551;*
> *(907) 243-5448*

Kniktuk runs "affordable Alaska" tent trips (wood floors, hot showers) for king, red, and silver salmon.

> *Kniktuk Outfitters, Inc., P.O. Box 882, Delta Jct., AK 99737.*
> *(907) 895-5285*

Located at the head of the Kenai River, where the world's record king salmon, at 97, pounds was caught in 1985, Osprey offers 1- to 7-day trips, provides gear and lodging and meals.

> *Osprey Alaska, P.O. Box 504, Cooper Landing, AK 99572 (summer).*
> *(800) 533-5364*

For a list of outfitters in Alaska:

> *Alaska Tourism Marketing Council, P.O. Box 110801,*
> *Juneau, AK 99811-0801. (907) 465-2010*

SALTWATER

From almost any point on the American coasts, saltwater fishermen surf-cast or fish from piers with baited lines. Check at local bait or gear shops. Some areas have daily fishing hot lines, such as the Outer Banks of North Carolina, (800) 446-6262.

Light-tackle fishing from the shore or from a boat, which is casting with a fly rod for shallow-water fish like bonefish, gives a deep-sea-fight feeling.

To fish in deeper, or blue, water takes planning. If you are after migrating fish, like rockfish or bluefish, how can you tell where they are? Reading weather patterns, knowing where to anchor, which are the best reels and lures, take experience. It pays to take a guide with a boat and the necessary gear if you're not 100 percent sure of what you're doing. Charter boat captains know the area and fish habits, and carry the necessary gear.

NORTH CAROLINA

In September the waters off Cape Hatteras are unrivaled for the number of species that pass each other when the south-flowing Labrador current meets the north-flowing Gulf Stream.

Leave at midnight Saturday and come back to port by 10 Sunday night. This 22-hour fishing marathon offered year round goes after bottom fish. Bring a sleeping bag to catch some z's aboard.

Carolina Princess, P.O. Box 1663, Morehead City, NC 28557.
(800) 682-3456; (919) 726-5479

FLORIDA

Fishing in Florida means blue water off the East Coast and the Keys, and shallower, tropical fishing in the Keys and the Tortugas.

The Keys are Hemingway country: man against fish and the love of the fight of the true sportsperson. Custom trips for bonefish, sailfish, permit, and tarpon off the Keys or in saltwater flats, where anglers fly-fish from a skiff and still catch 100-pound tarpon.

Cutting Loose Expeditions, P.O. Box 447, Winter Park, FL 32790-0447.
(407) 629-4700

The Yankee fleet runs 2-day fishing safaris to the Dry Tortugas for grouper, snapper, kings, and mackeral. Leaves every Tuesday and Friday at 11 P.M. from Stock Island.

The Yankee Fleet, P.O. Box 5903, Key West, FL 33040.
(800) 634-0939; (305) 294-7009

Anglers fish the ocean in deep-water excursion boats or surf cast from the beach, as this pair in Cocoa, Florida. *Photograph by Roger Archibald.*

Twenty-six backcountry guides stand ready to take you light-tackle fishing for bonefish and tarpon on the ocean or in the Everglades.

Bud N' Marys Marina, P.O. Box 628, Islamorada, FL 33036.
(305) 664-2461

ALABAMA

Capt. Rick Burns runs daily trips into the Gulf of Mexico for grouper and snapper, and father into blue waters for wahoo, dolphin, and marlin.

Capt. Rick Burns, Orange Beach, AL. (205) 981-3252

LOUISIANA

Venice runs daily trips 5:30 A.M. to 5:30 P.M. into the Gulf of Mexico for snapper, and offshore to the fish around the oil rigs—tarpon, marlin, and tuna.

Venice Marina, Inc., Aw Heck Charter Boat, P.O. Box 990,
Venice, LA 70091. (504) 534-9357

HAWAII

It doesn't take long to get to blue water off Kona, and this fast new boat accommodates lure and live-bait anglers, as well as fly fishermen after spearfish, tuna, and marlin. The fly tackle aboard is heavy-duty and able to take 150- to 200-pound fish. Half- and full-day excursions, year round.

Capt. Tom McNey, No Strings II, P.O. Box 4239,
Kailua, Kona, HI 96475. (800) 797-3474; (808) 329-6267

ANYWHERE

Name the place and the fish you would like to chase, and Fishing International will book your air, expedition, and hotel: (800) 950-4242.

FISHING FOR YOUR DINNER

If you want to play Robinson Crusoe, try it on a barren big barrier beach on Ossabaw Island in Georgia. Take your sleeping bag and spend 4 days roughing it. For dinner, run a crabline, learn how to pull a seine, and throw a cast net. Cook your catch on the beach. If you want to stay up and watch the moon, you will probably also see loggerhead turtles as they lumber out of the ocean, dig a hole, and lay their eggs, before slipping back into the sea.

Wilderness Southeast, 711 Sandtown Rd., Savannah, GA 31410-1019.
(912) 897-5108

ICE FISHING

Only the hardy need apply. Serious ice fishers cut a hole in the ice and set up a shelter where they can build a fire after they have slipped in a line hung from a rod that will twitch but not get pulled in when the fish strikes. No fights here: The snagged fish is simply hauled up. Most states have rules governing the size of the hole in the ice, how long your hut can stay up and how it should be identified, fish size and number limitations, as well as advice on how to stay out of the water.

Great Lakes

Walleye, northern pike, yellow perch, and bluegill are ready to be caught under the ice on the Great Lakes and surrounding rivers. Ice fishing is productive here: in Wisconsin it accounts for 21 percent of the annual catch, but only 13 percent of fishing activity. You will need a shelter, which you can rent, and a safe way of getting your gear to the center of the ice, which can be a toboggan. For rules, regulations, advice on gear, and a general how-to, get a copy of *Ice Fishing*, by Warren Downs, from:

> *University of Wisconsin Sea Grant Institute, 1800 University Ave.,*
> *Madison, WI 53705. (608) 262-0645*

Alaska

Northern lights and ice fishing are some of the attractions in this resort located in Wrangell/St. Elias National Park. They will fly you to lakes where the ice is several feet thick. A warm lodge with a roaring fire guaranteed after dark.

> *Ultima Thule Outfitters, 3815 Apollo Dr., Anchorage, AK 99504.*
> *(907) 333-2073*

SPEARFISHING

This has been called one of the most inefficient ways to fish: The average underwater catch per free-dive hour is less than 3 fish. But the sport uses all of your talents—holding your breath in a dive, you have to understand your equipment, your locale, and the fish you target. According to diver Bob Harding, "It's the satisfaction of an approach so perfect and a shot so accurate that death has no violence." Competitions are held regularly throughout the U.S. in dive clubs in lakes and the oceans. The caught fish are given to charity. *Note:* Spearfishing is outlawed in some areas. For information:

Underwater Society of America, Free Diving Committee,
Michael Montanez, 1452 Kooser Rd., San Jose, CA 95118.
(408) 265-5643

FISH WATCHING

Some premier aquariums offer fish from all water temperatures, all depths, and all parts of the oceanic world. Some have participatory tidal pools.

MASSACHUSETTS

The New England Aquarium has numerous exhibits on local Atlantic tidal ecosystems, and sends scientists on its research vessel with visitors to whale watch for the day off Stellwegen Bank. General information: (617) 973-5200. Whale watch trips (May to October): (617) 973-5277.

MARYLAND

The major attraction of the National Aquarium of Baltimore is its Marine Mammal Pavillion, but it also has both freshwater and saltwater creatures on seven levels for viewing. (410) 576-3800.

FLORIDA

Epcot's Living Seas Pavillion is a first-class way to see a coral reef, ocean ecosystems, huge tropical fish in a 4-fathom tank, a history of underwater exploration, a model of *Nautilus*, from the Hollywood version of *20,000 Leagues Under the Sea*, and the immersible robot, Jason. (904) 824-4321.

LOUISIANA

New Orleans is the home to the new Aquarium of the Americas, devoted to marine life in the western hemisphere, with rainforest, reef, and river environments. (504) 861-2537.

CALIFORNIA

Monterey Bay Aquarium, located in a major marine research station, benefits from the abundant migratory and resident sealife in Monterey. A huge fish tank, the Great Tide Pool, and a center to care for rescued sea otters make this a premier aquarium. (408) 648-4888.

FISH CONSERVATION

For information on fish conservation:

> National Audubon Society, Living Ocean Program, 550 South Bay Ave.,
> Islip, NY 11751
> Fisheries Conservation Program, Center for Marine Conservation, 1725
> DeSales St., NW, Washington, DC 20036. (202) 429-5609

OTHER SOURCES

A networking membership organization, the North American Fishing Club publishes *North American Fisherman* and sponsors Trade-a-Trip, in which a member in Maryland, for example, can trade smallmouth bass fishing in Maryland for trout fishing in Pennsylvania.

> North American Fishing Club, P.O. Box 3403, Minnetonka, MN 55343.
> (612) 936-9449

The Federation of Fly Fishers is an international nonprofit membership organization that seeks to cultivate the art, science, and sport of fly fishing as the most natural form of angling. Publishes magazine *FFF Quill.*

> Federation of Fly Fishers, P.O. Box 1595, Bozeman, MT 59771.
> (406) 585-7592

The largest fishing organization of its kind, the Bass Anglers Sportsmen Society publishes *Bass Master* magazine, has clubs around the country, and sponsors tournaments.

> Bass Anglers Sportsmen Society, P.O. Box 17900,
> Montgomery, AL 36141. (205) 272-9530

Recommended reading: Robert Gartner's *The National Parks Fishing Guide* (Globe Pequot, 1990), a complete list of where and how to fish in 50 states.

The Grand Canyon

Hiking up the steep and high Angel Trail in the Grand Canyon
looks easier than it is.

"**L**eave it as it is. You cannot improve upon it." So said President
Teddy Roosevelt when the Grand Canyon became a national
monument in 1908.

Getting your mind around the Grand Canyon can be a real
challenge. How do you relate to something as stupendous, humon-
gous, and breathtakingly beautiful as this? "I never knew what
awe-inspiring meant until I saw the fractured light on the walls of
the Grand Canyon," said Jo-Jo Salami, who helicoptered over the
canyon from Las Vegas just before sunset.

Native Americans called it *kaibab*, an inside-out mountain. Cut
through by the emerald Colorado River, the Grand Canyon is 10
miles across at its widest point, 1 mile of rust-and-lavender rocks
deep, 217 miles long, and almost 2 billion years old. After you've

stood on the South Rim and snapped pictures for half an hour, you might be ready for some greater involvement.

GETTING THERE

Probably the best way to arrive at the canyon is on the railroad that originally opened up tourism in the canyon in 1901. The two-and-a-half-hour trip starts in Williams, Arizona, near Flagstaff, and is accompanied by Wild West cowboys, wandering guitarists, and robbers on horseback. The train cars are furnished 1920s-style, pulled by a 1910 locomotive.

> Grand Canyon Railway, 518 E. Bill Williams Ave., Williams, AZ 86046. (800) 843-8724; (602) 635-4000

To fly over in a sightseeing plane or in a helicopter, you can book a flight at the Grand Canyon Airport, or from a variety of commercial operators south of the park in Tusayan. It is also possible to fly in from Las Vegas. For a list:

> Grand Canyon Chamber of Commerce, P.O. Box 3007, Grand Canyon, AZ 86023

GOING INTO THE CANYON

Mules

A traditional way to go into the canyon is by mule. The mules and the guides are well trained in the park, and equipped to carry everyone who is game for the ride down and up. The only requirements are height (more than 4 feet, 7 inches), weight (less than 200 pounds), and language (you must understand English). If you are pregnant, it must not be obvious. No age or physical ability restrictions apply.

South Rim Mules: You can take a 1-day trip that does not go to the river and returns before dark. The 2-day trip allows riders to spend the night at Phantom Ranch in the bottom of the canyon. Reservations for both mules and the ranch can be made as many as 11 months before your trip: (602) 638-2401.

North Rim Mules: On this side, you can take half-day or 1-day trips, but these never go to the river. Reservations: (602) 638-2292 (summer); (801) 679-8665 (winter).

Remember that mules are surefooted, but they are also tall. If heights trouble you, you will not enjoy being four or five feet above your normal eye-level on tiny narrow paths with precipitous drops and the bottom of the canyon in miniature below you.

Hiking Trails

Twenty hiking trials follow the rims and the river and crisscross the canyon, taking you into territory where you might see mule deer, pronghorn antelope, or mountain sheep. Each trail has its own level of difficulty; many are old miners' trails and remote. Remember that the Grand Canyon itself is between 6,000 and 8,000 feet high, and if you are not used to that altitude, you can develop headaches and shortness of breath. Drinking lots of water helps alleviate these problems.

Descending into the canyon is a lot easier and faster then climbing out. From the South Rim, it's possible to go down the Bright Angel Trail for as far as you want and return in a couple of hours, for a taste of Grand Canyon hiking. To go down to the river and back up comfortably takes 2 days.

To hike from the North to the South Rim (10 miles as the crow flies) is a challenging 21 miles that takes 2 or 3 days to complete. In all Grand Canyon hiking trips, allow not only for altitude but for heat: When it's 90 degrees on the South Rim, it can be 120 degrees in the bottom of the canyon.

SPECIAL TOURS

Hiking

The Grand Canyon Field Institute offers a banquet of natural history hikes within the Grand Canyon. Six-Day Geology Backpacks, for example, include a day in classroom lectures and five days hiking with two natural historians to identify and study the fascinating geology of the canyon.

> Grand Canyon Field Institute, P.O. Box 399, Grand Canyon, AZ 86023.
> (602) 638-2485

Hike from the North to the South Rim in a small group as part of a larger tour that includes Yosemite, Bryce Canyon, and Death Valley.

> Adventure Center, 1311 63rd St., Suite 200, Emeryville, CA 94608.
> (800) 227-8747; (510) 654-1879

Havasu Canyon and Falls have been compared to paradise. Located at one end of the Grand Canyon, the Havasupai Indian Reservation is a beautiful place for hikes. Spend 5 days hiking past blooming cactus and through steep sandstone gorges to the Native American village of Supai, the Eden of the Grand Canyon because of its waterfalls and blue-green pools. Camping offered in March.

Iowa Mountaineers, Inc., P.O. Box 163, Iowa City, IA 52244.
(319) 337-7163

Mountain Biking

In the spring and summer, the North Rim is a densely forested area with Douglas firs and ponderosa pines. Single-track terrain leads into hidden fire roads. Good for beginning mountain bikers. Four- and 5-day excursions include guides, food, camping, and mountain bikes.

Kaibab, 391 South Main St., P.O. Box 339, Moab, UT 84532.
(800) 451-1133

Photography Workshops

Spend 6 days rafting 188 miles down the Colorado with a professional photographer (with your camera safely stashed in a watertight container). Stops along the way for side hikes into the canyons. At take-out on the river, you will be helicoptered out of the canyon. *Friends of Arizona Highways* also offers a fall color trip to the North Rim in October.

Friends of Arizona Highways, P.O. Box 6106, Phoenix, AZ 85005-6106.
(602) 271-5904 (Travel Desk)

The Grand Canyon Field Institute offers 1- to 5-day photography workshops from May to October. Each includes slides and lectures that cover technical aspects unique to photographing the canyon, where the light creates completely different vistas hour by hour. Workshops range from easy rim walks to strenuous backpacking hikes into the canyon.

Grand Canyon Field Institute, P.O. Box 399, Grand Canyon, AZ 86023.
(602) 638-2485

Cross-Country Skiing and Snowshoeing

The North Rim is a 1,500-square-mile plateau. Snows come early in the Grand Canyon, and the Kaibab Lodge, located on the North Rim, has developed a good trail system. You can cross-country ski or snowshoe in 3-, 4-, or 5-day packages, starting at Christmas. The lodge provides instruction and has a super hot tub. Built as a cattle ranch in the 1920s, the lodge has rustic cabins for two and a group yurt that sleeps eight. Because there is no way to the lodge in winter except by their SnowVans, you must make arrangements to be picked up.

North Rim Nordic Center at Kaibab Lodge, Canyoneers, Inc.,
P.O. Box 2997, Flagstaff, AZ 86003. (800) 525-0924; (602) 526-0924

THE COLORADO RIVER

Rafting

Guides marvel that the Colorado River, one of the most difficult rivers in the world, is so "forgiving." Annually tens of thousands of tourists, many of whom have never been on a river before in their lives, raft some of the world's most dangerous rapids. Lava Falls, 250 feet wide and more than 900 feet long, looks like a hundred whirlpools going in different directions at the same time. All in all, 150 rapids are interspersed with deceptively calm emerald pools as the river follows a 2,200-foot descent through the 217 miles of the canyon. The riverbed, which varies in width from 50 feet to 900 feet, is between 6 feet and 110 feet deep. And the waters are almost uniformly cold.

Commercial rafting companies offer trips from 3 days to 3 weeks long, from April to October, in craft that range from motorized pontoon rafts that carry 16 people or more, to smaller rafts that are rowed by an oarsman. It is also possible to take standard 6- or 8-person paddle rafts and wooden dories, similar to those explorer John Wesley Powell used. If you're good and can prove it, you can rent or take your own kayak.

Each outfitter offers something different; Grand Canyon Dories, for example, rides Lava Falls in double-ended wooden dories, two passengers in back and two in front, with the oarsman in the middle rowing with two 10-foot oars, the gear stowed safely in hatches. Five- to 19-day trips.

Grand Canyon Dories, P.O. Box 216, Altaville, CA 95221.
(209) 736-0805

Grand Canyon Expeditions Company offers an astronomy rafting trip in September. These 8-day trips in 14-person motor pontoon rafts include rafting and hiking, plus an astronomer and several telescopes to take advantage of the clear skies visible from the bottom of the canyon.

Grand Canyon Expeditions Co., P.O. Box O, Kanab, UT 84741.
(800) 544-2691; (801) 644-2691

Just outside the park, the Hualapai Tribe offer 1- and 2-day 10-person motorized pontoon raft trips on the beautiful section of the

Colorado that runs through the Hualapai Reservation. Native American guides. Lots of stops for exploration.

>*Hualapai River Runners, P.O. Box 246, Peach Springs, AZ 86434.*
>*(800) 622-4409; (602) 769-2210*

The National Park Service publishes a list of 17 regulated commercial rafting companies. All trips require advance reservations.

>*ARA Wilderness River Adventures (800) 992-8022*
>*Arizona Raft Adventures, Inc. (800) 786-RAFT*
>*Arizona River Runners, Inc. (800) 477-7238*
>*Canyon Explorations, Inc. (800) 654-0723*
>*Canyoneers, Inc. (800) 525-0924*
>*Colorado River and Trail Expeditions, Inc. (800) 253-7328*
>*Diamond River Adventures, Inc. (800) 343-3121*
>*Expeditions, Inc. (602) 774-8176*
>*Hatch River Expeditions, Inc. (800) 433-8966*
>*Mark Sleight Expeditions, Inc. (801) 673-1200*
>*Moki Mac River Expeditions, Inc. (800) 284-7280*
>*O.A.R.S., Inc. (209) 736-4677*
>*Outdoors Unlimited (800) 637-7238*
>*Tour West, Inc. (800) 453-9107*
>*Western River Expeditions, Inc. (800) 453-7450*

The detailed list of river outfitters is available from:

>*The Grand Canyon National Park (602) 638-7888*

HOTELS

The Grand Canyon has been a national park since 1919. The original hotel that was built at the train depot is currently being converted to corporate offices and a new hotel is being built nearby, for completion in 1996.

Lodges on the North and South Rims provide about 900 rooms. But book early.

SOUTH RIM

>*Grand Canyon National Park Lodges (7 lodges), P.O. Box 699,*
>*Grand Canyon, AZ 86023. (602) 638-2401 (reservations)*

NORTH RIM

The North Rim is a thousand feet higher than the South Rim, or about 8,000 feet. It lies next to the Kaibab National Forest and is an excellent hiking area in the warm months, with ski-touring trails in the winter.

For lodging in the park on the North Rim, call TW Recreation Services, (801) 586-7686.

In winter two lodges outside the park on the North Rim remain open.

> *Kaibab Lodge (800) 525-0924; (602) 638-2389*
> *Red Feather Lodge (800) 538-2345; (602) 638-2414*

CAMPING

Several campgrounds on the less-crowded North Rim and very-crowded South Rim are open during the summer season (until mid-October); and several backcountry campsites are open year round. Make reservations well in advance of your trip.

For camping reservations, call MISTIX at (800) 365-2267. Or write:

> *Grand Canyon National Park, P.O. Box 129, Grand Canyon, AZ 86023.*
> *(602) 638-7888 (automated general information number)*

INSIDE THE CANYON

Phantom Ranch, a cluster of cabins, camping sites, and dormitories, lies at the bottom of the canyon, reachable only on foot or by mule. Reservations are required, (602) 638-2601.

OTHER SOURCES

Numerous specific trail guides and maps, books on history and natural history, and videos are available from the Grand Canyon Natural History Association. They offer a Trip Planning Package, with books on the natural history of the South Rim, North Rim, hiking guides, and map ($19.95, plus postage). For a catalog:

> *Grand Canyon Natural History Association, P.O. Box 399,*
> *Grand Canyon, AZ 86023. (602) 638-2481*

Grandparents- and-Grandchildren Adventures

No strangers to the natural world, kids can lead their grandparents
back to the simple pleasures of trying to climb a huge tree.
Photograph by Roger Archibald.

Grandparents and grandchildren come from different time zones,
but they can often hang out together more peacefully than parents
and children. Besides sharing a sense of adventure and exploration, they can pay reduced admission prices. The world is their
oyster.

Several companies organize tours especially for kids and their
grandparents. ($225–$500 per day for two.)

New York City

A 10-day trip to New York City and Montreal includes a horse and carriage ride in Central Park, and a helicopter ride over New York City; a train ride to Montreal, and a balloon ride over the countryside.

> Grandtravel, The Ticket Counter, 6900 Wisconsin Ave., Suite 706, Chevy Chase, MD 20815. (800) 247-7651; (301) 986-0790

Dude Ranch

Tours in the U.S., including a 5- or 8-day stay on a dude ranch.

> Generations, 835 W. Belden, Chicago, IL 60614. (312) 404-2400

Archaeology

Family Week in August gives grandparents a chance to spend archaeological time with grandchildren in grades 4 through 6, with a pottery course, simulated dig, and simulated lab. Includes a day trip to Mesa Verde.

> Crow Canyon Archaeological Center, 23390 County K Rd., Cortez, CO 81321. (800) 422-8975

South Dakota

In July and August, provides guided motorcoach tours for grandparents and grandchildren to Mt. Rushmore, with stops at Tipi Village Camp for hiking and learning Native American crafts, Badlands National Park to photograph buffalo herds, and the Rushmore Waterslide.

> Vistatours, 1923 No. Carson St., Suite 105, Carson City, NV 89701. (800) 468-6410

Farms

Today's grandparents may be the last generation to remember the family farm. Taking their grandchildren to visit a farm ensures that historical memories will not be lost.

Westfield Farm in Iowa welcomes grandparents and grandchildren on informal day tours. Kids are invited to take pony rides, play in the hay in the barn, feed the goats, give bottles of milk to baby calves, and collect eggs while they are still warm. At the end of the day, everyone can take a hayride and enjoy a wiener roast. No lodging, but several bed-and-breakfasts are nearby.

> Westfield Farm, 113 410th Ave., Grinnell, IA 50112-8145. (515) 236-3075

Green Meadows Family Farm in Wisconsin, an actively operating farm, is open for day visits during which you can milk a cow or a goat, feed the sheep, take a hayride together, or give the kids a pony ride. Free pumpkins if you go in October.

Green Meadows Family Farm, HWY 20, P.O. Box 182, Waterford, WI 53185. (414) 534-2891

OTHER SOURCES

For a guide to adventures with kids in the Four Corners area (Utah, Colorado, Arizona, and New Mexico), try *A Southwest Family Travel Guide* by Gayen and Tom Wharton (The Mountaineers, 1995).

Hang Gliding

A hang glider adjusts his harness before sliding his body forward for a flight over San Francisco Bay. *Photograph by Roger Archibald.*

S ome famous people—Daedalus, Leonardo da Vinci, and Wilbur and Orville Wright—have flown with a hang glider. Separated by several centuries, each still sought the same things: the right air for good lift, and control of their wings while they flew. The present shape of hang gliders derives from a design by Francis Rogallo in the 1940s, and changes since then have been refinements on the original design.

Hang gliding is the cheapest, simplest, and most accessible experience of flying with your own wings. Even pros who were among the first to fly in this country, in the early 1970s, describe it as "magical." Dave Baxter, director of Morningside Flight Park, who once flew for a half hour with a golden eagle, says teaching people to hang glide is giving them the freedom to explore a whole new world. But learning how to do it well is like learning how to play the piano: You can get the basics down in a hurry, but practice is what makes it all come together.

A hang glider has two wings which form a pointed boomerang shape separated by a central strut. A triangular frame hangs down from the center strut, and a harness hangs inside that. It weighs between 50 and 75 pounds. The flyer, wearing a helmet, with an altimeter on the frame and an emergency parachute, attaches himself to the harness, runs until he gains momentum, then shifts to a prone position, and holds on to the frame. In the air, the flyer, or *pilot*, controls his movement by shifting his weight: Pushing himself forward, he picks up speed; shifting backward, he slows down. To turn, he shifts in the desired direction.

Those are the basics. In some places you can learn what hang gliding feels like in a couple of hours, with an instructor at your side and a first jump only a few feet off the ground.

But the things you absolutely need to know about hang gliding are what your equipment can and can't do, and what the weather is doing and might do. Equipment gets refined every year, and over the years, hang gliders develop the ability to "feel" the weather. (Courses: 2-day beginner: $100–$200; 6-day novice: $400–$750; tandem jump: $85–$100.)

UNDERSTANDING THE AIR

Most hang gliders simply hang out once they are up: They find a *thermal*, or an updraft of warm air, and ride it around, often making no ground speed at all. Hang gliders avoid *rotors*, which are whirlpools of air that can be very dangerous. In mountainous areas, gliders can ride *ridges*, which is air that hits the side of a mountain and rises. Hang gliding has been called a mental sport because a pilot is always attending to the details of the weather as well as the ground landmarks that fix his position in the air. Average air speed is between 25 and 30 mph. But practice is what gives a pilot the gut feeling about his air. "Over the years, I've developed a sense of how the air feels near a thermal, which is one of those things that you can't explain," said Chris Arai, ranked second in the U.S., who has been flying since 1974. Ask a pilot what is the definition of a good flight, and he is likely to say a safe launch and a safe landing.

SCHOOLS

A good school teaches glider design, aerodynamics, and micrometeorology. First field experience is on level ground, and first jumps are on a shallow slope that might allow you to stay aloft for 10 or

15 seconds. The USHGA ranks pilots according to experience: beginner, novice, intermediate, advanced, and master. To progress from beginner to novice, a pilot needs ten 5-hour lessons. Then he spends 4 months during which he is expected to practice, making 15 to 100 flights.

Once you know your equipment, have an intuitive sense about the weather, are confident about your own skill, and are able to read your own mood, consider yourself a hang glider pilot. But it takes an initial commitment of time and serious focus to get there. An average flight cross-country is 30 or 40 miles.

Guidelines for spotting a good school:

- Do they use the best equipment?
- Does the manufacturer support them?
- Are the instructors available for all questions you have?
- Are there a lot of pilots there?

Remember that price is no indicator of their skill.

A lot of gliding schools and rental outfits exist around ski areas during the summer. Look for them also on the coasts, especially Kitty Hawk and Cape Cod, where steep sand dunes allow for good first-time experiences.

New Hampshire

Six lessons, says Dave Baxter, will teach the beginner "the light touch," how to use the body, how to focus on a target, do figure-eight turns, S-turns, slow, fast, and shallow bank turns, and how to glide to a target. But the beginner has to realize that those are just the stepping stones. "There's an ocean of air, an ocean of experience yet to come," he says.

> Morningside Flight Park, RFD 2, Box 109, Claremont, NH 03743.
> (603) 542-4416

New York

"If God had meant man to stay on the ground, he would have given him roots," is the motto of Mountain Wings, a USHGA-approved school in the Adirondack Mountains. For hang-gliding instruction, they offer a half-day introduction, 2-day beginner, 6-day novice, and a 10-day high-altitude flying program.

> Mountain Wings, 150 Canal St., Ellenville, NY 12428. (914) 647-3377

North Carolina

Kitty Hawk Kites, located on the famous Outer Banks of North Carolina, where the Wright Brothers made their famous first flight, is a real can-do kind of place. For serious hang-glider and paraglider students, they offer an intensive 7-day hang-gliding camp, and lessons leading to the USHGA Beginner status.

But for those who want to relate to the Sahara-high dunes on the Outer Banks, KHK provides a fly-and-jacuzzi package, with 2 nights in a hotel and a short hang-glider ride. Tandem instruction can take you 1,000 feet aloft, towed by a truck or a boat, with your instructor riding safely next to you in the harness. If you don't like hang or paragliding, you can try their rock gym, go in-line skating, parasail, or fly a kite.

Kitty Hawk Kites, P.O. Box 1839, Nags Head, NC 27959.
(800) 334-4772; (919) 441-4124

GEORGIA

Excellent winds allow this school to stay open 365 days a year. Offers many package programs from beginner to pilot.

Lookout Mountain Flight Park, Rt. 2 Box 215-H,
Rising Fawn, GA 30738. (800) 688-LMFP; (706) 398-3541

CALIFORNIA

North of San Francisco, Chandelle offers small classes, video-assisted classroom instruction, and a flight simulator for both hang gliding and paragliding. Packages include half-day introduction to 5 days of advanced flying, using thermals and ridge techniques. Tandem training, mountain trips for advanced pilots, and special clinics for the serious pilot.

Chandelle, 1595 East Francisco Blvd., Suite F, San Rafael, CA 94901.
(415) 454-3464

OTHER SOURCES

For a list of hang gliding schools and local chapters:

U.S. Hang Gliding Association, P.O. Box 8300,
Colorado Springs, CO 80933. (719) 632-8300

Hang Gliding magazine comes with membership in the USHGA. The annual New Pilots' Issue is a complete guide to schools and equipment.

Hiking

Hikers scale the rocky slopes of Mount Shasta, in Northern California. *Photograph by Roger Archibald.*

Some hikers develop favorite trails; others constantly seek new ones and will travel great distances to hike elsewhere. Some prefer the companionship of going in a group; others hike to be alone. Backpacking—carrying your own gear on your back—adds a dimension of weight to a hike, but allows hikers to explore backcountry sites. In the mountains, hut-to-hut hiking is possible in the snowless months.

All hikes are better with good maps, good shoes, and enough water. Dehydration and sunburn are principal concerns, but so are snakes, quicksand, and poison ivy. Check with local park rangers before you go to be aware of any potential dangers.

Also ask about numbers. National park trails tend to be very crowded in the summer, and some parks limit not only the number of people allowed in, but the duration of their stay. In fact,

Mount Marcy in Adirondack Park in New York has been so crowded that a local nonprofit group created a list of other area hikes and awards patches to those who complete three. For information on Adirondack Challenge II, contact:

> Adirondack Park Visitor Interpretive Center, P.O. Box 3000,
> Paul Smiths, NY 12970. (518) 327-3000

Leave no traces if you camp. Remember that American forests in the West tend to be tinder-dry in the summer, so watch your fires.

Several organizations publish maps and guides. (Three days with lodging, $100–$175 per day; Llama treks, $90–$190 per day.)

The Appalachian Trail, 2,100 miles long, begins in Georgia and ends in Maine. For a guide, *The Appalachian Trail Backpacker's Planning Guide*, by Victoria and Frank Logue, is available from:

> Menasha Ridge Press, 3169 Cahaba Heights Rd., Birmingham, AL 35243.
> (800) 247-9437

For easy trails along former railroad tracks, which can take you along often scenic routes in all parts of the country, buy the annually updated *500 Great Rail-Trails* ($9.95, plus $3.50 postage), or become a member:

> Rails-to-Trails Conservancy, Shipping Dept., P.O. Box 295,
> Federalsburg, MD 21632-0295. (800) 888-7747, ext. 11

Membership in Rail to Trails offers a pocket guide, *Sampler of America's Rail-Trails*.

> Rails-to-Trails Conservancy, 1400 16th St., NW, Washington, DC 20077

The Appalachian Mountain Club publishes AMC *Outdoors*, maintains a hut system in the northern forests, sponsors clubs, organizes tours, publishes books and maps, and gives discounts to members.

> Appalachian Mountain Club, 5 Joy St., Boston, MA 02108.
> (617) 523-0636

An outdoors club founded in 1906 to "explore, study, preserve and enjoy the natural beauty of the Northwest," the Mountaineers sponsors organized trips, publishes books and the periodical *The Mountaineer*, maintains ski lodges, is active in conservation, and offers discounts to members.

> The Mountaineers, 300 3rd Ave., W, Seattle, WA 98119-9914.
> (206) 284-6310

Organized in 1922, the Appalachian Trail Conference manages the 2,155 miles of the Appalachian Trail and enlists volunteers to keep it clean.

> Appalachian Trail Conference, Washington and Jackson Streets,
> P.O. Box 807, Harpers Ferry, WV 25425-0807. (304) 535-6331

The National Parks and Conservation Association is a nonprofit membership organization that has provided stewardship of the national parks since 1919 and watchdogs industrial encroachment. Publishes *The National Parks: Index* and *The National Parks: Camping Guide*, plus *The National Parks: Lesser-Known Areas*.

> *National Parks and Conservation Association, 1776 Massachusetts Ave., NW, Washington, DC 20036-1904. (202) 223-6722*

The American Hiking Society publishes an annual guide to volunteer work and internships in public lands, *Helping Out in the Outdoors* ($7.00). National Trails Day, the first weekend in June, sponsors cleanup events across the country.

> *American Hiking Society, 1015 31st St., NW, Washington, DC 20007. (703) 385-3252*

OUTFITTERS AND EXCURSIONS

New England

VERMONT

Hike through rolling fields and dense woods May to October, and spend the night at inns and lodges along the way. The Country Inns Along the Trail hiking package provides food, lodging, and pickup at the end of the trail on day hikes.

> *Country Inns Along the Trail, RR #3, Box 3115, Brandon, VT 05733. (802) 247-3300*

By the year 2000, Vermont hopes to have a Cross-Vermont Trail, 75 miles long. Several groomed hiking and walking trails already cross the state. For information and maps:

> *Green Mountain Club, RR 1, Box 650, Waterbury Center, VT 05677. (802) 244-7037*

NEW HAMPSHIRE

Three-Legged Tours offers six-day autumn excursions that include an Appalachian Trail hike in the White Mountains, with stays at Appalachian Mountain Club huts; biking in the foothills; and canoeing on Squam Lake.

> *Three Legged Tours, P.O. Box 3184, Copper Mountain, CO 80443. (303) 668-5521*

MAINE

Hiking Country Inn-to-Inn on the Maine Coast offers 4 days of challenging hikes in Acadia National Park and Mount Desert Island, with nights spent in elegant inns. Lobster dinners.

New England Hiking Holidays, P.O. Box 1648,
North Conway, NH 03860. (800) 869-0949; (603) 356-9696

If you like surf breaking against wild coasts and nobody there but
you and the puffins, try Earth Trek's 4-day hike on the undevel-
oped coastline of "Downeast Maine." The trail is described as
"spotty," but hiking is rated easy to moderate. Camping at night.

Earth Treks, RFD 2, Box 785, Thorndike, ME 04986. (207) 589-4311

Mid-Atlantic

NORTH CAROLINA

Hiking Holidays' inn-to-inn tour in the Blue Ridge Mountains
explores the summit of Grandfather Mountain, takes a loop on the
Appalachian Trail at 6,000 feet, passes cascades, rushing rivers,
wildflowers. In the spring and fall; 5 days.

Hiking Holidays, Box 750, Bristol, VT 05443. (802) 453-4816

Southeast

FLORIDA

It's possible to hike the whole length of Florida without going near
a beach. Open only to hikers, the Florida Trail is composed of private land and 300 miles of the National Scenic Trail. Start in the
Everglades, wear wading boots, and hike as far as Apalachicola
National Forest in the Florida Panhandle. This trip is usually done
in sections and is a lot more enjoyable from December to April.
Cypress swamps, pine flatlands, deer, maybe Florida panthers, and
lots of birds, some of them migratory, are part of the trek.

For information on this trail, you should join the Florida Trail
Association. They publish A Hiking Guide to the Florida Trail,
which is available only to members.

Florida Trail Association, P.O. Box 13708, Gainesville, FL 32604.
(904) 378-8823

For information on the federal part of the trail:

Florida National Scenic Trail, Forest Service, 227 N. Bronough St.,
Suite 4061, Tallahassee, FL 32301

Great Lakes

MINNESOTA

The Superior Hiking Trail is one of the most diverse and well-
maintained trails in the United States. For 200 miles, it winds
through forests, past cascading rivers, along a mountain ridge, and

around Lake Superior. From some points, you can look 50 miles across the lake's surface. Lots of wildlife, including moose and wolves. From May till October, hikers can have the best of both worlds, with hiking in the remote backcountry along the trail, and staying in lodges, historic inns, bed-and-breakfasts, and condos each night, while someone drives your car and transports your suitcases to you. Three- to 7-night trips with lodging and food (one to three meals a day) and all the information you need for the trail.

Lodge to Lodge Hiking, P.O. Box 2248, Tofte, MN 55615.
(800) 322-8327

Rocky Mountains

MONTANA

Glacier National Park, located on the Canadian border of Montana, is one of the country's largest (1,600 square miles) national parks. It tends to be cool (rarely above 80 degrees) and wet. Among its 50 glaciers, 200 lakes, and 10,000-foot peaks is a variety of plants, birds, trees, and wildlife, as well as black bears and grizzlies, mountain goats, wolves, bison, and bald eagles. Hikers can walk on some of the 700 miles of trails and camp at several campsites. Open from May to October, or at backcountry sites, open year-round.

Backpacking camping trips with guides and rented equipment are available from:

Glacier Wilderness Guides, P.O. Box 535-PS, West Glacier, MT 59936.
(800) 521-7238; (406) 888-5466

You can also go on day hikes with park rangers. Visitor centers stock free copies of *Nature With a Naturalist,* which lists ranger activities.

Glacier National Park, West Glacier, MT 59936. (406) 888-5441

For publications of trail guides and hikes, get a catalog from:

Glacier Natural History Association, (406) 888-5756

West

CALIFORNIA

The John Muir Trail is 211 miles from Yosemite Valley to the top of Mount Whitney. Spend 11 days hiking and backpacking with a guide.

Southern Yosemite Mountain Guides, P.O. Box 301,
Bass Lake, CA 93604. (415) 309-3153

If you want a lot more of California, try the Pacific Crest Trail, 2,600 miles from Mexico to Canada. Hike as much or as little as you want with guides and gear.

For more information on the Pacific Crest Trail:

> Pacific Crest Trail Association, Forest Service, Region 6, P.O. Box 3623, Portland, OR 97208. (800) 817-2243

The Anza-Borrego Desert State Park in southwestern California is 600,000 square miles of creosote desert, mud caves, narrow canyons, beautiful spring-blooming flowers, palm trees, bighorn sheep (or *borrego*; De Anza was an 18th-century Spanish explorer), and lots of hiking trails. Pioneers crossed here on the Southern Emigrant Trail in the 1850s and 1860s, but before them, Native Americans lived here and left artifacts. The Visitor Center provides maps and will issue permits to camp.

> Anza-Borrego Desert State Park Visitor Center, Palm Canyon Dr., Box 299, Borrego Springs, CA 92004. (619) 767-4205

There are a few privately owned hotels and restaurants in Borrego Springs, a tiny town in the middle of the park. For a motel in an oasis:

> Hacienda del Sol, 610 Palm Canyon Dr., Borrego Springs, CA 92004. (619) 767-5442

Desert Hiking, by Dave Ganci (Wilderness Press, 1993), is a backpacking guide to the desert.

Alaska

Alaskan wilderness is a natural for backpacking and hiking. Spirit of Alaska Backpacking offers a variety of day hikes and longer guided backpacking trips from easy to strenuous for all ages, beginning at age 8.

> Spirit of Alaska Backpacking, 5917 Camden Circle, Anchorage, AK 99504-3815. (907) 337-7707

For backpacking the Brooks Range, a 75,000-square-miles area located above the Arctic Circle, prepare for a more challenging trek. The only trails are those made by animals, and you might cover as few as 3 miles a day. But the wildlife and the variety of ecosystems are extraordinary—rosy finches, arctic warblers, caribou, marmots, grizzlies, and wolverines. Seven-day trips from June to August.

> Wilderness Alaska, P.O. Box 113063, Anchorage, AK 99511. (907) 345-3567

Hawaii

If you are in Hawaii, hiking a volcano is a must-do, and the 6,000-foot Haleakala Volcano (quiet since the 1700s) on Maui has both a Crater Trail and a Boundary Trail. The Boundary Trail on the southwestern slope is heavily forested and provides beautiful views of tropical Maui below. Campsites are available on both the lava-ash side and the forested side.

Haleakala National Park, P.O. Box 369, Makawao, Maui, HI 96768.
(808) 572-9306

LLAMA TREKS

Maybe it's their big brown eyes or their floppy ears, but most llamas steal hikers' hearts. Beasts of burden, llamas carry all the stuff, but they hum when they walk and seem to be lost in lofty thoughts, so they act more like thoughtful companions.

Mid-Atlantic

NORTH CAROLINA

The Pisgah National Forest in the Appalachian Mountains is about half a million acres of dense woods that turn brilliant colors

Llamas carry the gear and act as buddies on this wilderness trek.
Photograph by Roger Archibald.

in the fall. You can take 1- to 3-day guided llama wilderness treks or trout-fishing trips during the summer until November with Avalon Llama Treks. Avalon breeds and raises llamas and maintains a herd of between thirty and fifty. Avalon's staff will provide what they call a No-Brainer outing—they provide all the gear (including trout-fishing gear) and gourmet meals, and the llamas take care of the rest.

> *Avalon Llama Treks, 450 Old Buckeye Cove Rd.,*
> *Swannanoa, NC 28778. (704) 298-5637; (704) 299-7155 (phone/fax)*

Rocky Mountains

COLORADO

Three- and 4-day llama trips between Aspen and Vail give a family a wilderness experience, with fishing, camping, or hut hiking. Custom trips available too.

> *Paragon Guides, P.O. Box 130, Vail, CO 81658. (303) 926-5299*

WYOMING

You can llama-hike and camp Yellowstone National Park up to 8,000 feet with lots of wildlife, and the Jedediah Smith Wilderness in the Teton Range, between 8,000 and 10,000 feet. Four- to five-day trips, flexible itineraries, including fishing trips.

> *Jackson Hole Llamas, P.O. Box 7375, Jackson, WY 83001. (307) 733-1617*

Southwest

UTAH

Hike with your llama by your side past grottoes, deep canyons, and waterfalls in the Escalante Canyon Wilderness in southern Utah. Six-day trips in April, May, and October.

> *Sojourns of Discovery, P.O. Box 14057, San Luis Obispo, CA 93406.*
> *(800)736-TREK; (805) 438-5910*

Hike through Utah's Capitol Reef National Park, 70 miles of deep gorge, Anasazi rock art, nature, wildlife, and llamas. Four-day trips, camping.

> *Red Rock 'n Llamas, P.O. Box 1304, Boulder, UT 84716. (801) 335-7325*

Alaska

Take a moderate 7-mile, half-day hike with a llama and a native Alaskan guide to a scenic high point overlooking Knik Glacier. Then sweat in a sauna and stay in a log cabin with all amenities.

> *Knik Glacier Adventures, HC20 Box 7726, Palmer, AK 99645.*
> *(907) 746-5133*

If you want to know more about llamas, contact:

International Llama Association, P.O. Box 37505, Denver, CO 80237.
(303) 756-9004

Burro Treks

Burros are small donkeys with sure feet and the ability to help you carry your gear to high altitudes in the Sierras. The Sierra Club has several week-long trips for families and burros in Inyo Forest and Sequoia Park, between 10,000 and 12,000 feet altitude, with fishing, nature, camping, and hiking.

Sierra Club Outing Dept., 730 Polk St., San Francisco, CA 94109.
(415) 923-5522

OTHER SOURCES

Backpacker, Sierra, and *Outside* magazines are full of information on trails and hikes as well as tips on equipment and conservation.

History

Sailors aboard the historical tall ship HMS *Rose* get to do everything sailors did when the ship first sailed. Climbing the mast can take sailors as high as 130 feet above the deck.
Photograph by Roger Archibald.

History—that is, a written record—exists in the United States from the time of its European colonization. Exactly *when* the first Europeans came has been questioned: The Heavener Runestone in northeast Oklahoma, for example, is a 12-foot slab with eight runes thought to be a message left by Viking explorers sometime around A.D. 1,000. (A hiking trail goes by it. For more information: Heavener Chamber of Commerce, (918) 653-4303.)

But history in this country did not really begin until waves of immigrants arrived after 1600. Then all the bustle was on the East Coast, until the early 1800s, when Lewis and Clarke, under the direction of President Thomas Jefferson, found a river system that crossed the country to the West. In the 1860s, an estimated 350,000 people from all walks of life rode in covered wagons on the Oregon Trail to get free land and begin new and hopefully more prosperous lives in the West.

These trails, and many others, are commemorated, many of

them in Nebraska, where you can acquire an informational tape at public roadside stops. Narrated by Captain Nebraska, a TV personality, the tape gives you all the information a guide would if you passed through the state on a bus tour. (You "deposit" $12, which you get back when you return the tape. Or you can keep it.) (*For maps, see Covered Wagon Trips.*)

Battles from the Revolutionary and Civil wars are reenacted throughout the year in many states; living-history restorations of original settlements and their ships can be found at Jamestown, Virginia, Plimoth Plantation, Massachusetts, and Williamsburg, Virginia; of the Old West at Dodge City, Kansas, and other places. Check with state tourism offices for historical and cultural events.

HISTORICAL ARCHAEOLOGY

The National Park Service and the Association for the Preservation of Virginia Antiquities are conducting a five-year archaeological research project at *Jamestown, Virginia,* the site of the first English settlement in North America, in 1605. Contact William Kelso, (804) 229-1616, for more information on joining the dig.

George Washington's Virginia home, *Mount Vernon,* is also the site of several digs. Volunteers are accepted in July. Contact Dennis Pogue, (703) 780-2000.

The National Trust for Historic Preservation occasionally invites interested members to participate in archaeological or preservation projects in the summer as part of their Work/Study Program. Previous projects have included planting herbs at Woodlawn Plantation, George Washington's foster daughter's home, in Mount Vernon, Virginia; doing an archaeological survey at Belle Grove, a 1794 mansion in the Shenandoah Valley, Virginia; and excavating, identifying, and cataloging artifacts in an archaeological research center at Montpelier, the Virginia home of President James Madison. Projects include lectures, lodging, and food.

For more information, contact:

Aric Johnson, *National Trust for Historic Preservation,*
1785 Massachusetts Ave., NW, Washington, DC 20036. (202) 673-4138

COAL TOWNS AND RIVER RAFTING

West Virginia

Less than a hundred years ago, the New River National Gorge in West Virginia was under a cloud of smoke from coal-smelting furnaces. Trains hooted across the ridge, joining the towns, whose colorful inhabitants lived in little wooden houses, worked long hours, and played on Saturday nights in bars and big hotels. The rich lived in stone mansions. When oil replaced coal, workers went elsewhere, the rich left their mansions, and the buildings fell into ruins, today draped in vines and almost hidden by trees.

You can spend two days rafting down the challenging Class III to V New River rapids, with regular stops along the shore to hike up the luxuriant slopes of the gorge to view the ruins, while a guide fills in the rest of the story. Camping and gourmet cookout on the riverbank.

> *Class VI River Runners, P.O. Box 78, Lansing, WV 25862-0078. (800) 252-7784*

PENNSYLVANIA

Coal, iron, and steel drove the American economy for the better part of a century. The area around Pittsburgh, most recently a steel center, is a condensed history of the United States: colonial forts and battle sites, old farms, Civil War sites, famous rafting rivers, coal mines, iron and steel kilns, and the famous Johnstown Inclined Plane, a sort of vertical railroad. You can do it all, with guides, living-history projects, and lots of information from:

> *Southwestern Pennsylvania Heritage Preservation Commission, P.O. Box 565, Hollidaysburg, PA 16648-9904*

HIKING IN THE KLONDIKE

ALASKA

In the late 1890s more than 30,000 gold miners sailed to Skagway on the Klondike River, hoping to reinvigorate the search for gold after California was mined. What they left behind—a town with the necessary stores and the Chilkoot and White Pass Trails that collected everything from their shoes to liquor bottles—is being excavated by the National Park Service. Hikers (advanced on the difficult trails) get a real feeling for the tough life the gold seekers found. Skagway has many reconstructed buildings.

> *Klondike Gold Rush National Historical Park, P.O. Box 517, Skagway, AK 99840. (907) 983-2921*

SAILING

OLD IRONSIDES

The USS *Constitution*, 2-masted 44-gun frigate, was the terror of the seas from the time she was launched after the Revolutionary War in 1797. She fought several battles in the War of 1812, where she earned the name *Old Ironsides* because a French ship firing at her saw the cannon shells bounce off her side. In fact, she was built not of iron but of 22-inch-thick oak beams. The ship sits in Boston harbor.

Once a year on the 4th of July, the mighty ship hoists her sails, and to a fanfare of several-gun salutes, a harbor filled with tall ships and small yachts flying flags and pennants, sails out, turns around, and sails back to berth.

Several lucky people whose names are chosen by lottery get to sail on her historic decks on the Turnaround Cruise. To enter your name in the lottery, send a letter at least a month in advance to:

The Commanding Officer, U.S.S. Constitution,
Charlestown, MA 02129-1797

(Please note: The ship will be in dry dock for 1995; the next Turnaround is 1996.)

HMS ROSE

This is a trip for hardworking romantics who are as much in love with history as with tall ships. Patrick O'Brian fans especially appreciate the *Rose*, because the subject of many of his sea-loving novels is a ship very like her. The original *Rose* was built in England in 1757—before the Revolutionary War—to protect the American colonies during the French and Indian Wars. When the colonies rebelled against Britain, the *Rose* fought for Britain and sank off Savannah in 1779.

In 1970 an exact replica was built in this country, and today anyone can join her crew as she sails the Great Lakes throughout the summer.

The *Rose* is a 3-masted frigate, 135 feet long, with no less than 13,000 square feet of square sails. She has six watertight bulkheads and all new safety equipment. Three compartments with twelve bunks, each with a privacy curtain and reading lamp, accommodate adventurers, who are expected to haul sail, swab the decks, and stand watch (4 hours on, 8 hours off). The rigging, if you care to climb it, is 130 feet above the deck. Trips vary in length from a day to a few weeks. All ages are welcome.

HMS Rose Foundation, One Bostwick Ave., Bridgeport, CT 06605.
(203) 335-1433

RIVERBOATS AND CRUISES

The Mississippi River divides the country in half geographically and unites it commercially. To experience its river ports, historic sites, and folk festivals, take a tour on the *Mississippi Queen* or the

Delta Queen paddlewheel steamboat. Sleep-aboard 3- and 12-night cruises travel through Mark Twain country: St. Louis, Pittsburgh, Memphis, Cincinnati, and New Orleans.

> *The Delta Queen Steamboat Co., 30 Robin Street Wharf, New Orleans, LA 70130-1890. (800) 543-1949; (504) 586-0631*

THANKSGIVING DINNER

PLIMOTH PLANTATION

International relations were smoothly negotiated (according to legend) when resident Native Americans of the Wampanoag tribe offered corn to the starving, newly arrived colonists in Plimoth Plantation in the cold late fall of 1621. The Pilgrims accepted the invitation to dine, and a national holiday was born. Make reservations well in advance for one of the four sittings, and you can sit at a replica table in Plimoth Plantation with costumed actors reenacting the first Thanksgiving. Food is authentic and local: roast turkey, sausage stuffing, butternut squash, cranberry sauce, pumpkin bread, and apple cider.

Throughout October and November, Plimoth actors and musicians stage 17th-century harvest feasts, with such things as mussels steamed in beer, crimped cod, and Indian pudding.

The living-history replica plantation, located at the beginning of Cape Cod, is open April to November, as is the tiny ship *Mayflower II*, a replica of the one that transported the religious refugees to a new land.

> *Plimoth Plantation, P.O. Box 1620, Plymouth, MA 02362.*
> *(508) 746-1622*

AFRICAN-AMERICAN HISTORY

Many African Americans trace their history north from New Orleans to Chicago and New York, and many cities give black heritage tours (check with tourism offices).

For a real sense of the experience of many African Americans, linger in New Orleans and relive the music. A jazz tour (three and a half hours) of New Orleans's best jazz clubs, which includes dinner, is offered by:

> *Williams Tours and Transportation, 3301 Clearmont Dr.,*
> *New Orleans, LA 70122. (504) 945-9019*

For other tours in New Orleans, contact:

> *Greater New Orleans Black Tourism Network, Inc., 1520 Sugar Bowl Dr.,*
> *New Orleans, LA 70112. (800) 725-5652; (504) 523-5652*

Books on African-American historic sites include Henry Chase's *In Their Footsteps* (Henry Holt, 1994) and Marcella Thum's *Hippocrene U.S.A. Guide to Black America* (Hippocrene, 1991).

SMALL TOWNS

Wherever people in the United States moved in the West or South, they quickly set up small towns. Most had a schoolhouse, a general store, a post office, and a building that housed the regional physician, a lawyer, and maybe the newspaper. Many small towns fell into ruins when the railroad that sustained them moved elsewhere, or when the mine that residents worked was exhausted.

A move is on to revive some of these towns with tourism. Today you can visit places like Rugby, Tennessee, and Opelousas, Louisiana.

RUGBY, TENNESSEE

Rugby has a current population of 75, a reduction from the original 125 who lived in this small farm community in the Tennessee mountains about 100 years ago. Seventeen of its original buildings are restored and house a wealth of pictures, letters, and diaries from the original settlers. Two Victorian B&Bs take guests, who can have dinner at a road cafe.

> *Historic Rugby, Inc., P.O. Box 8, Rugby, TN 37733*

OPELOUSAS, LOUISIANA

Called the Capital of Creole and Cajun Food, rural Opelousas (an Indian name) is the home of French chef Paul Prudhomme, and famous as well for Cajun and Zydeco music. A few years ago, Cajuns (a corruption of *Canadiens*, which locals called the migrants from French Canada) invited descendants of Napoleon from France and descendants of Napoleon's soldiers from Louisiana to meet and help organize community activities for tourists. From that came music and folk festivals, the Cajun Joke-Telling Contest, restoration projects of old buildings and famous graves (Napoleon's soldiers), and walking tours. To visit this culturally interesting and rich area, contact:

> *The Opelousas Tourism and Activities Committee, P.O. Box 712, Opelousas, LA 70570. (318) 948-4731*

For more information on small towns being restored in the Tennessee area, contact:

> *Gale Trussell, Tourism Program, Old City Hall, 2C41B, Knoxville, TN 37902-1499. (615) 632-7410*

In the Southeast:

Bill Hardman, Southeast Tourism Society, P.O. Box 420308,
Atlanta, GA 30342. (404) 255-9472

THE OZARK FOLK CENTER

Located in an Arkansas State Park, the Ozark Folk Center not only encapsulates the Ozark Mountain culture of the late 1800s and early 1900s, but invites visitors to experience it. Staying at the Dry Creek Lodge, guests can learn how to blacksmith, make a piece of wood furniture, or weave.

October is harvest month, and the Center celebrates the harvest and prepares for winter by making shingles, splitting rails, making sorghum molasses and hominy, and preserving jellies.

The smell of peach cobblers, homemade pies, and Dutch-oven cooking, with daily demonstrations by author John Ragsdale, is everywhere. At night listen to a gospel concert or take part in the fiddle and dance jamboree.

Six nights a week from April to November, you can gather round for a concert by musicians on the hammered dulcimer, fiddle, acoustic guitar, mandolin, and banjo. Then dance.

The Ozark Folk Center, P.O. Box 500, Mountain View, AR 72560.
(800) 264-3655; (501) 269-3851

FESTIVAL OF AMERICAN FOLKLIFE

Each July hundreds of people gather on the Mall in Washington, D.C. for a celebration of folk arts and music. It's a real party with exhibits, crafts, and food sales, evening dances, and concerts. For information during the Festival, call: (202) 357-4700; before the Festival, contact:

Center for Folklife Programs, 955 L'Enfant Plaza, S.W., Suite 2600,
MRC 914, Smithsonian Institution, Washington, D.C. 20560.
(202) 287-3424

CROOKS' TOURS

A century ago, the most famous people in the Wild West were either bandits or sheriffs. They were immortalized in the American psyche in pulp fiction, serious histories, movies, and television. In some cases, art imitated life which imitated art: Buffalo Bill, a former Western scout, Pony Express rider, and Civil War soldier, was the hero in a dime novel from which a play was made. He starred in it, playing himself, and it was so successful that he then toured the country with his own Wild West Show.

Traveling west in the middle 1800s in search of new resources was truly an adventure. Once there, however, pioneer life was hard and tiresome; the economy was unstable; it was never clear who was really in charge; and haphazard parenting produced young men and women who often changed their names, chose to live by their wits, and opted for an easier life.

WYOMING: BUTCH CASSIDY

Butch Cassidy, born Robert Leroy Parker in the 1880s, assembled a gang of thugs, known as the Wild Bunch, in the remote reaches of northern Wyoming, called Hole in the Wall. There was no law in Hole in the Wall. The Wild Bunch robbed banks, stole horses, broke hearts, and became legendary, until Butch, his buddy the Sundance Kid, and his girlfriend escaped to South America, where the story has several endings.

If you are a reasonably confident horseman or -woman, you can participate in some reenactments from Cassidy's life in Wyoming. Great Divide Tours provides the Outlaw Trail Ride, 6 days or riding and camping in the foothills of the Big Horn Mountains, where you might accompany some members of the Wild Bunch and hear their stories directly.

If you want to play the other side of the law, you sign on for a Posse Ride and relive the ambushes between cattlemen and the new homesteaders in Wyoming. Count on camping and 5 hours of riding each day for 6 days.

For very strong riders: Ride With the Wild Bunch. For 6 days you ride 30 to 50 miles a day, driving roses across the same trail Butch Cassidy used to drive stolen horses and cattle home to Hole in the Wall.

Great Divide Tours, 336 Focht Rd., Lander, WY 82520. (800) 458-1915; (307) 332-3123

Butch Cassidy did manage to spend some quiet time in jail, at the Wyoming Territorial Prison, where he was sentenced in 1894 for stealing cattle. Now a restored museum, the prison is in a living-history park where you can experience life in a frontier town and meet Butch himself, as well as Calamity Jane.

Wyoming Territorial Park, 975 Snowy Range Rd., Laramie, WY 82070

NEW MEXICO: BILLY THE KID

Billy the Kid was born William Bonney in New York City in 1859. Little is known about his early years, but in 1877 he arrived in the town of Lincoln in the Rio Bonito Valley of New Mexico with a reputation as a killer. In Lincoln, cattlemen were fighting among themselves for the exclusive rights to provide beef to Civil War soldiers and Apache Indians. Billy worked as a cowboy for one of the cattle ranchers, who was killed. When the competing cattle-men took sides and shot it out in what became known as the Lin-coln County War, Billy did the unthinkable and shot the sheriff. Captured and held in prison, where he was sentenced to death, he somehow escaped, wrestled a gun from one of his two guards, and killed them both. He rode off free and remained at large for two months, until he was ambushed in his own house by the new sher-iff, Pat Garrett.

Billy the Kid died at the age of 21. In legend, the Kid is known alternately as a punk and hired killer, and as a sweet kid caught up in a ruthless battle among greedy and lawless men.

The town of Lincoln, not much bigger today than it was in 1880, is a living museum. It has preserved the places where the cattlemen worked and fought, where Billy the Kid rode out and shot the sheriff, and the courthouse from which he escaped. Lin-coln is located south of Albuquerque off Route 25 on Route 380.

> *Lincoln County Heritage Trust,*
> *(505) 653-4025*

Billy the Kid is buried by the gate of Fort Sumner State Monu-ment, a former Civil War military reservation for Apaches and Navajos, which had been bought by a cattleman who had given Billy a place to stay. Located 7 miles southeast of Fort Sumner via US 60 and NM 212. (505) 355-2573.

> *Billy the Kid Museum, 1601 E. Sumner Ave., Fort Sumner, NM.*
> *(505) 355-2380*

DEADWOOD, SOUTH DAKOTA: CALAMITY JANE

Born Martha Jane Canary in 1852, Calamity Jane was a Montana girl and a legend in her own time. Reputed to have been tall enough to pass herself off as a man when it suited her, she also hung out in mining camps, dabbled in prostitution to keep food on the table, and once rode a bull through the center of Rapid City. She, too, traveled in plays about herself, but took time to nurse children when a diphtheria epidemic all but ravaged South Dakota. Calamity Jane married someone named M. Clinton Burke, but when Wild Bill Hickok, a tall Nebraska marshal and Civil War scout, rode into Deadwood to try his hand as a goldminer, Jane and Bill became an item.

James Butler Hickok reinvented himself after a pulp novel made him into a ruthless seeker after justice named Wild Bill. Following his life as a marshal, he joined Buffalo Bill's Wild West Show and toured as himself. If he planned on running off with Calamity Jane and his poke full of gold after he arrived in Deadwood in June 1876, no one really knows. He was shot in the back while playing poker in Saloon #10 at the Deadwood Gold Camp in August of that year, two months after he arrived.

Jane died 27 years later. But today they rest side by side in the infamous Mt. Moriah Cemetery overlooking Deadwood Gulch—she as "Mrs. M. E. Burke"; he, as having been "killed by the assassin Jack McCall."

Today, Saloon #10 is preserved as the place where Wild Bill was brought down. The address: 657 Main St.; phone (605) 578-3346. The capture of Jack McCall, complete with shoot out, is acted out nightly on Main Street at 8:00 and is followed by a trial in a rowdy miners' court. (Call (605) 578-3583 for reservations.)

Mt. Moriah Cemetery is perched on a mountainside and contains many colorful tombstones, including that of Dora DuFran, a brothel madam, who is buried with her beloved Fred, a pet parrot.

For more information on Deadwood:

> Deadwood Visitors' Bureau, 460 Main St., Deadwood, SD 57732. (800) 456-2351

CHICAGO: AL CAPONE

The United States has produced many famous criminals, and Chicago in the 1920s and 1930s had more than its share. It was a time of Prohibition, when a lot of ordinary people mixed their own bathtub gin, and when organized criminals traded in illegal booze and operated out of gambling joints and bars, called speakeasies, behind blackened windows and guarded doors. Gangsters in tailored suits and natty fedoras did under-the-table deals with mayors and senators and made lots of money.

Al Capone, one of the most famous gang leaders, whose income exceeded $25 million a year, was responsible for the Valentine's Day Massacre, in which his men gunned down seven rival bootleggers on a street in Chicago. But Capone went to jail neither as a murderer nor as a gambler, but as a tax evader.

Fellow gangster, bank robber John Dillinger, whom the FBI called Public Enemy Number One, was ambushed and shot by agents after a date in a Chicago movie house with a woman known as the Lady in Red, who turned him over to the FBI for the $20,000 reward. Dillinger was so famous that crowds filed past his body in the morgue, although other gangsters claimed the FBI had shot someone other than Dillinger, who got away.

All of this history and more is available on a tour called The Untouchables, operated by Don "Dixie" Fielding and Rob "Dutch" Virmeulen, a pair of machine-gun-toting hotshots (the machine-gun fire is taped) in suspenders, wide ties, and broad-brimmed hats. Complete with anecdotes in the gangster language of the day, the tour takes a busload on a 2-hour tour to speakeasies, the movie house where Dillinger was framed, and the Lexington Hotel, where Al Capone held court above underground tunnels filled with illegal liquor traffic. Tours leave daily from Here's Chicago, 163 E. Pearson St. Reservations recommended.

Untouchable Tours, (312) 881-1195

Washington, D.C.: The FBI

A free one-hour tour of the FBI's Washington office is filled with historical mementos of the Chicago underworld, as well as those of many famous gangsters and criminals, and illustrates how present-day sheriffs catch their man or woman, with the latest forensic techniques. The tour includes an interview with a special agent who demonstrates his speed with a gun. And as if to settle doubts about whether or not the man they caught was in fact John Dillinger, the FBI proudly displays Dillinger's death mask.

Federal Bureau of Investigation Headquarters, 10th St., NW,
at Pennsylvania Ave., NW, Washington, DC 20535. (202) 324-3000

Horses

Riders get to know their mounts on horse pack treks. Here a rider coaxes a mule through the forest. *Photograph by Roger Archibald.*

WILD HORSES

You can still catch glimpses of some of the horses that once ran wild in parts of the U.S., playing in the wind, racing across fields and through streams. There are two places you can be sure of seeing them: One is in South Dakota, another in Virginia.

South Dakota

In South Dakota, the Black Hills Wild Horse Sanctuary is home to 300 mares for which the Bureau of Land Management was unable to find homes. The otherwise unadoptable horses would have been penned up if this sanctuary had not provided land for them to roam free. Last year a stallion was introduced with 80 of the mares.

The sanctuary, also called the Institute and Range of the American Mustang Horse and the Hell Canyon Horse Sanctuary, offers tours of the sanctuary, along the pine forest canyon of the Cheyenne River, past 11,000- to 14,000-year-old petroglyphs and original pioneer homesteads. You can be a guest at dinner, chuckwagon-style, and spend the night in a tepee.

> Black Hills Wild Horse Sanctuary, Box 998, Hot Springs, SD 57747.
> (800) 252-6652

Virginia

Thousands of ponies live on Assateague Island, on the Atlantic coast of Virginia. They are wild and have been there for as long as anyone can remember, and might be the descendants of the horses of early English explorers or settlers. Unchecked, the ponies would soon run out of grass on which to graze. Each year on the last Wednesday in July, members of the Chincoteague Volunteer Fire Company round up about 150 of the wild ponies and herd them across the water from uninhabited Assateague to the town on neighboring Chincoteague Island. There they are taken to the Carnival Grounds and auctioned off. Funds from the auction contribute to the wild ponies' care.

> Chincoteague Chamber of Commerce, P.O. Box 258,
> Chincoteague, VA 23336. (804) 336-6161

HORSEBACK TRIPS

Most dude ranches (see below) have horses which guests can ride on trails. Some ranchers and outfitters sponsor longer horseback trips into the wilderness; guests carry their gear in packs on the horse or on accompanying mules. Many trips in the Rocky Mountains or in the Sierras involve high altitude and very steep trails. Horses are surefooted. Riders should be calm. (7 days: $800–$1,100.)

South Dakota

The Badlands of western South Dakota, home of General Custer, Crazy Horse, and Buffalo Bill, were the backdrop for *Dances With Wolves*. The Husted Ranch, located on the old stagecoach trail, has been in the same cowhand family for almost a century. For a genuine cowboy experience, you can head off into the wilderness for 4 days on a horsepack trip, accompanied by a chuckwagon. Mounts are quarter horses, mustangs, or mules. Lots of wild horses, Indian lore, history, and fossils.

> Dakota Badlands Outfitters, Inc., P.O. Box 85, Custer, SD 57730.
> (605) 673-5363

COLORADO

On a 5-day pack trip in the Sangre de Cristo Mountains, riders rough it, having learned how to care for their mount and to appreciate the labor involved in camping. Hot springs and wildlife.

American Wilderness Experience, P.O. Box 1486, Boulder, CO 80306. (800) 444-0099; (303) 444-2622

ARIZONA

The high desert of the Superstition Mountains is filled with history of gold miners gone wrong, ghosts, and Anasazi archaeological sites. Spend 6 days camping and riding in the wilderness.

Weminuche Wilderness Adventures, 17754 County Rd. 501, Bayfield, CO 81122. (303) 884-2555; (303) 884-9235

VIRGINIA

A lot of eastern horses take western riders. Riding in the East lacks the expanse of the West, but gives a Daniel Boone–mountain man experience. The Blue Ridge Mountains, west of Lexington, Virginia, are good for riding in all seasons. Virginia Mountain Outfitters provides horses with western saddle for two days, with instruction. Nights are spent at Lavender Hill Farm, a working farm. Gourmet food.

Virginia Mountain Outfitters, Route 1, Box 244, Buena Vista, VA 24416. (703) 261-1910; (703) 464-5877

RAFTING AND RIDING

UTAH

Rivers in the West race past wilderness areas. Both are so attractive that if you're in the woods, you want to be on the river; if you're on the river, you wonder what is in the woods. Sensing that need to experience the West fully, several outfitters offer combination horse and raft trips.

The Colorado River in Utah runs through Canyonlands National Park, racing through steep red rock gorges with walls 2,000 feet high. Start on your horse at Pack Creek Ranch in the LaSal Mountains at 9,600 feet, and ride for two days, camping in an old cowboy camp. Then return to Moab and spend 3 days on a motorized raft in Cataract Canyon. Rapids are rougher in the spring, but gentle enough for the rest of the season. This trip invites families and kids, minimum age 9.

Adrift Adventures, P.O. Box 577, Moab, UT 84532. (800) 874-4483; (801) 259-8594

The Green River in Utah's Desolation Canyon runs some mighty rapids through canyons that once hid outlaws, among them Butch Cassidy. Spend 2 nights at the Rock Creek Ranch (whose owner's great-grandfather knew Butch Cassidy) overlooking Desolation Canyon from a 9,000-foot ridge, and trail ride through backcountry. Then spend 4 days paddling with a guide in a raft on the Green River.

World Wide River Expeditions, 153 East 7200 South, Midvale, UT 84047. (800) 231-2769; (801) 566-2662

MONTANA

South of Glacier National Park, in northern Montana, is some of the finest wilderness in the country, including Great Bear Wilderness. On this trip, you can spend 3 days riding, stopping to fish and to camp under the stars. Then you unpack your horse and spend 2 days rafting the Class III and IV rapids of the Middle Fork of the Flathead River.

Glacier Raft Co., P.O. Box 218D, West Glacier, MT 59936. (800) 332-9995; (406) 888-5454

DUDE RANCHES

The word *dude* appeared in a dictionary for the first time in 1880, meaning a dandy, or a person who always wore his best clothes. Before Patagonia, REI, and Levi-Strauss, when Easterners went West, they wore their city clothes, and it wasn't long before *dude* came to mean an overdressed Easterner, or a city slicker. City slickers believed cowboys were hayseeds who slept with their horses, and cowboys believed city slickers were not sure which end to face when they rode a horse. To bridge the cultural gap, dude ranches were born.

These days both dudes and cowboys have blended to the point where a city slicker can become the Marlboro Man, and Buffalo Bill can become the Cappuccino Cowboy. On dude ranches, golf ranges and pools are not an uncommon sight beyond the stables, and many ranches even run jeep tours to the best shopping spots.

Still, if you want an approximate experience of what life is like in the West, a dude ranch is the best way. You can ride the horses western-saddle along backcountry trails and learn how to swing a lasso in wrangling (calf-roping) activities. You can camp out overnight in the wilderness, watch cowboys prepare for rodeos, and go on a real hayride. The food is always good; steaming breakfasts served on the banks of the river where you have parked your horse have never tasted better. And people who spend their lives around horses in the West are friendly and funny, love music and dancing, and have stories that raise your hair or your curiosity.

For a guide to dude ranches in the West and Canada, call:

The Dude Ranchers' Association, (303) 641-1266

Request a copy of *Old West Dude Ranch Vacations* from:

American Wilderness Experience, P.O. Box 1486, Boulder, CO 80306.
(800) 444-DUDE; (303) 444-2622

Colorado has a big share of dude ranches. For a list of dude ranches and guest ranches, call:

The Colorado Dude and Guest Ranch Association, P.O. Box 300,
Tabernash, CO 80478. (303) 887-3128

It's not the Rocky Mountains, but this dude ranch in Wisconsin raises bison and horses, offers horse trail rides, covered wagon rides, sleigh rides in the winter, plus a Saturday-night square and line dance. For real dudes, there's tennis, swimming, and paddle boats on the pond. Lodging in log cabins.

Woodside Ranch Resort, Hwy 82, Mauston, WI 53948. (800) 626-4275;
(608) 847-4275

RODEOS

If you want to match wit for wit and muscle for muscle with a jumping bronco or a snorting steer, and you have your own roping equipment and know how to use it, you can try out at any of the numerous rodeos held throughout the West in the summer. The champions move on to the National Finals Rodeo in Las Vegas in December. For information, contact:

Professional Rodeo Cowboys Association, 101 Pro Rodeo Dr.,
Colorado Springs, CO 80919

BECOME A COWBOY

Nobody does it better than cowboys when it comes to horses and cattle. Leon Harrel, World Champion Cowboy, runs a program that includes instruction on caring for and riding the American Working Cowhorse, rounding up cattle, sorting, team penning, and the master art of cutting the herd. The final day is Ranch Rodeo Competition Day, with competitions between cowboys and cowgirls. Chuck wagon food is served, followed by guitars and cowboy melodies. This is no dude ranch: Harrel's motto is "The best thing for the inside of a man is the outside of a horse." Open from February to November.

> Leon Harrel's Old West Adventure, The Harrel Ranch, 1120 Spur 100, Kerrville, TX 78028. (210) 896-8802

CATTLE DRIVES AND RANCHING

Cattle drives provide a down-and-dirty experience of the Old West. Because cattle spend the summer grazing at a cooler high altitude, they need to be guided back in their spring and fall migrations. Sometimes cattle herds are moved from one state to another. As a rider in a cattle drive, you will help keep the herd together, rounding up rebels and making sure the herd is safe for the night.

Caution: It pays to be a self-confident rider with some experience on roundups, because you won't have time to think about how to control your horse: Horsemanship should come naturally. Plus, you have to love being on the range: The days in the saddle will be long and dusty.

COLORADO

If you are an experienced rider and can take steep terrain, the Wilderness Trails Ranch looks for 16 skilled riders to round up its cattle in the last 2 weeks of the fall. You spend your days riding

The excitement of the roundup is in the dust, the herd, and a lot of good riding. Photograph by Roger Archibald.

through the San Juan Mountains behind and beside the baying cattle, but your nights at the ranch include a hot tub, good food, and some civilized time in front of a big fireplace.

> *Wilderness Trails Ranch, 776 County Rd. 300, Durango, CO 81301.*
> *(800) 527-2624; (303) 247-0722*

ARIZONA

North of Phoenix on the Agua Fria River, Horseshoe Ranch has been a working cattle ranch for more than a century. Tenderfoots are invited to help "search, drive, sort, rope, brand, castrate, ear-notch, dehorn, and doctor cattle." Daily chores depend on the cattle and the weather ("God sets our schedule"), but you can begin each morning by catching, grooming, and saddling your own mount before you help in any of the activities mentioned above, or repair damaged fences. It's open year round, and you can spend 3 nights or as long as you choose. Comfortable lodging, good southwestern food, and a pool that looks good at the end of the day.

> *Horseshoe Ranch, Bloody Basin Rd., HCR 34, Box 5005,*
> *Mayer, AZ 86333. (602) 632-8813*

WYOMING

On these "Lonesome Dove Cattle Drives," riders spend 2 days getting back in the saddle and learning how to handle their horse and the peculiarities of riding with cattle, safety being the first concern. The final 4 days are spent camping and driving the cattle.

> *Lozier's Box R Ranch, Box 23, Cora, WY 82925. (307) 367-4868*

Bring your sleeping bag and your own towels when you stay at the High Island Guest Ranch in Wyoming, where you can choose to sleep in a bunk in the lodge, in a tent, or under the stars. Days include cattle work on this working cattle farm near the Rockies. From May until September the ranch offers branding and roundup weeks for families with kids 12 and older; and cattle drives, including one that rides the Oregon Trail 1800s-style, for families with teenagers 16 and older.

> *American Wilderness Experience, Inc., P.O. Box 1486,*
> *Boulder, CO 80306. (800) 444-0099; (303) 444-2622*

TENNESSEE

Not all cattle ranches are in the West. Sugar Ridge Ranch in the mountains near Nashville welcomes horse lovers to their working cattle ranch on 1- and 4-day rides. On a quarter/stock horse, riders can learn roping and team penning, or just move or work with the cattle. Camping is in cowboy range tents; country cooking includes steak cookouts, followed by country music. Bring your own guitar, or just your singing voice. April to November.

Sugar Ridge Ranch, 1786 Cayce Springs, Thompson Station, TN 37179. (800) HOS-CAMP; (615) 794-6953

RIDING SCHOOLS

CALIFORNIA

In the breathtaking John Muir and Minarets Wilderness areas of the High Sierras in eastern California, you can spend a week learning how to pack a mule properly and ride with your pack mule in tow along a 9,000-foot-high trail. At night, you will let your mule and your horse graze, and in the morning you will be expected to round them up and get them ready for the trail again. Instruction will be given in pack loading, knot tying, horseshoeing, and the care of mules and horses, as well as safety on the trail and wilderness permits and government regulations in public wilderness areas.

Red's Meadow Pack Station, Box 395, Mammoth Lakes, CA 93546. (800) 292-7758; (619) 934-2345

WYOMING

In true horse country between Cheyenne and Laramie, Wyoming, the Sodergreen Horsemanship School offers 10-day live-in, intensive horse-riding training. Learn everything you could want to know about horses, from foaling, feeding, and managing their stables, to showmanship, jumping, and dressage. Both English and western saddle are taught.

Sodergreen Horsemanship School, William or Eleanor Prince, Buford, WY 82052. (307) 632-7954

RACING

A competitive endurance race takes a good horse and a basic rider over a course that is 25 or 50 miles long. The race involves maximizing your horse's capabilities and employing the best tactics. On this 7-day horse adventure, you can spend a week north of San Francisco, with riding expert Donna Snyder-Smith. You train for 2 days with your horse, a mustang, which is slightly smaller and slightly more wild than other horses. Then, well prepared, you take part in the daylong race on Saturday. Even if you lose, you're a better rider. If you like mustangs, this is the place for you.

FITS Equestrian, 685 Lateen Rd., Solvang, CA 93463. (800) 666-FITS; (805) 688-9494

HORSE CENTERS

KENTUCKY

Lexington, Kentucky, is the home of the Kentucky Derby and numerous horse parks, horse farms, thoroughbred racing, and harness racing. For a list of events and places, contact:

Greater Lexington Convention and Visitors Bureau,
430 West Vine St., #363, Lexington, KY 40507. (800) 84-LEX-KY

VIRGINIA

Lexington, Virginia, in the Shenandoah Valley, is the site of a state-of-the-art Virginia Horse Center. Jumping, horse fairs, and miniature horse events are scheduled throughout the year.

Lexington Visitors Bureau, 106 East Washington St.,
Lexington, VA 24450. (703) 463-3777

POLO

CALIFORNIA

Clinics and private instruction are available for beginners and intermediates in Palm Springs at the Eldorado Polo Club.

Ludwig Polo Clinics, 74-350 Primrose Dr., Palm Desert, CA 92260.
(619) 773-3558

The U.S. Polo Association publishes a list of polo schools located throughout the country.

U.S. Polo Association, Kentucky Horse Park, 4059 Iron Works Pike,
Lexington, KY 40571. (606) 255-0593

Polo matches are held at various sites, usually every weekend. To find a game in the area where you will be staying, pick up a copy of *Polo Magazine,* which lists events. (Courses: 3 days, $250–$450; 2 weeks, $675–$1,935.)

House-Building

Two participants in a timber-framing workshop prepare the timbers that will frame an entire house. *Photograph courtesy Bear Mountain Outdoor School, Hightown, Virginia.*

The concept is this: You'll build a house from the ground up, using only natural materials. Or you'll design the perfect structures for people otherwise homeless. Or you'd just like to know how to plug a leak in the roof. For any of these reasons, you're willing to spend your vacation learning how to design and build a home.

Most design-and-build outfits offer programs that include a combination of lectures and hands-on, hammer-and-nail experience. You will know how to find wells; how to site your house in the most energy-efficient way; how to install electricity; what's toxic, what's not; how to use recycled materials; how to lay bricks straight on a wall or a path; as well as how it feels when you place a sturdy timber at the correct angle for support and nail it in.

Information on house repairs, timber framing, how to build a log cabin, and how to build with stone is included in the five-day

137

courses at Bear Mountain Outdoor School, located in the high hills in western Virginia at the source of the Potomac River. Weekend seminars are given in passive solar design, home building, and the use of recycled materials.

But Bear Mountain also offers such things as blacksmithing, maple sugaring, and spinning and dyeing. Or you can take your family for woodland ecology and natural history hikes or for a weekend of Appalachian folklore. Lodging is dormitory-style in the main lodge, or in smaller bunkhouses.

Bear Mountain Outdoor School, Inc., Hightown, VA 24444.
(703) 468-2700

Heartwood offers a three-week intensive course on house building for the "keen to learn." One-week courses are available in renovation, timber framing, home framing, home design, cabinetmaking, and carpentry. You can also learn landscape design and masonry skills.

Heartwood is located in the Berkshires Hills in western Massachusetts. The Mount, Edith Wharton's summer home in nearby Lenox, is now a museum [(413) 637-1899]. Lots of local bed-and-breakfasts, or camping at any of several campgrounds.

Heartwood, Johnson Hill Rd., Washington, MA 01235. (413) 623-6677

Located on the coast of Maine, Shelter Institute offers housebuilding courses that cover everything from financing to solar heating, and emphasizes way to cut costs. Their 5-day Purely Post and Beam program allows novices to design, cut, assemble, an erect an entire frame of a small post-and-beam house. Shelter Institute also offers a 2- and a 3-week design-and-build course.

On the Maine coast, you can camp in nearby state parks or stay in bed-and-breakfasts, summer cottages, or motels which offer a reduced rate for institute participants.

Shelter Institute, 38 Center St., Bath, ME 04530. (207) 442-7938

Located in a big Victorian house in Atlanta, Southface Energy Institute offers a 9-day intensive house-building course, in which you can actually build a complete small structure from the concrete slab to the roof, with electricity and plumbing, passive solar design, and new energy technologies.

A shorter, weekend course, from Thursday night through Sunday, gives you everything you need to know about housebuilding without actually doing it.

Southface Energy Institute, P.O. Box 5506, Atlanta, GA 31107.
(404) 525-7657

Yestermorrow is staffed with architects and offers a 1-week home-design course and a 2-week home-design-and-build course stressing resource-efficient building at minimal costs. The staff recently gave a course at the Pine Ridge Reservation in South Dakota for members of the Oglala Lakota tribe.

Yestermorrow owns 38 acres of rolling fields in the valley below the Sugarbush ski area in the Green Mountains. The White Horse Inn in nearby Fayston provides lodging with three meals a day. The Inn has a studio in the basement where you can practice at night what you learn during lectures at the main studio during the day.

Yestermorrow, RR Box 97-5, Warren, VT 05674. (802) 496-5545
CompuServe: Go HOMING Forum

With Habitat, you can get experience in building while you help provide shelter for low-income families. Habitat's Global Village Project, with a thousand affiliates in North America, has 200 work-camp teams. These enlist people who are willing to spend 1 or 2 weeks helping repair, build, and maintain houses in such communities as Coahoma, Mississippi, the South Bronx of New York City, or on Native American reservations in the Great Plains. Jimmy Carter offers his help and name in June each year to publicize Habitat for Humanity.

You will receive basic instruction. Work includes installing electricity, painting, raising walls, putting in windows, giving simple financial advice, or fixing problem areas. Lodging is usually dormitory-style. Call the main number above, or check out your regional office in the white pages of your phonebook.

Habitat for Humanity, Habitat and Church Streets,
Americus, GA 31709-3498. (912) 924-6935

Las Vegas

Gambling aside, Vegas's attractions are its spectacular hotels, like
the Excalibur, where knights on horseback engage in jousting
matches every hour. *Photograph by Jo-Jo Salami.*

*There is only one Las Vegas. Unique to the United States, Las Vegas is
an adventure composed of a little Monte Carlo, a little DisneyLand, but
mostly Las Vegas.*

Hollywood writer Adam Barr admits to loving Las Vegas almost
as much as he hates it. Las Vegas is like that.

Viva Las Vegas!
by Adam Barr

I am not a "gambler." I live a fiscally responsible life, free from
high-stakes chances and impulsive flights of fancy. Yet, put me in
Vegas, and I transform instantly into a freewheeling, money-burn-
ing gangster of frivolity. The same will happen to you, if you are
at all human.

Vegas is divided in two. There is Downtown, Glitter Gulch, a neon canyon of mostly older hotel/casinos. Then there is The Strip, a 2-mile stretch of Las Vegas Boulevard, home to the newer, glitzier Vegas, with the ten largest hotels in the world.

Each hotel on The Strip has its own outrageous theme. Caesar's Palace is a sprawling Roman bacchanalia; Treasure Island has a high-seas pirate adventure out front, with a pirate ship gun battle enacted every hour; the Mirage is home to live white tigers and a volcano that erupts every 15 minutes; the Luxor has a pyramid and a Nile boat river ride in the lobby; the Excalibur has jousting matches; Circus Circus has swinging trapeze artists; and MGM is possibly the biggest building on the planet.

Step inside, out of the scorching desert heat and into the air-conditioned comfort of the 100,000-square-foot casino, and you are transported into another dimension with neither day nor night. It's a grand sociological field trip into the belly of humanity: thousands of tourists, conventioneers, rich businessmen, Texans with their glamour girlfriends, and the desperate regulars who come all the time, their life's earnings in their back pockets. They swirl together with the thousands of casino staffers: the money changers, carnival hawkers, cocktail waitresses in skimpy theme costumes, baggy-eyed dealers, and sharp-eyed pit bosses.

But stay awake. Notice the psychology of the place. Everything and everyone is designed to pull money from your pocket. There are no windows, no clocks, no easy ways to exit. Luxury cars (That could be yours!) litter the floor. Bright boards display accumulating jackpots (It could be yours!). Bells, whistles, the sound of coins emptying a slot machine and clanging into the winner's tin bucket (A quick $100! Or is it $1,000?) Sit at a gaming table or at a slot machine, and there's a free drink in your hand. (Want another? Stay longer!)

Note the festive color patterns of the wallpaper and the carpeting. They've done studies: Red inspires a sense of victory and wealth. Olfactory specialists have designed special smells that are being pumped through the air-conditioning system. There's plenty of food, and it's cheap.

Find an empty seat at a blackjack or poker table, or a spot at craps or roulette, and the real fun begins. Hand the dealer your cash, and you're in. Your money disappears into a black box beneath the table, and in exchange you get gaming chips—don't think of it as real money! Hey, lose some, get some more! Need a drink? They'll take care of you. Have to go to the bathroom or get a bite to eat? They'll gladly save your place. Spend more than 4 hours playing, hey, they just might give you a free hotel room (on your next visit). Can't remember how long you've been playing?

Just ask. They've been keeping track of your gambling from the moment you sat down.

There are also 90,000 slot machines throughout the casinos, in the airport, in laundromats, in the 7-Elevens. But as you pump in your nickels, quarters, or $5 pieces, consider this: Each slot machine costs the casino about $6,000. They operate nearly trouble-free 24 hours a day, year-round, pulling in an average of $50,000. Multiply that by 90,000, and you get a figure that is more than chump change.

There *are* other things to do in Vegas. In the last few years, the city has undergone reconstruction to attract families. Now MGM has a theme park in its backyard, and Circus Circus offers Grand Slam Canyon, a 5-acre water theme park under a dome.

And there's live entertainment. Each night there are a half dozen "big shows," glitzy stage spectaculars with familiar music and a hundred topless feather-headed showgirls. Or get tickets to a headliner, like Tom Jones, Sinatra, magician David Copperfield, Jay Leno, Diana Ross.

For sports fans, some hotels host world-class boxing matches; many have pro golf courses. Or you could spend some time in the sports and racing caverns within each casino, devoted to betting, where you slip into a chair, have a drink, and watch a giant TV screen playing a game or a race in progress from somewhere in the world.

Hotel rooms are forever scarce (though there are more than 90,000). If you book 4 months in advance, you might find a place on The Strip, where rooms range from $30 to $50 a night. And don't worry about getting there: More than 600 flights a day pour into McCarren Airport.

Vegas must be experienced, not merely for the thrill of the spectacle, but for the insight into human nature, what happens when humankind is unleashed, given free reign and easy access to unlimited cash. You will leave this desert city, built by mobsters, with considerably less money than when you arrived, but you will have had an adventure unlike any other. And you will return. Oh, yes. You will return.

****

If the casino and the entertainment aren't enough, try some white-knuckle adventures. Former California surfer and stuntman Rich Hopkins, owner of the Adrenaline Vacation Company, will help you live on the edge by day, enjoy Las Vegas by night. A 5-day vacation package includes bungee jumping from a jump tower, fire-walking over hot coals (part of a personal confidence seminar), a tandem skydive, a beginner's rock climb and rappel down, and paragliding with 2 to 3 hours of ground school. Stay longer, do more. Includes hotel, gourmet lunch each day, and a video of what you did.

Thrillseekers Unlimited, 3172 N. Rainbow Blvd., Suite 321, Las Vegas, NV 89108. (800) 8THRILL

Mountaineering

Climbing steep ice, a mountaineer negotiates a secure grip against the perils of verticality and intense cold on Frankenstein Cliffs, Crawford Notch, New Hampshire. *Photo courtesy International Mountain Climbing School, North Conway, New Hampshire.*

Climbing up mountains on terrain that can include frozen waterfalls and single columns of ice is probably one of the most rugged activities you can engage in. Danger levels flash red in some places on the high peaks, which makes this a sport you should never do alone, or do without instruction. Plus, you have to like being outdoors in the cold: A lot of unhappy ice climbers have converted to rock climbing. Although some snowy mountains have exposed rock, and ice climbers have to switch to rock climbing, surprisingly, very few climbers regularly do both.

Mountaineering ranges from ascents up simple snowy slopes to vertical ice faces. Climbers who do extreme mountaineering usually have a lot of time to devote to doing it right. Experienced mountaineers must learn self-rescue and the rescue of others, as well as emergency medical treatment for serious problems such as high-altitude pulmonary edema.

This is not a sport to take lightly. ($100–$150 per day per person [depends on group size] Alaska is more expensive.

East

NEW HAMPSHIRE

The White Mountains in the Appalachian Chain are famous for the highest peak in the Appalachians—Mount Washington, 6,288 feet—and three peaks in the Presidential Range that are more than 5,000 feet. Mount Washington is also the windiest spot in the Lower 48 states.

At the International Mountain Climbing School, you can start out on the basic course with instruction in crampons and ice axe and move onto advanced mountaineering across the Presidential Range. IMCS also sponsors day climbs, and nights in February and March spent at the Mount Washington Observatory, after a day's climb up, where climbers can learn about weather data collection on a peak with some of the most exciting weather in the world. IMCS also gives a course in everything you need to know about avalanches.

> *International Mountain Climbing School, Box 1666,*
> *North Conway, NH 03860. (603) 356-7013*

NEW YORK

The Adirondacks are good learning slopes, safe enough to climb without ropes. There are no glaciers, but at some levels, mixed rock and ice. Alpine Adventures nevertheless gives beginner and advanced courses in Frozen Walls and Waterfalls, using ropes and ice screw belays. Courses take 2 to 7 days. Alpine Adventures also gives a course in winter camping.

> *Alpine Adventures, Inc., Route 73, P.O. Box 179, Keene, NY 12942.*
> *(518) 576-9881*

Rocky Mountains

COLORADO

Mountaineering in the West involves peaks that are 14,000 feet high (or "fourteeners," as they are called), which means that in addition to learning where to put your feet and hands, your body has to adapt to the thin atmosphere. Generally, any level above 9,000 feet can create discomfort or altitude sickness. Drink lots of water, and if you feel sleepy or ill, immediately descend to 9,000 feet. "Climb high, sleep low" is the motto of mountaineers, because the body does not adapt as well to new altitudes in a relaxed state.

For a beginner course in the Rockies, Fantasy Ridge recommends learning in the San Juan Range in southwestern Colorado. In small groups in 5-day sessions from a base lodge, new climbers learn knot tying, rope handling, belaying, rappelling, and anchoring, as well as glacier travel and crevasse rescue. Then the climber has the option of climbing Mount Sneffils or Teakettle.

Fantasy Ridge Mountain Guides, P.O. Box 1679,
Telluride, CO 81435-1679. (303) 728-3546

This unique 1-day course introduces newcomers to mountaineering. At the Mountain Skills Workshop in the Beaver Creek/Arrowhead ski areas, you will learn skills in backcountry travel, weather reading, understanding avalanches, map and compass reading—everything to make you more comfortable in backcountry snow. Combination lecture/skiing.

Mountain Skills, Paragon Guides, P.O. Box 130, Vail, CO 81658.
(303) 926-5299

WYOMING

The lordly Grand Tetons in Wyoming, arguably among the most beautiful mountains in the world, are also among the toughest mountains to climb. Exum Mountain Guides has been in existence since 1931 and is the only outfitter allowed on all park routes and peaks all year by the National Park Service. Base camp is at 11,600 feet, and many routes are both snow and rock. Exum teaches all levels of ice climbing and mountaineering, from 1-day trips to ski traverses. They also teach a course on avalanche safety.

Exum Mountain Guides, Grand Teton National Park, Box 56,
Moose, WY 83012. (307) 733-2297

West

CALIFORNIA

When the snows on Mount Shasta melt, much of California is watered. But while they are frozen, Mount Shasta's 14,651-foot peak presents a challenge for mountaineers. If that's not enough challenge, you should know that Shasta is also considered an active volcano. Shasta Mountain Guides have been climbing it for more than 26 years and offer instruction and guides in easy, slow, fast, and hard ascents, glacier climbing, ice climbs, and mountaineering, plus telemark and cross-country skiing. They provide food and expertise; you rent equipment. No one under 14 on summit climbs, but ask about special trips for kids, as well as the disabled.

Shasta Mountain Guides, 1938 Hill Rd., Mt. Shasta, CA 96067.
(916) 926-3117

WASHINGTON

The northern Cascades Range in Washington is excellent training ground for alpine climbing. Six- and 12-day mountaineering courses with guides and instructors from the American Alpine Institute will teach you the fundamentals and techniques of rock, ice, and snow climbing. When you have mastered these skills, plus rescue operations, you are ready for an expedition on the challenging peaks of the Alaska Range (*see below*). American Alpine also teaches rock climbing and gives a 10-day intensive course in advanced wilderness first aid.

American Alpine Institute, 1515 12th St., Bellingham, WA 98225. (206) 671-1505

Mount Rainier, at 14,411 feet, is an excellent mountain on which to learn and to polish your mountaineering skills. Experts in the field since 1938, REI offers summer and winter trips. Summer trips teach snow and ice techniques, with climbing by day, lectures by night. Winter seminar teaches snowshoeing, snow cave construction, avalanche rescue, carrying heavy loads, and crevasse rescue. Weather permitting, there will be an attempt at the summit. Beginners or advanced must be in excellent shape and have a physician's release. Billed as strenuous.

REI Adventures, 1700 45th Street East, Sumner, WA 98390. (800) 622-2236; (206) 891-2631

Alaska

Mount McKinley, or Denali (which means "the great one"), is the highest point in North America, at 20,320 feet. If you're a serious ice climber, it's probably on your list. In May and June, IMCS guides lead climbers up the West Buttress, which is moderately difficult, and the West Rib, for those who have climbed at high altitude before.

International Mountain Climbing School, Box 1666, North Conway, NH 03860. (603) 356-7064

Mount McKinley and St. Elias, which has routes that have never been climbed, are only two of several challenging peaks in Alaska, where mountaineers bring their advanced expertise. The Alaska Range also offers excellent downhill, cross-country, and alpine touring skiing, especially in the summer when the days is 24 hours long, and you can strip to a bathing suit in the noonday sun.

American Alpine Institute, 1515 12th St., Bellingham, WA 98225. (206) 671-1505

You can also climb Denali with guides from Fantasy Ridge, an authorized concessionaire in Denali National Park, who climb in association with Exum Mountain Guides.

Fantasy Ridge Mountain Guides, P.O. Box 1679,
Telluride, CO 81435-1679. (303) 728-3546

OTHER SOURCES

For a list of mountaineering guides in the U.S.:

American Mountain Guides Association, 710 10th St., Suite 101,
Golden, CO 80401. (303) 271-0984

The AMGA provides a professional review of climbing schools. Certification guarantees a certain level of expertise.

For mountaineering in the Northwest, join up with The Mountaineers, an outdoors club since 1906, which maintains ski lodges and ensures that appropriate conservation measures are taken on the slopes. Membership links you up with places, people, and trips.

The Mountaineers, 300 3rd Ave., W, Seattle, WA 98119-9914.
(206) 284-6310

Recommended books: *Mountaineering: The Freedom of the Hills* (The Mountaineers, 5th ed., 1992). James A. Wilkerson, ed., *Medicine for Mountaineering* (The Mountaineers, 1994).

Rock and Ice magazine and *Climbing* magazine offer abundant information on trips and places to climb.

Ask for a copy of *AAI's Most Highly Recommended Mountaineering Books*, from American Alpine Institute (*address above*).

Native American Tours

In dazzling full dress, a youthful member of the Nez Perce tribe dances in Idaho.

Following a Canadian trend, many Native Americans are organizing tourist trips, centers, and experiences for non–Native Americans. Native American culture varies from tribe to tribe throughout the country, and many tribes have maintained a lot of original colorful traditions, some of which are easily shared with visitors. Ways to gain a serious appreciation of the culture are through Native American guides or by taking an educational venture with a non–Native American interpreter. (3–12 days: $650–$1,750 per person. Alaska is more expensive.)

NATIVE AMERICAN GUIDES

Rocky Mountains

MONTANA

Hike and camp on the Blackfeet Indian Reservation with a local guide who will fill you in on the history and meaning to the Blackfeet of the Mission Mountain peaks and wilderness.

> Curly Bear Wagner, Blackfeet Historical Site Tours, P.O. Box 238, Heart Butte, MT 59448. (406) 338-7406

WYOMING

The Wind River Reservation (2.3 million acres) is the homeland shared by two different tribes, the Shoshone and the Arapaho. At a 3-day August seminar, tribal elders, artists, politicians, and young people from both tribes present aspects of their culture, from ancestor stories, ancient uses of botany, arts, and government to sacred sites.

> Snake River Institute, P.O. Box 128, Wilson, WY 83014.
> (307) 733-2214

COLORADO

Near the Anasazi site of Mesa Verde in the Four Corners area, the Ute Mountain tribe has set aside 125,000 acres on its reservation. Here, Ute guides lead guests into the backcountry to understand the history, culture, and art of several ancient cliff dwellings reached by ladder, and "to walk on dirt the Anasazi walked on," according to Park Director Ernest House. Day and half-day trips in vehicles or on foot leave daily from snowmelt to snowfall, about April to late October.

> Ute Mountain Ute Tribal Park, General Delivery, Towaoc, CO 81334.
> (800) 847-5485; (303) 565-3751 (main office, Ute tribe)

Southwest

ARIZONA

More than eighty trained Navajo guides lead tours of Canyon de Chelly (pronounced "shay"), a vast area gutted by washes and surrounded by high mesas that contain underbellies of red sandstone cliffs, many of them carved with beautiful ancient pictographs. On horseback or in four-wheel-drive vehicles (yours or theirs), guides explain the meaning of Home, which the canyon is, not only to the Navajo but to the Hopi and, before them, the Anasazi.

> Canyon de Chelly Guide Association, Box 588, Chinle, AZ 86503.
> (602) 674-5436

West

WASHINGTON

The Pacific Catalyst, a 74-foot wooden luxury yacht 60 years ago and a research vessel today, plies the San Juan Islands. In September, Thlackmish guide Kenneth Cooper takes people interested in marine life, birds, botany, and Indian song and ritual on a trip through the San Juans, with kayaking and hiking sidetrips.

> *All Adventure Travel, 5589 Arapahoe, Suite 208, Boulder, CO 80303. (800) 537-4025*

In informal cultural exchanges, Earth Treks provides two trips to tribes in the Southwest. Visitors will meet with tribal elders and artisans, visit ruins, and understand the meaning of trees, mountains, rivers, and ocean. In northeast Arizona, a small group will visit Navajo healers and artists and participate in a sweatlodge. Lodging is in camps; reasonable fitness required for hiking. All profit is given back to Native American programs for cultural survival.

> *Earth Treks, RFD 2, Box 785, Thorndike, ME 04986. (207) 589-4311*

Alaska

Ten miles north of the Arctic Circle, at the gateway to the Arctic National Wildlife Refuge, the Caribou People invite summer day-trippers to spend a day getting to know how they live. As part of Alaska's Cultural Rural Wilderness Project, the Caribou People offer guided walks, canoe trips, and tribal songs and dances. This Athabascan tribe, led by Chief Trimble Gilbert, derive 75 percent of their diet from wild animals and use the caribou for clothing, food, and tools. Tourism is new to the area, and some homes are open for visitors; others will be in the future. "We want to show tourists our arts and crafts and let them see our country," said the chief. "We want to make them happy." The only way in is by plane from Anchorage.

> *Arctic Village Tours, P.O. Box 82896, Fairbanks, AK 99708. (907) 479-4648*

River raft the Kobuk River in Kobuk Valley National Park and stop along the way to spend time with villagers in three to five small villages. Wildlife and nature; camping. A Native American guide and a guide from Alaska Discovery accompany this tour.

> *Alaska Discovery Tours, 5449 Shaune Dr., Suite 4, Juneau, AK 99801. (907) 780-6226; (907) 586-1911*

Huslia is a fishing village of 260 people in the Koyukuk National Wildlife Area, 200 miles northwest of Fairbanks. Take a riverboat in to the village, then live with an Indian family for 4 days. Gather food, visit archaeological sites, take pictures of lots of wildlife.

> *Athabascan Cultural Journeys, P.O. Box 10, Huslia, AK 99746.*
> *(800) 423-0094; (907) 829-2261*

Join an archaeologist for 9 days at a site on Kodiak Island, while you stay in an Afognak village. The Afognak culture dates from 10,000 years ago, so the site could be exciting. On nondig hours, join villagers in dances and watch a potlatch ceremony.

> *Mary Patterson, Afognak Native Corporation. (800) 770-6014*

Take a small boat on the Yukon River after you leave the highway that runs from Fairbanks to Prudhoe Bay, and a native guide will introduce you to villagers in a fish camp near the Athabascan Stevens Village.

> *Yukon River Tours, 214 Second Ave., Fairbanks, AK 99701.*
> *(907) 452-7162*

If you would just like to sit awhile and chat with some folks, take a village excursion to the Eskimo village of Kiana, a half-hour small-plane shuttle from Kotzebue. The guide will show you how he makes wood sleds. You can also opt for an overnight and take a boat to a remote fish camp.

A 1-day bus tour of Kotzebue with NANA guides is an introduction to Eskimo culture, complete with a blanket toss, a dance, storytelling, and a tundra tour ("like a big sponge") where vegetables are harvested on the permafrost.

> *Guy Adams, NANA Development Corporation, Tour Arctic,*
> *Kotzebue, AK 99752. (907) 442-3301*

Please note: The above two trips can be booked through Alaska Airlines, as well: (800) 426-0333.

The Kodiak Alutiiq Dancers not only give brilliant performances with drums, headdresses, and "snowfalling" parkas trimmed with ermine and Arctic fox, they also represent part of a culture that was rescued by a modern Kodiak native who interviewed the few remaining elders and researched historical records. Daily performances except Sunday are given in a *barabera*, a replica of a traditional Alutiiq home, near downtown Kodiak. Call (907) 486-4449.

For information on visiting the Sitka Tribes, contact Keith Perkins, (907) 747-3207.

For more information on tribal sites and activities, request a copy of *Alaska Native Journeys* from:

> *Alaska Native Tourism Council, 157 "C" St., Suite 304,*
> *Anchorage, AK 99501. (907) 274-5400*

NON–NATIVE AMERICAN GUIDES

Great Plains

OKLAHOMA

Anthropologist Robert Vetter, an "adopted" Native American who has worked with several tribes in Oklahoma, offers 5-day "full immersion" trips, during which you can meet tribal elders, priests, and families, learn Native American songs and dances, participate in ceremonies, eat and celebrate with them, and visit museums and craft centers. Camping is in tepees. Groups are limited to twenty; also offers trips to Native American groups in southern Arizona and Massachusetts.

Journeys Into American Territory, P.O. Box 929,
Westhampton Beach, NY 11978. (800) 458-2632

Rocky Mountains

UTAH

Spend 5 nights in a remote Navajo village, in Navajo Mountain, Utah, with non–Native American cultural interpreters. Herd sheep, learn to prepare frybread, weave, make pottery, talk, and share stories.

Four Corners School of Outdoor Education, P.O. Box 1029,
Monticello, UT 84535. (801) 587-2156

COLORADO

On weeklong cultural explorations, Crow Canyon Archaeological Center hosts Native American artisans who share their skills. Debbie Silversmith, a Navajo, teaches hands-on silver bead making. Santa Clara potters Jody Folwell and Rose Naranjo, famous for their Pueblo pottery, will teach you everything from clay preparation to pot building, design, and firing.

Crow Canyon Archaeological Center, 23390 County Rd. K,
Cortez, CO 81321-9995. (800) 422-8975

Southwest

ARIZONA

Onshore/Offshore runs a 9-day cultural exchange program to the Hopi and Navajo reservations in July. Having been briefed in lectures, museums, and by a storyteller, visitors then visit and talk with members of the Hopi in their mesa home near the San Francisco Mountains. Spending nights in the reservation's hotel, guests participate in arts and crafts, share ideas with elders and experiences with villagers, and observe sacred kachina dances. This is followed by a horseback trip to Canyon de Chelly on the Navajo Reservation and a camp stay in the canyon on a Navajo farm. This outfitter also designs custom trips for families or extended families.

> *Onshore/Offshore Explorations, P.O. Box 3032, Flagstaff, AZ 86003.*
> *(800) 947-4673*

THE TRAIL OF TEARS

NORTH CAROLINA

The Trail of Tears is the route taken by Cherokees in 1837–38, when the U.S. government forced 16,000 members of the tribe to move from the Great Smoky Mountains in North Carolina to settle in Oklahoma. Today the Cherokee tribe is divided between descendants of Cherokees who settled in Oklahoma and descendants of Cherokees in the Great Smoky Mountains who hid in the homeland and escaped evacuation. You can visit museums in North Carolina and Oklahoma to see artifacts of the Trail of Tears, not yet a marked trail.

> *Cherokee Tribal Travel and Promotion, P.O. Box 460,*
> *Cherokee, NC 28719. (800) 438-1601; (704) 497-9195*

The Cherokee Reservation has cultural events and lots of fly fishing on 30 miles of stocked streams. Permits ($5) and a brochure on fishing are available in local shops.

> *The Cherokee Nation, P.O. Box 948, Tahlequah, OK 74464.*
> *(918) 456-0671*

For information on the trail:

> *Trail of Tears National Historic Trail, Southwest Region,*
> *National Park Service, P.O. Box 728, Santa Fe, NM 87504*

SPAS

NEW MEXICO

Ojo Caliente Mineral Springs is fed by five hot, bubbling healing waters containing iron, soda, lithia, sodium, and arsenic. The iron spring feeds a large pool; the arsenic (good for arthritis) is fed into tubs; the other spring waters are served as drinks. Long revered by Native Americans, the sacred waters are thought to come from an opening to the dwelling place of the Great Spirits.

> *Ojo Caliente Mineral Springs, P.O. Box 468, Ojo Caliente, NM 87549.*
> *(505) 583-2233*

OREGON

> Hot springs and mineral baths are the central draw to Kah-Nee-Ta. The resort is run by a confederation of tribes to whom the springs are sacred and for whose deity the springs are named. Stay in a modern lodge or in a tepee, play tennis, or take a nature hike or river raft with a Native American guide.
>
> *Kah-Nee-Ta Resort, Box K, Warm Springs, OR 97761. (800) 831-0100; (503) 553-1112*

OTHER SOURCES

> Oklahoma is home to sixty-seven different Native American tribes, of which thirty-seven maintain tribal headquarters. For information on events:
>
> *The Oklahoma Indian Affairs Commission, 4545 Lincoln Blvd., Suite 282, Oklahoma City, OK 73105. (405) 521-3828*

> The Oklahoma State *Calendar of Events* lists powwows and other events of the many Native American tribes. Free. Also request a state map. (800) 652-6552 or (405) 521-2409.
>
> Many other states have separate Native American Tourism Offices, with listings of activities.

ARIZONA

> *Native American Tourist Center (602) 945-0771*
> *Navajo Nation (602) 871-6659*

COLORADO

> *Southern Ute Tourist Center (800) 876-7017*
> *Ute Mountain Ute Indian Tribal Parks (303) 565-3751*

MONTANA

> *Office of Indian Affairs (406) 444-3702*

NEVADA

> *Indian Territory (702) 623-5071*

NEW MEXICO

> *Navajo Land Tourism Department (602) 871-6659*

NORTH DAKOTA

> Ask for the brochure *Native American Events*, (800) 435-5663.

SOUTH DAKOTA

Bureau of Indian Affairs (605) 773-3415

UTAH

Ask for an *Events Calendar*, (800) 200-1160

WYOMING

Ask for a *Calendar of Events*, (800) 225-5996

A recommended book on Native American sites: Eagle/Walking Turtle: *Indian America* (John Muir Publishers, 1993).

Natural History

Adjusting to the snow, bison in Yellowstone National Park walk
along the side of the road, indifferent to visitors on foot or in cars.
Photograph by Roger Archibald

"You have to pay attention to all things, large and small. You can't
take anything for granted, including help. But those are the
only moments when you're truly alive, when you're paying attention to the present moment. . . . To me, that's an exhilarating feeling."

Naturalist and author Peter Mathiessen was talking about the
Everglades in Florida, but what he said can apply to any wilderness experience. Most natural history tours take you deeper into
the connection with your environment so that while you canoe or
hike or raft, you understand where you fit. ($50–$100 with a guide
per day; $100–$400 with lodging per day. Alaska is more expensive.)

157

Mid-Atlantic

Pierre DuPont set out in 1908 to tame nature on his sprawling estate outside Philadelphia, planted originally in 1798. The result is 6,500 species of plants, arranged seasonally by color among numerous species of trees and several fountains, on more than a thousand nurtured and manicured acres.

Longwood Gardens represents the perfect order of culture imposed on nature. Creating a garden like this is like assembling a symphony orchestra. To learn at the feet of the master some of the complex intelligence that must go into gardening, many people spend their vacation taking an intensive 1-week course in everything anyone needs to know about perennials. The gardens are open year-round and offer lectures and courses on such things as seed germination and replanting plants from Greenland and the Falkland Islands.

> *Longwood Gardens, P.O. Box 501, Kennett Square, PA 19348-0501.*
> *(215) 388-6741*

South

FLORIDA

The Everglades   There have been almost as many sightings of Bigfoot in the Everglades as in the Pacific Northwest. This indicates, if nothing else, that the Everglades are big and dense. In fact, the Everglades are so rich in plants and animals on land and in the water that half of them are hidden. Hidden, too, are some of the ecological problems threatening this 500-square-mile area in southern Florida, composed of fresh and salt water, coral reefs, and mangroves and prairies. To better understand the Glades, you can spend 3 or more days traveling with a former Everglades National Park ranger, now a naturalist, who will help you identify birds and sealife. Snorkle, swim, and help operate a 36-foot houseboat on your journey through the American subtropics. If you have very good eyes, you might catch a glimpse of one of the almost-extinct American crocodiles which inhabit the southern reaches of the Glades.

> *Chic Charney Enterprises, P.O. Box 295, Key Largo, FL 33037.*
> *(305) 852-4553*

Gulf Coast   On the Gulf Coast of Florida is as great a diversity of life as you'll find anywhere. Wading birds and manatees inhabit the waters near Tampa; Sanibel Island and the Ding Darling National Wildlife Refuge offer a multitude of sea and land creatures. Spend a week in the winter with two naturalists who will open your eyes to it all.

The Natural History Travel Program, Massachusetts Audubon Society, Lincoln, MA 01773. (800) 289-9504; (617) 259-9500

Florida's Gulf Coast was once the exclusive home of the Seminole Indians, who fished and hunted in the swamps, cypress wetlands, and freshwater marshes that comprise the coastline. Beyond are forests and dense palmetto prairies. You can travel 25 miles of this area with a naturalist guide on a train trip that takes less than 2 hours, from Fort Myers to Bonita Springs. The guide points out the ecosystems at work on the coast.

Seminole Gulf Railway, 4110 Centerpointe Dr., Suite 207, Fort Myers, FL 33916. (813) 275-8487

GEORGIA

The Okefenokee Swamp in southern Georgia is the last refuge of the American alligator, which has been hunted almost to extinction. This dense cypress swamp is also home to songbirds, beautiful hawks, and ibises. Canoeing through the swamp with a naturalist, you can experience its primordial life-pulse, visit its trembling prairie (actually peat mounds), and see snakes, turtles, armadillos, and deer. This 7-day excursion also includes time spent on Cumberland Island, Georgia's unspoiled barrier reef.

Victor Emanuel Nature Tours, P.O. Box 33008, Austin, TX 78764. (800) 328-8368; (512) 328-5221

Great Lakes

MINNESOTA

Lake Superior, the largest of the Great Lakes, is surrounded by interesting landforms, from sheer cliffs to thousands of islands. The "Land of Gitche Gumee" has a storehouse of shipping and trading history from the earliest explorers and Native Americans to modern barges. In fact, many ships rest on the lake floor, visible through the clear waters. On this naturalist-guided 8-day cruise, you can look at the lake's geology, including the dramatic forms of Isle Royale, retrace historical routes, and track wildlife on the shores.

Marine Expeditions, 13 Hazelton Ave., Toronto, Ontario M5R 2E1. (800) 263-9147; (416) 964-2569

Ozarks

The Ozark Mountains are no more than a beautiful blip on the flat plain of the Midwest, yet they are a rewarding adventure because of their little-known whitewater rivers, caves, waterfalls, dense forests, and songbirds, as well as local folk music and dance.

On an 11-day spring tour of the Ozarks and prairies in Missouri and Arkansas, a local naturalist guide will point out the secret beauty and ecosystems of the area.

Victor Emanuel Nature Tours, P.O. Box 33008, Austin, TX 78763.
(800) 328-8368

Great Plains

OKLAHOMA

The 8-foot-tall grass prairies of the Great Plains seem to stretch to infinity and are home to 250 bird species, from prairie chickens to eagles; 80 species of mammals, including deer, pronghorn antelopes, and bobcats; and an astounding 500 plant species. These grasslands, described by early homesteaders as "oceans of grass," once covered portions of fourteen states of America's bread-basket. Today less than 10 percent remains, in Kansas and the northern Oklahoma highland. The Nature Conservancy, which maintains the area, has reintroduced bison in an effort to reestablish the original ecosystems.

This is a self-guided hike, excellent for photographers and nature lovers. The Nature Conservancy provides a free guide and map of the 36,600-acre preserve.

The Tallgrass Prairie Preserve, P.O. Box 458, Pawhuska, OK 74056.
(918) 287-4803

Rocky Mountains

COLORADO

If you have ever wondered what wildlife is creaking through the underbrush on the sides of the river you are rafting down, or which dinosaurs might have walked the path you are horseback riding on, you can travel for a week with one or more scientists who will fill you in on the mysteries as they join you in your adventures. Lodging is in cabins or camps; activities also include fishing and hiking.

Science Adventures, P.O. Box 51, Paonia, CO 81428. (800) 686-8667

WYOMING

Spend 4 days with a geologist who will take you on field trips and lecture on such things as why different plants tend to grow on top of different rocks and what elements compose a hot spring. This adventure studies geology unique to the West and includes looking at the Oregon Trail 150 years later and seeing how the land has restored itself after early homesteaders' grazing cattle left it almost grassless.

Snake River Institute, P.O. Box 128, Wilson, WY 83014. (307) 733-2214

Hiking in the wilderness means much more if you can read the clues and traces of animals who live there but remain hidden most of the time. Animal Tracks and Signs: Signatures on the Land, a 2-day adult seminar in the Greater Yellowstone Ecosystem, of which Yellowstone National Park is a part, teaches you how to interpret tracks, spore, sheddings, teeth marks, and other signs of animals.

Teton Science School, P.O. Box 68, Kelly, WY 83011. (307) 733-4765

Summer and winter, Yellowstone National Park is a living laboratory of steamy hot springs, big lakes, sagebrush and flowers, herds of elk and bison, elusive wolves and coyotes, and bears. Study them in the backcountry on horseback or hiking with a llama, on cross-country skis, and in wilderness camps.

Yellowstone Institute, P.O. Box 117, Yellowstone National Park, WY 82190. (307) 344-2296

MONTANA

The Greater Yellowstone Ecosystem comprises seven national forests with eleven wilderness areas, from prairies to mountains, mountain lakes, and the world's largest geyser system. This is also where the Yellowstone Grizzly Foundation does field research on bears. A 7-day naturalist-guided tour includes hikes, lectures about Yellowstone issues, such as forest fire ecology, and visits to field research stations.

Sojourns of Discovery, P.O. Box 14057, San Luis Obispo, CA 93406. (800) 736-TREK; (805) 438-5910

See Yellowstone National Park the way you would like to see it, with a guide who will arrange a private 3- to 5-day excursion that can include rafting, fishing, horseback rides, and trips to see it all, with lodging in hotels or camps. Go alone or go with your group. Special gear is provided.

Yellowstone Guidelines, 16634 Bridger Canyon, Bozeman, MT 59715. (406) 586-2876

Southwest

TEXAS

Spend 10 days touring Texas's wild Big Bend wilderness area. This naturalist-guided tour takes you through the Davis and Guadalupe mountains, across deserts, through canyons, and down the Rio Grande on a raft. Part of the learning adventure takes place in Carlsbad Caverns and in McDonald Observatory to identify stars crisply visible in the West Texas night.

> *Questers Worldwide Nature Tours, 257 Park Ave. South, New York, NY 10010. (800) 468-8668*

West

CALIFORNIA

Off the coast of central California, the Channel Islands, remote and removed, are filled with interesting natural history. Santa Cruz Island, which the Nature Conservancy calls the "crown jewel" of preserves, harbors forty-two plant species, including the Island bush poppy, and thirteen animal species, such as the tame Island fox. These, plus volcanic peaks and deserted beaches, are part of a 5-day boat, jeep, and foot trek with a naturalist.

> *Kurt Rademacher, Director of Field Trips,*
> *The Nature Conservancy of California, 3152 Paradise Ave., #203,*
> *Tiburon, CA 94920. (415) 281-0423*

Yosemite National Park, in the Sierra Nevada Range, has some of the most dramatic landscape in the country, much of it captured in Ansel Adams's photographs. Yosemite Falls, the longest water-fall in the continent, groves of giant sequoias, and the sheer gran-ite face of El Capitan or Half Dome are familiar sights to millions of people. In fact, human impact on Yosemite is threatening the health of the park. A 5-day off-season tour with naturalists lets you explore the efforts to preserve the park while you hike in the wilderness, walk on a glacier, and study the sequoias' ecology and the park's geology.

> *Smithsonian Institution, Study Tours and Seminars, 1100 Jefferson Dr.,*
> *SW, MRC 702, Washington, DC 20560. (202) 357-4700*

OREGON

The volcanic eruption at Mount St. Helens in May 1980 devas-tated forests and animal and human habitats as molten lava raced down its sides and mud streamed through the valley. But the mir-acle was that life came back so quickly. On this 1-day guided tour, you can see the charred remnants of the forest interspersed with new growth of grass, trees, and flowers, listen to lectures, and see a video of the eruption. Some of the battered houses are still vis-ible in the valley.

> *EcoTours of Oregon, 1906 SW Iowa St., Portland, OR 97201.*
> *(503) 245-1428*

Alaska

You can spend 5 days around the summer solstice hiking (at midnight), boating, fishing, talking with your naturalist guide about the interdependence of river ecosystems, the life cycles of salmon, and how to identify signs of wolves, lynx, and beaver, and looking for wildflowers and marsh plants near a glacier. This Eco-Adventure II includes hot tubs and saunas at Kulik Lodge in the Katmai National Park.

Angler's Paradise Lodges, 4700 Aircraft Dr., Anchorage, AK 99502.
(800) 544-0551; (907) 243-5448

Tread lightly with naturalists through the rainforests of Kenai Fjords, mountainous Denali and Katmai national parks, and Prince William Sound. Here you will see all the wildlife Alaska has to offer, including fishing bears, calving glaciers, spouting whales, plus some wondrous plant life. Two weeks include stays in park lodges.

North Star, P.O. Box 1724, Flagstaff, AZ 86002. (800) 258-8434;
(602) 773-9917

Hawaii

Volcanoes created the Hawaiian Islands, and exist in all forms of development, from empty craters to active, lava-spewing explosions, on Maui. On a 7-day trip in Hawaii Volcanoes National Park, the National Wildlife Federation and volcanologists from the University of Hawaii will explain some of the fascinating geology and varied plant life that are associated with volcanoes, and how they affect wildlife that live near them. National Wildlife's Conservation Summits are also offered in the Colorado Rockies and the Blue Ridge Mountains. All ages.

National Wildlife Federation, Conservation Summit, 1400 16th St., NW,
Washington, DC 20036. (800) 245-5484; (703) 790-4265

For camping information:

Hawaii Volcanoes National Park, Hawaii National Park, HI 96718

Orienteering

An orienteer plots his way on the map before racing through the woods in York, Pennsylvania, to the next station. *Photograph courtesy Orienteering North America.*

C alled the thinking sport, orienteering requires skills in map reading and following a compass. Using detailed contour, or topo, maps, contestants enter an area where certain trees, rocks, and other features, some of them hidden, are tagged with numbered markers. Each team puts its own stamp on the marker, then scopes the best route to get to the next numbered point. The trick is to think and act fast in challenging circumstances, because the course involves trail-less terrain through thick stands of trees, swamps, boulders, and dense underbrush. The first to arrive is the winner. Then everybody gets together and celebrates, usually with a barbecue or potluck supper.

Mastering the skill of orienteering means you will never be lost. The key to success is being so adept at map reading that you can plot the fastest way to the next point, avoiding ponds and other nontraversable obstacles, in the fewest possible minutes.

In addition to being a great workout, orienteering brings team members and families together. Kids love it. In winter, devotees do it on cross-country skis. Other clubs stage running races or orienteer on horseback. (Instruction and maps: $10–$15; race fee: $1–$3.)

Contact the United States Orienteering Federation for a list of clubs; almost every state has one. Clubs provide instruction, stage meets, and have regular social get-togethers. There is a $25 membership fee.

> United States Orienteering Federation, P.O. Box 1444,
> Forest Park, GA 30051. (404) 363-2110

MOUNTED ORIENTEERING

If you have a horse, pony, or mule that is conditioned for back-country travel, join one of the clubs in the twenty-two states that sponsor mounted orienteering meets. Mounted orienteers do exactly the same thing as orienteers on foot, but a lot faster: Winners in a 9-mile, 16-point course, for example, complete the race in less than 2 minutes. The only other differences are that the orienteer has to wear a helmet and carry the compass around the neck to keep it from being joggled. Mounted orienteers add other levels of involvement: Easter egg hunts and coded messages. Letters from station markers, when put together correctly at the end of the race, spell out a line from a poem.

For a list of clubs and how to join:

> National Association of Competitive Mounted Orienteering,
> 503 171st Ave., SE, Tenino, WA 98589-9711.
> (800) 354-7264; (206) 264-2727

SKI ORIENTEERING

In ski orienteering, orienteers wear cross-country skis or snowshoes and follow the complex network of signs on packed-snow trails, rather than plow through deep, boulder-strewn backcountry snow, where they would leave footprints. Leaving in staggered starts, teams race to complete the course, choosing what they think is the most efficient trail to lead them to the end. "When you know there's supposed to be a flag around the boulder, and you come around the boulder, and there's a flag, *that's* a rush," says Larry Berman, chairman of the Ski Orienteering Committee of the USOA. Most ski orienteering competitions are held in New York

State or in New England and take about one and a half hours to complete. For information on ski orienteering, contact the United States Orienteering Association, *above*.

OTHER SOURCES

Orienteering North America contains schedules of events in the U.S. and Canada, plus maps and other information. Ten issues a year/$23.50, from:

Larry Berman, 23 Fayette St., Cambridge, MA 02139. (617) 868-7416

Paragliding

Paragliding looks like sky diving, but the canopy is almost twice as
long, and the paraglider takes off after a short run down the hill.
Photograph by Roger Archibald

In paragliding, you put on your harness and spread out a 15- or 20-
pound canopy behind you, constructed of several baffles that catch
air. Then you run until the air fills the canopy. Once in the air,
you hang in a vertical position and control your movements with
a handbrake in each hand connected to the trailing edge of the
canopy. This adjusts the angle of the baffles to the air.

A lot different than hang gliding, paragliding is closer to the
parachute ride in skydiving, but the canopy is completely different—almost twice as wide, with 26 to 28 baffles to catch the air.
Once in the air, paragliders rarely exceed 20 mph, but piloting still
requires what Dean Leyerle of the U.S. Hang Gliding Association
calls "intelligent use of air." The danger in paragliding is canopy
collapse.

Fred Stockwell, publisher of *Paragliding Magazine*, a Brit who opened the first paragliding school in the U.S. in the early 1980s, laments the fact that the U.S., with only 2,000 paraglider and 8,000 hang glider pilots, lags way behind the rest of the world. In fact, the American Paragliding Association was absorbed a couple of years ago by the U.S. Hang Gliding Association. Some pilots do both; most do not.

Like hang gliding, paragliding depends on the weather and the equipment, which, Stockwell said, is now "fine-tuned," but you have to know how to use it and maintain it. You can take a quickie run in tandem with an instructor, or you can taste what it's like by jumping (or flying) off a 6-foot incline.

As in hang gliding, practice and attention to details will allow you to be in control in the air. "Learning to paraglide is like learning to kayak," said Stockwell. "In kayaking, you learn to avoid turbulence called eddies; in paragliding, you learn to avoid turbulence called rotors. A ten-to-fifteen-mile-an-hour wind is good; but a twenty-to-twenty-four-mile-an-hour wind is dangerous. If you're careless about learning, you could be dead or seriously injured. If you take the time to learn properly, you'll enjoy it for many years."

To choose the right school, Stockwell advises spending some time at one to watch the instructor and students as they interact. (Beginner, 1 day: $60–$125; Class I, 5 days: $500–$650; Tandem: $95–$100.)

MICHIGAN

Great place to begin—on 450-foot sand dunes. Also teaches advanced paragliding.

Traverse City, 1509 E. 8th St., Traverse City, MI 49684.
(616) 922-2844

IDAHO

Located at the base of thermally blessed Bald Mountain, Sun Valley Paragliding specializes in private tandem instruction.

Sun Valley Paragliding, P.O. Box 5715, Ketchum, ID 83340.
(208) 726-3332

UTAH

The wind and weather in Utah are almost perfect for paragliding with winds steady and clear, and the first school opened here in 1978. Above and Beyond teaches introductory to advanced, gives tandem first jumps, and offers a course on weather.

Above and Beyond Paragliding School, 3314 West 11400 South,
South Jordan, UT 84095. (801) 254-7455

TEXAS

Beginning and advanced paragliding taught in cowboy Hill Country; ridge soaring and motorized paragliding.

Hill Country Paragliding, Inc., 4800 Whispering Valley Dr.,
Austin, TX 78727. (800) 664-1160

OTHER SOURCES

To get more information on paragliding, contact:

United States Hang Gliding Association, Inc., P.O. Box 8300,
Colorado Springs, CO 80933. (719) 632-8300

Paragliding: The Magazine publishes an annual Special New Pilots Edition which lists paragliding schools.

Paragliding: The Magazine, 8901 Rogue River Hwy,
Grants Pass, OR 97527. (503) 582-1467

Photography

Photography travel courses take photographers to wildlife in the backcountry or to natural wonders like the waterfalls in Yosemite National Park.

Even professional photographers need help if they have never photographed in the wild. There are technical differences in filters for changing light, the use of close-up lenses for tiny things, and film speed for wild animals and wind. The outdoors also requires a special mind-set that allows for patience, as well as for treks into difficult spots. (1 day: $95–$145.)

South

TENNESSEE

Northeast of Chattanooga is an area called the Tennessee Overhill. It's a dream place for photographers because it has forest wilderness, historic mines and tiny villages, a retired copper-smelting plant, and the whitewater Ocoee River. For a guide to the best spots, with photo tips on the best times for photos, ask for a free copy of *Images of the Tennessee Overhill Photography Tour* from:

> *Linda Caldwell, Tennessee Overhill Experience, P.O. Box 193, Etowah, TN 37331. (615) 263-7232*

GEORGIA

Okefenokee Swamp and the area around Sapelo Island are rich in flora and fauna. Light is languid, birds abound, alligators snooze on the banks. All of this is accessible from a canoe, with a professional from Nikon. Lodging, depending on the trip you choose, is in cabins or a restored plantation.

> *Wilderness Southeast, 711 Sandtown Rd., Savannah, GA 31410-1019. (912) 897-5108*

Rocky Mountains

WYOMING

Much of nature photography focuses on small things: insects, shells, flowers, small animals. The Snake River Institute gives a 1-day course in photographing nothing "farther away than your hand."

Snake River also gives a 4-day course on photographing wilderness in Yellowstone and Grand Teton parks in autumn, and a weeklong course on understanding light in the wilds of northern New Mexico with nature photographer Jim Bones.

> *Snake River Institute, P.O. Box 128, Wilson, WY 83014. (307) 733-2214*

A weeklong course, Outdoor Photography: Tools and Techniques of the Photonaturalist invites photographers to field trips, lectures, and assignments in and around Jackson Hole, Wyoming. A Primer course of 2 days is designed as a review session for the experienced photographer. Lodging and meals are included.

> *Teton Science School, P.O. Box 68, Kelly, WY 83011. (307) 733-4765*

Southwest

ARIZONA

Space and distance in Canyon de Chelly defy everything you've ever learned about judging distance. This canyon is incomprehensibly vast, not only on a horizontal level, but on a vertical level. Two- to 6-day photo workshops year-round include canyons, prehistoric sites, silhouetted cacti, and old towns in Arizona.

> *The Friends of Arizona Highways, Photo Workshops and Scenic Tours, P.O. Box 6106, Phoenix, AZ 85005-6106. (602) 271-5904*

NEW MEXICO

The Bisti Badlands in northwestern New Mexico is a geologically unusual region where unique clay-and-rock shapes rise out of the desert. On a 3-day photo workshop, join two professional photographers.

> Southwestern Travel Photo Adventures, Santa Fe Workshops,
> P.O. Box 9916, Santa Fe, NM 87504. (505) 983-1400

West

CALIFORNIA

Few other places on earth are as satisfying to a lens as desert dunes lit by a setting sun. In Death Valley, stark sand hollows contrast against distant mountains. On a 6-day photo trip to Death Valley and the Eastern Sierras, photographers will also get to frame Mono Lake, a super-salted lake with strange pillars, and a ghost town. Camping gear supplied. Ecosummer offers several other photo expeditions.

> Ecosummer Expeditions, 936 Peace Portal Dr., P.O. Box 8014-240,
> Blaine, WA 98230. (800) 688-8605; (604) 669-7741

The old, huge trees in northern California's redwood forests exude a quiet dignity. Exotic mushrooms grow at their roots, along with flowers and rhododendrons. Light in this dense forest is dramatic and misty. Redwood Exposure offers daily excursions or 2- to 7-day trips with a naturalist and photographers, to the redwoods or to tidal pools and birds on northern California's coastline. Lodging is in bed-and-breakfasts; gourmet food.

> Redwood Exposure, P.O. Box 525, Arcata, CA 95521. (800) 995-8688;
> (707) 839-0216

Ansel Adams found the High Sierras intriguing: hidden lakes, reflected clouds, distant snow-covered peaks. Hike or horseback ride the trials of the Minaret Wilderness with a photographer-guide. Flexible camping, 4 days.

> Red's Meadow Pack Station, P.O. Box 395,
> Mammoth Lakes, CA 93546. (800) 292-7758; (619) 934-2345

UNDERWATER

Spend a weekend competing with others on a Beach Photo Dive, held at various beaches on coasts in the U.S. All divers compete on the same day in the same water with the same ASA film (which they are given) for 4 to 5 hours. The film is turned in after the event, processed overnight, and judged the next day. Then everybody enjoys an awards dinner and dancing. This is one of many underwater film competitions.

Underwater Society of America, P.O. Box 628, Daly City, CA 94017.
(415) 583-8492

OTHER SOURCES

If you are seriously interested in nature photography, join the pros and learn about the problems in this new membership organization. ($50 membership.)

North American Nature Photography Association, 10200 West 44th Ave.,
Suite 304, Wheat Ridge, CO 80033-2840. (303) 422-8527

River Rafting

Eight paddlers follow the commands of the guide who shouts instructions above the roar of the rapids on the Gauley River, West Virginia. *Photograph courtesy Class VI River Runners, Inc., Lansing, West Virginia.*

For most people, riding river rapids in an inflatable craft is like learning how to ride a bicycle: After a certain amount of trepidation, it becomes addictive. Digging a paddle into churling waters to the commands of a guide who sits in the back of the raft gives a weekend adventurer the sense that he or she is in control. Waves can be high, everyone will get soaked, the roar of the rapids can be frightening, but the thrill of being tossed up and down and spun around and surviving it whets the appetite for another trip. (1 day: $55–$95; 6 days including food and camping: $1,100–$1,550.)

THE GUIDES

Only a couple of decades old, the sport grows increasingly safe with the accumulated experience of guides and the improvement of the rafts. Good guides create a mood of adventure as well as safety, because they know the river, which changes daily, and are able to read the flow of the sometimes confusing whirlpools that gather around rocks. Guides run through safety precautions like flight attendants: If you are washed over, point your feet in the direction of the flow and lie on your back until you come to a pool or a break in the rapids. Then swim to shore so that you can be picked up. Most guides cherish their professional status, and some move on to rivers in the southern hemisphere when the season ends in the U.S. Others do Clark Kent–type things, like teaching or school counseling. Their outfitters, in league with national organizations, make sure that they are informed on risk management and safety precautions.

THE RAFTS

Inflatable rafts usually sit four to eight people who paddle, after initial instruction. The best rafts are self-bailing and sturdy—and heavy, as paddlers learn when they carry theirs to the waiting truck at the end of the trip. Rafts are equipped with a first-aid kit and a dry bag where paddlers can keep their cameras. Large and popular rivers, like the Colorado, accommodate larger rafts that sit sixteen or more safely in the center. Some rafts are motor assisted; others are oar driven by a guide. Individuals can ride rapids in kayaks, inner tubes, and duckies, which are inflatable kayaks.

THE OUTFITTERS

Most outfitters run scheduled trips or will create custom trips if you ask in advance. They provide the rafts, guides, hard hats, life jackets, and transportation to the put-in at the river and at the take-out at the end of the day. Because most rivers often change daily in volume, speed, and in some cases, rapids configurations, outfitters usually send out a scout and post the current conditions.

Outfitters rent cold-weather wet suits and windbreakers. You can usually buy socks and river sandals or shoes at the outfitters' store, or you can wear old sneakers. Bring a visor cap to keep out the sun or the rain. Trips last for a half-day or for a week, and can include camping or staying in bed-and-breakfasts along the way. Generally it's a sport for all ages. Most outfitters start with kids over 7, although some do run trips for 5-year-olds with adults.

THE BROCHURES

The elaborate color brochures outfitters publish all look alike. How can you tell a good outfitter? America Outdoors (*see below*), which holds annual conferences for outfitters to raise the level of professionalism in the sport, suggests guidelines for identifying the right outfitter for you:

- What is the company philosophy? Are they interested primarily in having a good time? Conservation? Daring sport? Safety?
- Are they licensed by their state or by the federal government?
- How long have they been in business?
- How much experience do their guides have?
- Do they specialize in one or more rivers?
- What are their base facilities like?
- Can they reference past participants?

THE CLASSES OF RAPIDS

Rapids are broken into six classes, which require a judgment call to identify. Generally:

- Class I: Easy, gentle ripples
- Class II: Ripples and waves
- Class III: Bigger waves and deeper holes, or drops
- Class IV: Very challenging waves, holes, whirlpools
- Class V: Extremely challenging: rushing, churning water and lots of rocks
- Class VI: For experts only or unnavigable: waterfalls, deep drops, hidden rocks, or unavoidable rock overhangs

Some rivers have long stretches of rapids which can challenge newcomers and require a high level of fitness. Others have rapids of various classes interspersed with pools, or quiet water, when paddlers have time to relax and look around. Whitewater rivers descend, and the rate of descent affects the size of the rapids:

Some calmer river trips take passengers in rafts with a guide who negotiates rapids with two long oars, like this one on the Colorado River near Moab, Utah. *Photograph by Roger Archibald*

Sharp descents are waterfalls. The speed of the water is measured in cubic feet per second. A cubic foot is the amount of water that would fit into a basketball. Gauges on the banks measure the number of feet passing by per second; in the spring runoff or when dams are opened, the rate can range from 12,000 to 36,000 cfs, which is a lot of very fast basketballs.

Water speeding over rocks gets sucked into whirlpools. When waters whirling around rocks go in different directions, the river is said to have technical rapids, which requires thoughtful negotiation on the part of the guide to avoid. Most Class IV, V, and VI rapids are checked out by spotters from land or in kayaks before rafts with paddlers hit the river, so the guide can know which direction to go in to minimize being sucked into whirlpools. But decisions on the river tend to be well-calculated judgment calls by the guide, whose final decision also depends on the experience and attitudes of the paddlers in his or her raft.

THE RIVERS

The Colorado River in the West and the Gauley River in the East are the premier whitewater sites. Many veteran rafters say the best way to do the Colorado in the Grand Canyon is on a 5- to 7-day trip. But the Gauley in West Virginia gives an equally intense challenge in a 1-day sprint, especially in late September when the Army Corps of Engineers opens the nearby Summersville Dam.

Also in the East, experienced whitewater rafters rave about the Youghiogheny and the Cheat, which run through Pennsylvania and Maryland, and the Ocoee in Tennessee, site of the 1996 Olympic Whitewater Competition. In the West, favorites are the South Fork of the American and the challenging Tuolumne in California; the Middle Fork of the Salmon, the Snake, and the Selway in Idaho; the Flathead in Montana.

For family trips, experienced rafters say you can't beat the Upper New River in the New River National Gorge, West Virginia; the Middle Fork of the Salmon River in Idaho; and the Rogue River in Oregon. The smooth and easy flow of these rivers, their gentle rapids and pools and accessible beaches, give an excellent introduction to whitewater rafting.

Throughout the summer, gear manufacturers and dealers hold festivals on some rivers to demonstrate their wares as well as the expertise of local rafters. They hold competitions, stage stunts, and offer free rides and lots of food, music, and other goings-on.

The Wild and Scenic Rivers Act in 1978 designated several rivers as endangered or threatened by pollution from industrial wastes, herbicides, and pesticides, and laid out guidelines for their preservation. Some of these rivers, such as the Lower and Middle Forks of the Flathead in Montana, run through true wilderness; others are scenically beautiful, like the North Fork of the Salmon in California. Most have at least some sections set aside for recreational use.

Tourism is an excellent economic replacement for other industry, but only so long as tourists carry out what they bring in and respect campgrounds on riverbanks. For tourists, rivers are not only challenging but a good place to think: The power of a river, with the distant sound of rapids, the stillness of its forests, and the activity of its living residents, insect, flora, and fauna, is humbling.

Once a year, in May, America Outdoors, in association with several other river organizations, coordinates National River Cleanup Week. They provide cleanup kits and trash bags and enlist the services of volunteers who help remove some of the trash and debris from rivers across the country. If you are interested in helping out, call (615) 524-4814.

Please note: Rivers do not obey state boundaries, and outfitters usually specialize in more than one river. The following list is only a sampling. It's surprising how many states have *some* whitewater in rivers at different times of the year; the list below covers only the major rafting rivers.

Northeast

Maine: Annual Kennebec Festival Race (August).
Massachusetts: Deerfield River Festival, Charlemont (August).
Contact AWA, (914) 688-5569, for dates.

MAINE

The Kennebec is gentle downstream, the Dead is continuous
rapids in the spring, and the Rapid is Class IV. The West Fork of
the Penobscot is a challenging Class IV–V.

> *Moxie Outdoor Adventures, Lake Moxie Camps, The Forks, ME 04985.*
> *(800) 866-6943; (207) 663-2231*
> *New England Whitewater Center, P.O. Box 21, Caratunk, ME 04925.*
> *(800) 766-7238; (207) 672-5506*

MASSACHUSETTS

Rivers here are better for canoes, and the coast is better for kayaks.
But the Deerfield River is great family whitewater, at Class I–II.

> *Crab Apple Whitewater, Inc., P.O. Box 295, Charlemont, MA 01339.*
> *(800) 553-7238; (413) 339-6660*
> *Zoar Outdoor, P.O. Box 245, Charlemont, MA 01339. (800) 532-7483*

What might be the most unusual whitewater trip in the country
happens in the city of Lowell, called the Venice of America
because the city is crisscrossed with rivers and manmade canals.
From April to the end of May, paddle-raft or kayak on whitewater
through the center of the city for 1 to 2 miles over Class III and
IV rapids.

> *Gerald Gilday, Lowell Parks and Conservation Trust, P.O. Box 7162,*
> *Lowell, MA 01852. (508) 934-0030*

Mid-Atlantic

NEW YORK

The Hudson races through a gorge at Class IV, with some hair-raising moments; the Moose is a rough Class V. Some experience is
required here.

> *Adirondack River Outfitters, P.O. Box 649, Old Forge, NY 13420.*
> *(800) 525-RAFT; (315) 369-3536*
> *Middle Earth Expeditions, HCR 01 Box 37, Lake Placid, NY 12946.*
> *(518) 523-9572*

PENNSYLVANIA

The Lower Youghiogheny (called the Yok) is Class III and IV. The
Middle Yok, Class I–II, is a popular family river. The Delaware and
the West Branch of the Susquehanna have easy rapids. The

Lehigh is challenging in May, and Pine Creek, which runs through a wild gorge called the Grand Canyon of Pennsylvania, has gentle rapids in the spring and fall.

Laurel Highlands River Tours, P.O. Box 107, Ohiopyle, PA 17470.
(800) 4 RAFTIN; (412) 329-8531
Pocono Whitewater Adventure Center, Route 903, Jim Thorpe, PA 18229.
(717) 325-3656

Whitewater clinic:

Whitewater Challengers Guide School, P.O. Box 8,
White Haven, PA 18661. (717) 443-9532

MARYLAND

The Upper Yok, with Class V rapids, poses difficult challenges even for experts. The Savage and the Cheat also require prior expertise.

Upper Yough Expeditions, P.O. Box 158, Friendsville, MD 21531.
(800) 248-1UYE; (301) 746-5808

WEST VIRGINIA

The Lower New is good for beginners and families, the Upper New has some tricky Class V rapids, and the Gauley is for experts. Many river outfitters in West Virginia offer speciality trips: rafting and ecology or history or birdwatching.

The Gauley River Festival is held in September.

Class VI River Runners, P.O. Box 78, Lansing, WV 25862-0078.
(800) 252-7784
ACE Whitewater Ltd., Box 1168, Oak Hill, WV 25901. (800) 223-2641

NORTH CAROLINA

The Nantahala, mostly Class II, runs through the Great Smoky Mountains National Park.

Carolina Outfitters Whitewater Rafting, 12121 Hwy 19 W,
Bryson City, NC 28713. (800) 468-7238
Nahantala Outdoor Center, 13077 Hwy 19 W, Bryson City, NC 28713.
(800) 232-7238

Ozarks

TENNESSEE

The Ocoee, site of the 1996 Olympic Whitewater Competition, is continuous Class III–IV.

The Ocoee Whitewater Rodeo is held in Ducktown in June.

Ocoee Inn Rafting, Inc., Route 1, Box 347, Benton, TN 37307.
(800) 272-7238; (800) 221-7238 (in Tennessee)
Wildwater Limited, P.O. Box 507, Ducktown, TN 37326. (800) 451-9972

Rocky Mountains

COLORADO

The most popular river is the Arkansas; its Class III run through Brown's Canyon attracts lots of rafters. The Animas is rough in parts and very gentle in others. The Gunnison runs Class II to IV through a rugged gorge a mile below the road.

The Arkansas River Festival takes place in Salida in July.

Bill Dvorak's Kayak and Rafting Expeditions, Inc., 17921 U.S. Hwy 285, Nathrop, CO 82136. (800) 824-3795; (719) 539-6851

(Ask about rafting trip with a string quartet.)

Wilderness Aware, P.O. Box 1550, Buena Vista, CO 81211.
(800) 462-7238; (719) 395-2112

River Runners, 11150 Hwy 50, Salida, CO 81201.
(800) 525-2081; (719) 539-2144

IDAHO

The Middle Fork of the Salmon River is popular because of its great variety of rapids along the 100-mile course. The Snake goes through Hell's Canyon at Class IV and V; and the Selway, Class III to IV, with short and intense rapids, gives a sense of being in true wilderness.

Salmon River Outfitters, P.O. Box 32, Arnold, CA 95223. (209) 795-4041

(Ask about their magician/rafting trip.)

Action Whitewater Adventures, P.O. Box 1634, Provo, UT 84603.
(800) 453-1482

ECHO: The Wilderness Co., 6529 Telegraph Ave., Oakland, CA 94609.
(800) 652-3246; (510) 652-1600

(Offers yoga and rafting.)

Middle Fork River Co./Far and Away Adventures, P.O. Box 54, Sun Valley, ID 83353. (800) 232-8588; (208) 726-8888

WYOMING

The Snake River, Class III and IV, flows through Yellowstone and Grand Teton national parks.

Mad River Boat Trips, Inc., 1060 S. Hwy 89, Box 2222, Jackson, WY 83001. (800) 458-7238

Snake River Kayak and Canoe School, P.O. Box 3482, Jackson, WY 83001. (800) 529-2501

Yellowstone Raft Co., P.O. Box 46, Gardiner, MT. (800) 858-7781; (406) 848-7777

MONTANA

True western country, Montana has several rivers, but one of the most wild and scenic of the Wild and Scenic is the Lower Flathead, which runs through steep canyons, yet is a warm 75 degrees in summer. For a trip that starts on the broad expanse of Flathead Lake and goes upriver:

> Glacier Raft Company-Polson, Box 945D, Polson, MT 59860.
> (800) 654-4359; (406) 883-5838

Southwest

ARIZONA

Here, the Colorado River cuts through the Grand Canyon (*See the chapter on the Grand Canyon for a list of outfitters*). Arizona has other rivers, the Salt, Gila, and Verde, which run through some exotic desert terrain, Class I and II.

> Cimarron Adventures and River Co., 7714 East Catalina,
> Scottsdale, AZ 85251. (602) 994-1199

NEW MEXICO

The Rio Grande and the Rio Chama provide beautiful passages through gorges and canyons. Some parts of the Rio Grande are Class VI in the spring, but the Lower Rio Grande and the Rio Chama are mostly Class III.

> Kokopelli Rafting Adventures, 1702 Medio, Sante Fe, NM 87501.
> (505) 988-5799
> New Wave Rafting Co., Route 5, Box 302A, Santa Fe, NM 87501.
> (505) 984-1444

UTAH

The Green River passes through beautiful gorges and has Class I to IV rapids. The San Juan is unsurpassed in its collection of geological wonders. Many of the cliffs have petroglyphs, accessible only from the river.

> Adventure Bound, Inc., River Expeditions, 2392 H Road,
> Grand Junction, CO 81505. (800) 423-4668; (303) 245-5428
> Moki Mac River Expeditions, Inc., P.O. Box 21242,
> Salt Lake City, UT 84121. (800) 284-7280; (801) 268-6667

For a free copy of the *Raft Utah Vacation Planner*, which includes a list of Utah river outfitters, contact:

> Raft Utah, 153 East 7200 S, Salt Lake City, UT 84047. (801) 566-2662

West

CALIFORNIA

The Middle Fork and South Fork of the American, near Sacramento, with Class III and IV rapids, run through gold country; the Stanislaus and the North Fork of the Stanislaus, east of San Francisco, are Class III and IV. The Tuolumne goes through Yosemite with Class IV rapids, but the Cherry Creek/Upper Tuolumne is Class V and for experts. The Lower Kern, near Los Angeles, has Class IV rapids.

A good school in which to learn everything you need to know about whitewater rafting.

O.A.R.S., P.O. Box 67, Angels Camp, CA 95222. (800) 346-6277; (209) 736-4677

American River Touring Association (ARTA), 24000 Casa Loma Rd., Groveland, CA 95321. (800) 323-2782; (209) 962-7873

Access to Adventure, P.O. Box 2014, Woodland, CA 95776. (800) 441-9463 (only in California and Nevada); (916) 662-7296

An experienced company, run by William McGinnis, who has taught many guides. Instruction and trips on the Kern, American, Merced, Stanislaus, Tuolumne, Yuba, Klamath, and California Salmon rivers. Requires prior experience of participants for some rivers.

Whitewater Voyages, P.O. Box 20400, El Sobrante, CA 94820-0400. (800) 488-7238; (510) 222-5994

OREGON

The Rogue has something for everyone and is a great family river.

Sundance Expeditions, Inc., 14894 Galice Rd., Merlin, OR 97532. (503) 479-8508
Wild Water Adventures, P.O. Box 249, Creswell, OR 97426. (800) AT-WILD-H2O; (503) 895-4465
Running Wild Whitewater School, P.O. Box 658, Ashland, OR 97520. (503) 482-9283

Alaska

Rivers in Alaska include wildlife, fishing, and glaciers and often need to be accessed by plane. The Talkeetna, near Denali National Park, has Class III and IV rapids. The Alsek and the Tatshenshini run through almost virgin wilderness near Glacier Bay, and have Class I to III rapids.

Adrift Adventures, P.O. Box 192, Jensen, UT 84035. (800) 824-0150
Wilderness Alaska, P.O. Box 113063, Anchorage, AK 99511. (907) 345-3567
National Audubon Society Travel, 700 Broadway, New York, NY 10003. (212) 979-3066
(Offers rafting on the Tatshenshini.)

Alaska River Journeys, P.O. Box 220204, Anchorage, AK 99522.
(800) 349-0064
Adventure Alaska Tours, Inc., 2904 W. 31st Ave.,
Anchorage, AK 99517. (800) 365-7057
Mountain Travel-Sobek, 6420 Fairmount Ave.,
El Cerrito, CA 94530-3606. (800) 227-2384; (510) 527-8100

OTHER SOURCES

The oldest river conservation group in the United States, American Rivers creates the list of Wild and Scenic Rivers with both houses of Congress.

American Rivers, 801 Pennsylvania Ave., SE, Suite 400,
Washington, DC 20003. (202) 547-6900

America Outdoors holds annual conferences on whitewater risk management, raises public perception of the industry, and increases the professionalism of guides. Publishes an annual *Directory of Backcountry Outfitters*.

America Outdoors, P.O. Box 1346, Knoxville, TN 37901.
(615) 524-4814

American Whitewater Affiliation is a river conservation and preservation group that makes sure rivers are healthy and accessible to recreational activities. Publishes a whitewater safety code and *American Whitewater* magazine and sponsors manufacturers' festivals.

American Whitewater Affiliation, P.O. Box 85,
Phoenicia, New York 12464. (914) 688-5569; CompuServe 72732,401

Paddle America, by Nick Shears (Washington, D.C.: Starfish Press, 1994) contains a state-by-state list of rivers and outfitters and is considered to be the bible of river paddling. *White Water Rafting in North America,* by Lloyd Armstead (Globe Pequot, 1994), is also recommended.

For a daily reading of selected river level gauges, to find out how fast and how high your river is running, call (800) 945-3376.

No complete list of outfitters exists. However, good lists can be found in *Paddle America (see above),* and *Directory of Backcountry Outfitters,* published annually by America Outdoors *(see above).* Individual companies advertise in travel and outdoors magazines, such as *Outside, EcoTraveler, Men's Journal,* and other magazines.

Rock Climbing

Two climbers plan strategy in a crack climb in the Shawaugunk
Mountains, known as the Gunks, New York State.
Photograph by Roger Archibald

Early cliff dwellers in the American Southwest were rock climbers
out of necessity. They scampered up and down using little inden-
tations in the cliff face and probably did not consider it a sport.
Nor does the military, when getting from one place to another
without using a road is imperative to their strategy.

But today sport rock climbing is one of the fastest-growing
recreational adventures in the country. All you really need is to be
fairly limber and not easily subject to vertigo. Many skilled rock
climbers were never good at any other sport, and it's a sport that
a climber has a lifetime to perfect—age is no barrier.

One of rock climbing's attractions is the sense of moment-to-
moment control. A veteran climber described it as "a combination
of ballet, gymnastics, karate, and chess. You have to know your

center," he said. Where you put each hand and foot in your upward movement takes planning and balance; as in a good strategy game, you must think several moves ahead.

The basic rock climbing challenge is to go up like a fly and bounce down using a rope, called rappelling. Most pictures show climbers clinging like flies to a vertical rock face miles above the earth. In fact, two days of good instruction can take a novice up a fairly steep incline and teach him how to rappell safely down with the help of his partner, or belayer. It has its dangers. Some rocks, because of overhanging ledges, are difficult to rappel down from; others have eroded sections or are subject to falling rocks. A major player is the weather: Extreme cold or heat sap your energy; sudden severe storms find you very vulnerable. (1 day: $65–$200; 5–7 days: $600–$1,000.)

THE GEAR

In addition to having flexible rubber shoes and chalk to make fingers stick, climbers need a hard hat and a harness. Plus, they need to know how to tie good knots, to do a lot of homework on the rock about to be climbed, and to keep the body lean and limber enough to stretch it into excruciating angles. Climbers need extremely strong fingers, toes, arms, and legs, concentration, and a lot of guts.

ROUTES AND DIFFICULTY LEVELS

Climbers have a special vocabulary: they use words like *crags*, *knobs*, *chickenheads*, *domes*, and *chimneys* to describe a rock. Paths that climbers use are called *routes*. Routes have *pitches*. Most routes are named, maybe descriptively, but certainly unforgettably, such as The Magical Chrome-Plated Semi-Automatic Enema Syringe in the Lumpy Ridge, in Rocky Mountain National Park in Colorado. Technical climbs are *free* climbs, using only hands and feet; and *big wall* climbs, using stirrups temporarily drilled in the stone. The difficulty of routes is graded in the U.S. according to the Yosemite Decimal System, which goes from 1 to 6, or easy to impossible. Technical climbing is graded on that system in the 5s: from 5.0 to 5.14. Another grading, from I to IV, involves how long it takes to scale a route, with I taking as little as 1 hour, and IV taking 2 or more days.

Crack climbs require jamming all or parts of the body into cracks in the rock face. *Wall* climbs that take more than 1 day to complete require a lot of prior planning to carry food and drink and a sleeping bag and to pace the climb to arrive at a ledge by dark.

If you have never done it before, or if you are uncertain about your skill, take a course and go with a guide. Many areas with good climbing rocks have good schools which offer basic instruction and take climbers up easy slopes to learn techniques. It is not just that rock climbing can be dangerous; it is a sport that has its own language, one which has been refined over the years so that a good guide can give you the subtle hints about technique that will make all the difference in the level of your enjoyment.

Outfitters provide the gear, hard hat, harness, rope, a ball of chalk, and metal aids. Shoes can be rented, but, unlike bowling shoes, climbing shoes are important, and it's better to own your own.

With so many rock-climbing schools to choose from, how do you tell the good guys from the bad guys? Check out their licenses. To climb in national parks or forests, outfitters must be licensed for certain areas, and they must publish their territory. A stamp of approval from the American Mountain Guides Association means guides have completed certain requirements to be guides.

The best climbing areas in the U.S. are the White Mountains in New Hampshire, the Adirondacks in New York, the Appalachians in West Virginia and North Carolina, the Tetons in Wyoming, the Rockies in Colorado, Idaho, and South Dakota, the Sierras and Joshua Tree National Monument in California, the Cascades in Washington, and Mount McKinley in Denali National Park, Alaska.

OUTFITTERS, GUIDES, AND SCHOOLS

The White Mountains

Eastern Mountain Sports Climbing School offers daily, 3-, and 4-day instruction programs, plus guided climbs, and specialized instruction in such things as leading and self-rescue.

> *Eastern Mountain Sports Climbing School, Main St.,*
> *North Conway, NH 03860. (603) 356-5433*

International Mountain Climbing School offers 3-day advanced, 4-day beginner, and many specialized programs in the White Mountains.

> *IMCS, Inc., P.O. Box 1666, North Conway, NH 03860.*
> *(603) 356-7064*

The Adirondacks

Alpine Adventures teaches everything from beginning climbing to rescue techniques for leaders. It has two schools, one in the Adirondacks, the other in the White Mountains in Jackson, New Hampshire.

> Alpine Adventures, Inc., Route 73, P.O. Box 179, Keene, NY 12942. (518) 576-9881

Diamond Sport offers climbing instruction in the popular Shawangunk Mountains, called the Gunks. Offers special kids' program. New Paltz is a good town for climbers to unwind in after a climb.

> Diamond Sport, 3 Crispell Lane, New Paltz, NY 12561. (800) 776-2577; (914) 255-4085

Complete instruction is available through High Angle Adventures; offers special women's program and custom-designed trips.

> High Angle Adventures, Inc., 5 River Rd., New Paltz, NY 12561. (800) 777-CLIMB; (914) 658-9811

Zen Mountain Monastery offers a weekend that is a combination Zen retreat and rock-climbing instruction for beginners with experienced guide.

> Zen Mountain Monastery, P.O. Box 156MR, South Plank Rd., Mt. Tremper, NY 12457. (914) 688-7993

The Appalachians

Seneca Rocks is a favorite of climbers because of its two challenging routes: Ecstacy, which is a 5.7 bare face; and Shipley's Shivering Shimmy, a 5.8 double face.

> Seneca Rocks Climbing School, Inc., P.O. Box 53, Seneca Rocks, WV 26884. (304) 567-2600

Hard Rock Climbing Services offers half-day and 1-day instruction on one of 1,400 routes on rocks of the New River Gorge. Custom-designs courses for special groups.

> Hard Rock Climbing Services, 131 S. Court St., P.O. Box 398, Fayetteville, WV 25840. (304) 574-0735

Wisconsin

One-week intensive climbing and outdoor leadership courses on the granite bluffs in Devil's Lake State Park are offered by Devil's Lake Training Center. Covers everything you could ever need to know. May through September.

> Devil's Lake Outdoor Training Center, P.O. Box 44156, Madison, WI 53744. (800) 33CLIMB

The Tetons

Exum Mountain Guides offers climbing instruction and guided climbs on several routes on the Grand Teton Range, including the 13,766-foot Grand Teton peak, generally reserved for experts or climbers out for a heavy-duty challenge.

Exum Mountain Guides, Grand Teton National Park, Box 56, Moose, WY 83012. (307) 733-2297

Authorized for Grand Teton National Park, Jackson Hole Mountain Guides offers instruction and guides from 1 to 8 days.

Jackson Hole Mountain Guides, Box 7477, Jackson, WY 83001. (307) 733-4979

The Rockies

South Dakota

Sylvan Rocks Climbing School and Guide Service offers guides, instruction, and special classes for kids. Also offers advanced climbs on Mount Rushmore and The Needles, the famous (much-photographed) peaks in South Dakota's Black Hills.

Sylvan Rocks Climbing School and Guide Service, Box 600, Hill City, SD 57745. (605) 574-2425

Colorado

Many climbers who live near Boulder love Eldorado Canyon in the Flatiron Mountain Range. (Contact: Boulder Chamber of Commerce, (800) 444-0447.)

Fantasy Ridge offers guides and 5-day courses on the granite walls of Black Canyon in Gunnison National Monument and 1-day course in Telluride.

Fantasy Ride Mountain Guides, P.O. Box 1679, Telluride, CO 81435. (303) 728-3546

An outdoor school which offers a 2-hour introduction to climbing as well as 1 or more days of advanced instruction in the San Juan Mountains in southwest Colorado.

SouthWest Adventures, P.O. Box 3242, 780 Main Ave., Durango, CO 81302. (303) 259-0370

Utah

Tower Guides offer beginner and advanced ascents and instruction on Castleton Tower, Utah. Also climbs Indian Creek, Six Shooter Peaks, and Devil's Tower, Wyoming.

Tower Guides, P.O. Box 3231, Grand Junction, CO 81502. (303) 245-6992

Iowa Mountaineers, Inc., P.O. Box 163, Iowa City, IA 52244.
(319) 337-7163

Iowa Mountaineers' guides offer climbing trips in Rocky Mountain National Park, the Sawtooth Range in Idaho, Castleton Tower, and beginner instruction in Wisconsin.

California

There is no place quite like Joshua Tree. Rising out of the desert east of Palm Springs, its sandstone rock outcrops look like something from another planet. Lots of climbers, but lots of routes too. For assistance, contact:

Joshua Tree National Park, Visitors' Center, (619) 367-7511
Wilderness Connection, P.O. Box 29, Joshua Tree, CA 92252-0029.
(619) 366-4745

Also near Los Angeles is Tahquitz, an 8,000-foot granite rock in the cool hills near Idyllwild.

Vertical Adventures, P.O. Box 6548, Newport Beach, CA 92658.
(714) 854-6250

The Wall at El Capitan in Yosemite is a sheer 3,000 feet. Other routes are more leisurely; one is a crack climb with four ledges.

Yosemite Mountaineering School and Guide Service,
Yosemite National Park, Yosemite, CA 95389. (209) 372-1244

Southern Yosemite Mountain Guides offers weekend climbs, lots of wilderness, camping, gourmet meals, campfires. Also offers tours for more advanced climbers.

Southern Yosemite Mountain Guides, P.O. Box 301,
Bass Lake, CA 93604. (415) 309-3153

South of Mount Shasta is Castle Crags State Park, a collection of granite towers, one of which, the Cosmic Wall, is 1,000 feet high. Climb this, or learn the basics on other Castle Crags rocks from March to October with experienced Shasta Mountain guides and instructors.

Shasta Mountain Guides, 1938 Hill Rd., Mt. Shasta, CA 96067.
(916) 926-3117

Washington

The northern Cascades in summer are a rugged collection of granite peaks, leftover snow, and fields of heather. For challenging climbs with beginning, intermediate, and master's rock instruction and guides, contact:

American Alpine Institute, 1515 12th St., Bellingham, WA 98225.
(206) 671-1505

OTHER SOURCES

For a list of climbing guides:

American Mountain Guides Association, 710 10th St., Suite 101,
Golden, CO 80401. (303) 271-0984

The AMGA provides a professional review of individual instructors and climbing schools. Certification ensures expertise.

The AMGA provides a list of members, but no complete list of outfitters exists. *Rock and Ice* magazine, *Summit* magazine, and *Climbing* magazine can provide many contacts.

Recommended books: *Mountaineering: The Freedom of the Hills* (The Mountaineers, Seattle, 1992), John Long's *How to Rock Climb!* (Chockstone, 1989), and Royal Robbins's *Basic Rockcraft* (Siesta Press, 1989). Many excellent guides to specific rocks and their routes can be found in outdoors outfitting stores. For a broad database, try Fantasy Adventures of Earth, Inc. (800) 836-4675 ($2.00 per minute).

ROCK GYMS

Within the last few years, rock gyms have sprung up by the hundreds across the country. These are huge warehouse-type spaces with wood walls covered with simulated rock holds. One climber described them as "a human puzzle. I ask myself, 'How can my body fit into it?'" While their belayers feed them rope, climbers climb up steep or inclined walls, or upside down across the ceiling, or use the bouldering area, which simulates difficult horizontal climbs without rope, but is only a few feet off the ground. Others try their skill at a crack climb, which is usually a vertical break in the wall.

"This is no substitute for nature," said a rock gym instructor. "It's probably impossible to build a strong interior wall thirty feet high with a jagged crack."

Climbing in a rock gym is a different experience than climbing outdoors. For one thing, the simulated rock holds are in place. Although some climbers feel safer taking initial instruction in a rock gym, and many rarely or never climb outdoors (some rock gyms have scheduled meets), instructors emphasize that, although floor mats or gravel break falls, rock gyms are only as safe as a climber's own safety precautions.

But rock gyms are terrific strength-builders. Even four hours a week in a rock gym provides a climbing workout that climbers

A belayer holds the rope while his buddy negotiates the ceiling at the Boston Rock Gym.

rarely get outdoors. They are also good places to make contacts with other climbers to learn the best places to climb.

For a list of rock gyms in the United States, see *Rock and Ice* magazine.

John Long's *Gym Climb!* (Chockstone Press, 1994) explains the differences involved in climbing in a rock gym.

Rowing

Rowing on a quiet river early in the morning gives a pair of scullers the time and place to practice.

Rowing is what slaves did for the Romans and the Vikings, pumping huge ships at racing pace across large bodies of water. Rowing is different than paddling: The slim, tapered craft are propelled by long oars, and the sport has a long tradition of panache. Ivy League crews compete traditionally in 4- and 8-person shells. But more and more, single-person shells are turning up on city rivers, and rowing, called sculling, is becoming a recreational adventure. This is in part because of its extraordinary cardiovascular and calorie-burning (400 in 20 minutes) benefits, but it's also because, as one rower said, "sculling alone on a beautiful river is good for the soul."

Single-person craft, called shells, have a sliding seat that moves the rower forward and backward with the strokes of the 9-foot, 9-inch oars. Although they weigh less than 30 pounds, recreational shells range from 16 to 22 feet long and are 15 to 21 inches wide. Racing shells are even longer and narrower.

The biggest race is the Head-of-the-Charles Regatta, which is held every October in Boston and attracts hundreds of collegiate, professional, international, and amateur singles and crews. For information, call (617) 864-8415 or (617) 354-1623.

But if you just want to row for recreation, and don't know how to scull, contact a school for lessons, then join a local club where you can rent a shell.

The US Rowing Association is a membership organization. Joining will give you access to a list of clubs as well as races and rowing events. (Lesson: $40–$50. Club membership usually includes one lesson.)

> US Rowing Association, 201 S. Capitol Ave., Suite 400,
> Indianapolis, IN 46225. (800) 314-4769; (317) 237-5656

Following is a list of instructors and schools, compiled by the US Rowing Association.

New England

VERMONT

In the warm months, Craftsbury Sculling Center runs week- and weekend-long sculling camps.

> Craftsbury Sculling Center, Box 31, Craftsbury Common, VT 05827.
> (802) 586-7767

Three-day courses for all levels are offered here with video feedback, troubleshooting.

> Sparhawk Sculling School, 222 Porters Point Rd., Colchester, VT 05446.
> (802) 658-4799

NEW HAMPSHIRE

Durham Boat Co. offers 2- and 5-day sculling packages in New Hampshire, where they have an indoor tank, and in Florida in the winter.

> Durham Boat Co., RFD #2 Newmarket Rd., Durham, NH 03824.
> (603) 659-2548

MASSACHUSETTS

Northeast Sculling and Rowing Center maintains a rowing camp in Maine.

> Northeast Sculling and Rowing Center, P.O. Box 2060,
> Duxbury, MA 02332. (508) 934-6192

Mid-Atlantic

NEW YORK

Private instruction at four areas in the New York region.
*East Arm Rowing Centers, P.O. Box 648, Sterling Rd.,
Greenwood Lakes, NY 10925. (914) 477-3076*

Instruction in sculling at winter location in Palm Beach County.
*Florida Rowing Center, 1140 Fifth Ave., New York, NY 10128.
(212) 996-1196*

NEW JERSEY

Beginning and intermediate instruction.
*Rowing Systems, 4905 Atlantic Ave., Ventnor, NJ 08406.
(609) 822-0736*

Southeast

FLORIDA

Lessons for individuals and groups, racing and recreational.
*Shells for Rowing, 53302 Clifton Rd., Jacksonville, FL 32211.
(904) 725-7573*

Midwest

MINNESOTA

Workshops and lectures in mind-set techniques, plus injury prevention and reconditioning.
*Aqua-Tymz: The Body-Mind Connection,
1304 West Medicine Lake Rd. #107, Plymouth, MN 55441.
(612) 920-3317*

West

WASHINGTON

Instruction in open-water shells.
*Rowing Northwest—Seattle, 3304 Fuhrman Ave. East,
Seattle, WA 98103. (206) 324-5800*

Sculling lessons for open-water racing or recreation.
*Rowing Northwest—Spokane, North 10711 College Place Dr.,
Spokane, WA 99218. (509) 466-8158*

Offers instruction and coaching for all ages and special needs.
> Rowing Unlimited, Metropolitan Park District of Tacoma,
> 1602 South K St., Tacoma, WA 98405. (206) 591-5314

CALIFORNIA

Sculling instruction for all levels, with clinics for rough-water rowing.
> Open Water Rowing, 85 Liberty Ship Way #102, Sausalito, CA 94965.
> (415) 332-1091

Part of UCal Berkeley, Cal Adventures offers an introduction to sculling in San Francisco Bay. Also offers recreational sculling rental boats if you know how to scull.
> Cal Adventures, 2301 Bancroft Way, Berkeley, CA 94720.
> (510) 642-4000

OCEAN ROWING

Ocean sculling requires craft that are heavier and longer for rougher water. Rowing with long oars requires managing the delicate balance of rower, craft, and oars in sometimes turbulent seas. The 7-mile Isle of Shoals Race, which starts in Kittery Point, Maine, has been held for two decades. For information on the race:
> Alden Ocean Shell Association, P.O. Box 368, Eliot, ME 03903.
> (207) 439-1507

OTHER SOURCES

Recommended reading: Joe Paduda's *The Art of Sculling*. It can be ordered from:
> The Rower's Bookshelf Catalog, P.O. Box 440C, Essex, MA 01929.
> (508) 468-4096

INDOOR ROWING

Indoor rowers, who number in the tens of thousands around the world, can compete in February in Boston with several thousand others in the C.R.A.S.H.-B Sprints World Indoor Rowing Championships. Concept II Rowing Ergometers, invented by two former Olympian rowers, are indoor rowing machines that have a computer on which the rower can monitor and store his rowing data and compare the data directly with scores on other Concept II Ergometers.

Rowers at home self-report their times and speeds to the main database at Concept II headquarters and are logged into an international pool of rowers' best times and distances. From a published list, a rower in Winnetka, for example, can check his or her times against someone in the same weight and age group in Japan or France.

World-ranked since 1982, the C.R.A.S.H.-B Championship, sponsored by Concept II, is the largest of 80 to 90 indoor rowing races. Most meets compete in 2,500-meter speed and 30- and 60-minute distance races, as well as round-the-clock marathons at clubs.

Ages range from 6 to 99; data are logged for kids, men, women, the disabled, lightweight, heavyweight, and those who have done more than a million meters.

Concept II, Inc., RR 1, Box 1100, Morrisville, VT 05661-9727.
(800) 245-5676; (802) 888-7971

Sailing

Two-masted schooners, like the *Spike Africa*, take passengers on windjammer cruises. *Photograph by Roger Archibald.*

More than most adventures, sailing gives you a sense of freedom and yet of being in control. The feel of the tug of the ocean current on the keel, the rush of the wind in the sail, and the spray of salt water on your face are powerful tonics. (Beginner weekend: $200–$450; live-aboard cruising course, 5-day: $1,100–$1,900.)

LEARNING HOW

Most sailing schools run accessible weekend courses which will give the novice a feeling for being on the water in a boat moved by the wind and currents. By Sunday night you should be able to take the tiller, hoist the sails, and tack and jibe.

If you stay for the week or go for a series of weekends, you will

Sailing the predictable winds in San Francisco Bay is a good way to learn the boat, the water, and the wind, like these sailors on the brigantine *Rendezvous*. *Photograph by Roger Archibald.*

also learn something about knot tying, docking, reading the weather, spotting wind direction, how to navigate using a chart with hundreds of little numbers on it, and even chart a course to a desired destination. Above all, the practice will make you feel confident on the water.

Then you can move on to celestial navigation, emergency medical practices at sea, and bareboat cruising, which will allow you to skipper a rented yacht and go to Fiji, for example.

Sailing has some interesting spin-offs: You learn to duck the boom, coil the ropes into perfect circles on deck, and fold your clothes into little squares so that everything can go in its proper place. That's known as being *shipshape*.

RHODE ISLAND

J Boats are fast and sleek, and the designers of these boats offer them to beginners and advanced sailors to learn and to polish their skills on the water. They operate out of Key West, San Diego, and the famous waters of Narragansett Bay off Newport, Rhode Island, where America's Cup races began. J World Sailing School offers weekend beginner courses, racing courses, and live-aboard cruising.

J World Sailing School, P.O. Box 1509, Newport, RI 02840.
(800) 343-2255; (401) 849-5492

MARYLAND

The first school to teach sailing to the general public, Annapolis
Sailing School runs programs in the Chesapeake Bay and in
Tampa Bay out of St. Petersburg, Florida. Offers weekend beginner
courses, 5-day sailing courses, and cruises. Advanced students learn
coastal and celestial navigation, piloting, and bareboat chartering.
The Become a Sailing Family course offers a 24-foot sloop for up
to six family members for a weekend of beginning courses.
Annapolis Sailing School, P.O. Box 3334, Annapolis, MD 21403.
(800) 638-9192; (410) 267-7205 (in Maryland)

FLORIDA

Offers beginner weekend courses through to performance sailing,
introductory and advanced racing, as well as live-aboard cruising
and catamaran handling and cruising. Works out of four U.S. sites:
Captiva Island and St. Petersburg, Florida, Newport, Rhode Island,
and the San Juan Islands, Washington. Also offers special family
packages that include care for kids 3–11, and courses for teens.
Offshore Sailing School, 16731 McGregor Blvd., Fort Myers, FL 33908.
(800) 221-4326; (813) 454-1700

CALIFORNIA

Operating out of San Francisco Bay, where the winds are predictable and steady, this club certifies sailors through their Accelerated Learning System, which builds from weekend courses on
20-foot boats to bareboat charter cruising on more than 30-foot
yachts. Also rents boats and gives refresher courses.
Offshore Circle Sailing Club, 1 Spinnaker Way, Berkeley Marina,
Berkeley, CA 94710. (510) 843-4200

Special Course   An important part of any sailing trip is knowing
what to do if a member of the crew is injured or sick. This special
4- or 6-day Emergency Medicine at Sea program takes place at the
Monterey Bay Marine Sanctuary. Novices will learn a lot about
sailing, and advanced sailors will enhance their seamanship.
Ocean Voyages, 1709 Bridgeway, Sausalito, CA 94965. (415) 332-4681

SAILING TRIPS

Sailing Safaris has four yachts, 30 to 44 feet, which you can charter with a skipper or with you at the helm (if you are certified for
bareboat cruising). The territory is the coast off Chugach National

Forest, with lots of land and ocean wildlife. Also offers guided natural history tours, with side trips in kayaks to watch wildlife.

Alaska Wilderness Sailing Safaris, P.O. Box 1313, Valdez, AK 99686. (907) 835-5175

Huntley Yacht Charters brokers yachting trips with or without a skipper and crew in many places around the U.S. Ask for a catalog.

Huntley Yacht Charters, RD #1, Box 301, Wernersville, PA 19565. (800) 322-9224; (215) 678-2628

WINDJAMMER CRUISES

MAINE

Sailing on a 2-masted gaff-rigged schooner—a windjammer—is a lot different than sailing on a single-masted sloop. For one thing, the schooner's broad beam means you can stroll around the deck when the wind is quiet and the loudest sound is a seagull's flapping wings. For another, when the several thousand square feet of sail catch a breeze, every romance novel you have ever read about the sea comes to life. Windjammers were the fleet of schooners built in the 19th century to carry freight until sail was replaced by coal power, and windjammers became fishing boats or pilot boats or simply fell into disuse.

Not all of Maine's passenger windjammers are the original 19th-century ships: Some were built recently. All are approved by the U.S. Coast Guard and outfitted for passengers and their comfort and safety, with bunk beds and bath facilities and a big galley. Food takes on extra importance at sea, whether you are out for the day or for a week.

A typical 3- or 6-day windjammer cruise in Maine involves 5 or 6 hours a day of sailing Maine's intricate island-strewn cobalt blue waters. In summer and fall the weather tends to be crystal clear, and the towns along the way look like calendar pictures. Each ship accommodates at least twenty passengers, who can help hoist and lower the sails, as well as swim, snorkle, explore islands, and look for seals and birds when the ship anchors. The final night at sea is a Down East lobster bake cooked over a fire on a beach. The season is late May to mid-October. (3 days: $300–$445; 6 days: $575–$600.)

The Maine Windjammer maintains a fleet of ten ships that vary in length from 64 to 130 feet: *Angelique, Grace Bailey, J&E Riggin,*

Mary Day, Mercantile, Nathaniel Bowditch, Roseway, Timberwind, and *Victory Chimes.*

> *The Maine Windjammer Association, P.O. Box 1144 F,*
> *Blue Hill, ME 04614. (800) 807-WIND*

Maintains three windjammers: *American Eagle, Heritage, Isaac H. Evans.*

> *North End Shipyard Schooners, P.O. Box 482, Rockland, ME 04841.*
> *(800) 648-4544*

Lewis R. French is the oldest windjammer afloat, built in 1871. She has been a passenger boat since 1976.

> *Schooner Lewis R. French, Capt. Dan and Kathy Pease, P.O. Box 992,*
> *Camden, ME 04843-0992. (800) 469-4635; (207) 594-9141*

MICHIGAN

The *Manitou* is a 114-foot 2-masted topsail schooner that sails on Lake Michigan and Lake Huron and stops at Mackinac and other islands to allow passengers to beachcomb and hike. Three- and 6-day cruises, June to October.

> *Traverse Tall Ship Co., 13390 S.W. Bay Shore Dr.,*
> *Traverse City, MI 49684. (800) 678-0383; (616) 941-2000*

CALIFORNIA

The *Duen* is a 72-foot gaff-rigged ketch with an interesting past. Built in Norway in 1939 as a fishing boat, she was sailed in the Pacific as a world cruiser until she was bought in 1986 and outfitted as a coastal sailer. A 10-day tour in late May takes guests through the Pacific Northwest to southeast Alaska. The owner and his wife are veteran sailors, and she is a good cook. Book early.

> *Ocean Voyages, 1709 Bridgeway, Sausalito, CA 94965. (415) 332-4681*

WORKING CRUISES ON TALL SHIPS

The crew on a square-rigged tall ship needs to work like a well-oiled machine to make the ship run. Yards and yards of sail, miles and miles of line, plus the daily maintenance duties of keeping the ship on course and shipshape requires around-the-clock attention. In the process of tending to the ship's duties, the crew members, often without realizing it, form a synchronous unit: The ship needs them to operate, and they need each other to keep it going.

For these reasons, sail-training organizations specialize in taking high school students to help them learn to pull together as a group by contributing their individual skills. Many ships also take interested adults who have always wanted to know what it feels like to sail on a historic sailing ship and who are not afraid of getting calluses. (*See the chapter on History for a description of HMS* Rose.)

Expedition length varies from 1 day to several weeks. Ships are of different sizes and ply the Great Lakes, the Atlantic, and the world. Expect to keep a night watch, wash the decks, tie knots, toss the hawsers, and even cook. Going aloft to climb the rigging is not required, but those who do it, 100 feet or more above the deck, report a rush of excitement.

The American Sail Training Association publishes an annual *Directory of Sail Training Ships and Programs*, free with membership, or separately for $8.00. This lists (with photos) the tall ships that take passengers on working tours.

ASTA is the umbrella organization for 130 tall ships and sail-training programs in North America. A membership organization, ASTA provides scholarships to students in sail training and publishes a newsletter, *Running Free*. (1 day: about $100.)

> *The American Sail Training Association (ASTA), P.O. Box 1459, Newport, RI 02840. (401) 846-1775*

Sea Education Association runs six 12-week programs a year, called SEA Semesters, for college students who study for 6 weeks onshore at Woods Hole and 6 weeks at sea sailing the Caribbean aboard the 125-foot staysail schooner *Windward* or the 134-foot brigantine *Corwith Cramer*. Each SEA Semester gives 17 college credits.

For teachers, SEA runs a summer SEA Experience of 3 weeks ashore studying oceanography, nautical science, and maritime history and literature, followed by 1 week applying the knowledge at sea on a cruise in the North Atlantic.

In conjunction with Elderhostel, SEA runs Lifelong Learners, with lectures in the field, ashore.

> *Sea Education Association, Inc., P.O. Box 6, Woods Hole, MA 02543. (800) 552-3633; (508) 540-3954*

OTHER SOURCES

For a list of sailing schools, contact:

> *American Sailing Association, 13922 Marquesas Way, Marina del Rey, CA 90292. (310) 822-7171*

Sail magazine, *Cruising World*, and *Sailing* contain information on boats and sailing.

Scuba

Coral reefs, shipwrecks, millions of small fish and a few huge fish, plus sponges, caves, rock formations, and mysteries are all part of the underwater adventure.

Scuba diving is one of the premier technological advances of the 20th century. These days, any certified diver can do night dives with the mantas, or underwater photography, or take extra courses to do deep-water wreck diving or cave diving.

Certification from a reputable instructor is mandatory for a serious diver. Quickie courses, usually in warm-water resorts, introduce previous novices to the underwater in 1 to 3 days, which enables a vacationer to take a couple of shallow water dives to see what it's like.

A certified diver is one who has had at least 28 hours of classroom and pool experience and at least one open-water dive. Certified divers keep logbooks and log in each dive, usually at diveshops, where divers get tanks filled with air. A diver is only as good as his most recent dive, because repetition gives experience. C-cards (certification cards) are provided by Scuba Schools International, which has begun issuing silver, gold, and platinum cards for divers who have made 500 to 5,000 dives. The cards are held in great esteem.

Scuba is dangerous: You are not in your natural environment, and you are breathing a canned mixture of oxygen and nitrogen. Nitrogen accumulates in the blood, and if the diver goes too deep for too long or rises too fast, physical complications can result. This is only one of the reasons why you should take the time and scout out a good course before you go on a trip, because then you will learn how to read dive tables that tell you safe diving durations, safe ascent practices, and the amount of surface time your body needs to rid itself of excess nitrogen.

You won't be alone. Between 300,000 and 400,000 people get certified annually, joining the other estimated 5 million certified divers in the U.S.

Dive shops are the place to start. They have instructors, sell gear, give advice, provide guides, and in some cases, organize trips. Check the telephone book, or call any scuba organization for a list of affiliates. If you become hooked on diving, try a live-aboard dive boat, where you and your shipmates will do nothing but dive every day, several times a day. (1-day boat dive: $60–$80; live-aboard, 4–7 days: $1,300–$1,700.)

The following organizations will mail you a list of dive instructors who use their teaching technique:

National Association for Underwater Instruction (NAUI),
P.O. Box 14650, Montclair, CA 91763.
(800) 553-6284; (714) 621-5801
Professional Association of Dive Instructors (PADI), 1251 East Dyer Rd.,
#100, Santa Ana, CA 92705. (800) 729-7234; (714) 540-7234
National YMCA Scuba Program, 5825-2A Live Oak Parkway,
Norcross, GA 30093-1728. (404) 662-5172
Scuba Schools International, 2619 Canton Court,
Fort Collins, CO 80525-4498. (800) 892-2702

GEAR

Diving gear is bulky and heavy to travel with, but you can rent the heaviest things at the dive site—air tanks and belt weights which keep you underwater. If you plan to dive often, it pays to invest in a buoyancy compensator (BC) vest that fits you, a breathing regulator that goes in your mouth and attaches to the tank, a computer that reads depth, time elapsed, and air pressure, a face mask, and any other gadget that you need. (Rinse well after saltwater dives to keep equipment in good working order.) Then you're ready to hoist up the tank and somersault into the ocean. Beneath is another world—quiet, mysterious, beautiful.

WRECK DIVING

Advanced divers can receive special instruction in wreck penetration diving, which is often deeper than 130 feet and involves longer stays down, carrying two tanks of air, and wearing a bulkier drysuit rather than a wetsuit. Most divers carry tools to wedge them out of difficult situations. On very deep dives, team diving is recommended. It is important to know something about the layout of the sunken ship so that you won't get stuck in a hallway, and how not to panic in silt clouds, that are created by divers entering rooms that have been untouched since the ship sank.

Wrecks exist wherever there have been commerce, and storms or enemies to bring down the ships—in Lake Michigan off Isle Royale, off Cape Cod, New York, New Jersey, the Channel Islands in California, and strewn throughout the Florida Keys. Wrecks are fascinating historically, and are sometimes gruesome, if skeletons are still in place. Check with the dive shop in the area for laws governing souvenir taking.

For wreck-penetration diving courses:

> *National Association for Cave Diving, Wreck Penetration Branch,*
> *P.O. Box 14492, Gainesville, FL 32604*

CAVE DIVING

According to the National Association for Cave Diving, "Cave diving is caving using scuba gear," which means that no amount of open-water diving experience is preparation for the peculiarities of swimming through the maze of roofed underwater rooms. Diving in caves, divers risk getting lost or trapped, losing their tanks or regulator hoses, running out of air, getting cold, and panicking. Plus, some caves are in deep water. Special courses include learning how to dive wearing a dry suit and a helmet and carrying two tanks, three lights, and extra regulators, and diving with a team. Rewards are high: Underwater caves are as fascinating as below-ground caves, with the added bonus of unusual fish residents, such as moray eels.

For a list of cave-diving certification courses, from shallow-water cavern diving to specialty cave-diving courses, contact:

> National Association for Cave Diving, P.O. Box 14492,
> Gainesville, FL 32604
> National Speleological Society, Cave Diving Section, P.O. Box 950,
> Branford, FL 32008-0950. (813) 528-4202

For technical underwater diving in deep-water wreck penetration and caves, involving mixed gas (often nitrogen, hydrogen, and oxygen) for longer and deeper underwater dives, IANTD will send a list of instructors for $5.75:

> International Association of Nitrox and Technical Divers,
> World Headquarters, 1545 NE 104th St.,
> Miami Shores, FL 33138-2665. (305) 751-4873

REEF DIVING

Coral reefs are complex architectural structures intermingled with fantastic sponges in all colors and shapes and are home to hundreds of species of fish. Florida's coral reef has suffered through several years of careless boat anchoring, land pollutants, and boat oil and paint. Most dive shops will emphasize responsibility in reef diving. Don't break the coral—it kills it.

Artificial reefs are formed when deliberately sunk vessels provide good habitat for reef fish.

DIVES AND DIVE SHOPS

New England

Side-wheel steamships used to ferry passengers between resorts on Lake Winnipesaukee, New Hampshire. Storms sank a few; now divers look for their wrecks. Dive from the diveship, Lady-Go-Diva. This company also gives scuba courses.

> Dive Winnipesaukee Corp., P.O. Box 2198, Wolfeboro, NH 03894.
> (603) 569-8080

Forty wrecks, from World War II submarines to tugboats to passenger vessels, are 50 to 250 feet beneath the surface of the ocean off Cape Cod. Most of what divers can carry back they can legally keep. From May to November, Erik Takakjian's Grey Eagle will carry you to the wrecks for the day or the weekend. His crew of four is trained in emergency medical procedures, and the boat carries 400 cubic feet of oxygen. Bring your own gear and C-card.

Grey Eagle Charters, Erik Takakjian, P.O. Box 42,
Yarmouthport, MA 02675. (508) 362-6501

New York and New Jersey

The waters from Long Island to the tip of the Jersey coast are full of wrecks, from rowboats to the Italian cruise ship *Andrea Doria*, which sank in 1957. The USS *San Diego*, a World War I cruiser, was sunk by a German mine in 1918, leaving it upside down and armed. No legal restraints prevent divers from keeping what they can carry from the ship, which is 110 feet down, off Long Island, but diving to it requires two tanks as well as some familiarity with its layout. Try Island Scuba Centers, Freeport, Long Island, (516) 546-2030; or Scuba Shop, Medford, Long Island, (516) 289-5555.

North Carolina

The Union's Civil War ironclad ship, USS *Monitor*, one of the first metal ships and a forerunner of the battleship, sank in a storm off Cape Hatteras while it was being towed south, a few months after having done battle with the South's USS *Merrimac*. More than 80 years later, a depth charge apparently from a German U-boat during World War II blew up a good portion of the ship. "It's still big, both in size and in history," says Arthur Kirchner, the only concessionaire diver approved by NOAA, which oversees the wreck as a marine sanctuary.

But diving on it is not easy. Using National Oceanic and Atmospheric Association (NOAA) specifications, veteran diver Kirchner handpicks divers who have made at least five dives deeper than 200 feet, with three years of diving, minimum. Teams of four, each with two tanks of mixed gas, spend 20 minutes 240 feet down at the wreck. The long ascent is aided by an oxygen hose 70 feet for the surface, where divers can stop for their last decompression stop.

If you qualify and have DAN insurance (*see Insurance section in the Appendix*), contact Kirchner for a September/October dive. *Warning:* Aborts are possible because of adverse weather conditions and strong currents which affect the oxygen hose and the placement of the 35-foot dive boat, *Margie II*. Check weather reports and allow for extra time.

Arthur Kirchner, Atlantic Wreck Diving, Teach's Lair Marine,
Cape Hatteras, NC. (919) 986-2460 (April–October),
(201) 361-3018 (winter), (919) 986-2832 (Margie II)

Florida

THE KEYS

Key Largo and Looe Key, off the upper and lower Florida Keys respectively, are two world-class coral reef habitats, with spiny lobsters, sea turtles, and brain, pillar, elkhorn, and staghorn corals. Between South Miami and the Dry Tortugas are American Shoal, Aligator Reef, and Sombrero Reef. All of these are National Marine Sanctuaries, which means they are protected.

For information on visiting them:

Marine and Estuarine Management Division, National Oceanic and Atmospheric Administration, 1825 Connecticut Ave., NW, Suite 714, Washington, DC 20235. (202) 673-5122

For a PADI 5-star dive shop with courses, certification, nitrox for deep-water dives, and a nearby hyperbarics center:

Ocean Divers, 522 Caribbean Dr., Key Largo, FL 33037. (800) 451-1113; (305) 451-1113

THE SPRINGS

In north central Florida and the panhandle, Ponce de Leon's Fountains of Youth inundate the land with freshwater springs. The water is a cool 70 degrees year-round and fairly clear. Divers report having found mastodon bones, fossils, and some carved pillars, thought to date from about 2,000 years ago. Several deep caves require technical training, but easy caves, some with permanent guidelines, at Ginny Springs, and artificial caves at Vortex are open to noncertified cave divers.

Dive shop, cave-diving instruction, camping facilities, wilderness activities are available at:

Ginny Springs Resort, 7300 N.E. Ginnie Springs Rd., High Springs, FL 32643. (800) 874-8571; (904) 454-2202

Dive shop, cavern instruction, hotel, motel on site of Vortex Springs.

Vortex Springs, Inc., Route 2, P.O. Box 650, Ponce de Leon, FL 32455. (800) 342-0640; (904) 836-4979

MANATEES

Sea Ventures will certify you as a PADI Open Water Diver in 4 days on Crystal River, where in winter, you can dive with manatees when they migrate. Hotel included in package. (*See also Manatees, in the Wildlife chapter.*)

Sea Ventures, Marine Education Institute, P.O. Box 23931, Jacksonville, FL 32241. (904) 268-0956

LIVE-ABOARD

The *Nekton Pilot* is an unusually stable dive boat built like an oil rig outside, with luxury fittings inside. You'll never get seasick, and you can travel for a week throughout the waters off Florida. Families are invited for beach exploration and snorkeling. Diving amenities include tanks, air, and belts.

> *Florida Adventures, Inc., P.O. Box 677923, Orlando, FL 32867.*
> *(407) 677-0655*

Michigan

Lake Superior's Isle Royale, the largest of a 200-island archipelago, is famous for its abundant moose. The surrounding shoals have wrecked dozens of ships over the years. For a list of dive outfitters as well as diving preserves:

> *Michigan Underwater Preserves Council, 11 S. State St.,*
> *St. Ignace, MI 49871. (906) 643-8717*

For camping reservations:

> *Isle Royale National Park, 87 N. Ripley St., Houghton, MI 49931*

Texas

The Flower Garden Banks are flower-like coral reefs in the Gulf of Mexico. The 41 square miles provide tropical beauty for divers. Dive boats are available from the Texas or Louisiana coasts. For information, contact:

> *Flower Garden Banks National Marine Sanctuary, Texas A&M Sea Grant*
> *Program, 1716 Briarcrest Drive, #702, Bryant, TX 77802.*
> *(409) 847-9296*

California

The Channel Islands, above and below water, are a National Marine Sanctuary. Divers here find wrecks and prehistoric Chumash Indian artifacts.

> *Channel Islands National Marine Sanctuary, 113 Harbor Way,*
> *Santa Barbara, CA 93109. (805) 966-7107*

For a dive shop with guided beach dives on the Channel Islands as well as the kelp beds off San Diego:

> *Rick's Diving Locker, 945-L W. Valley Parkway, Escondido, CA 92025.*
> *(619) 746-8980*

How underwater systems work is not always evident to divers. The University of California at San Francisco gives a course called Marine Biology for Scuba Divers, on weekends in September and October, with diving off Monterey Peninsula.

Millberry Programs and Services, University of California.
(415) 476-1115

Researchers are interested in mapping and cataloging marine life around Monterey Bay's subtidal habitat. No experience mapping is needed; divers must prove their underwater ability. Then you can spend 6 hours a day for 3 days on a 40-foot dive boat.

Oceanic Society Expeditions, Fort Mason Center, Building E,
San Francisco, CA 94123. (800) 326-7491; (415) 441-1106

Hawaii

Hawaiian volcanic activity left sharp lava pinnacles and caverns underwater. Beyond the coast, the open Pacific is home to some huge residents, including humpback whales. For diving packages, some with instruction, others with night dives, all with lodging and a rental car; and a Blue Water Experience, a 1-day dive away from the coast among jellyfish, whale sharks, pilot whales, and whatever else is there, contact:

Eco-Scapes, 75-5626 Kuakini Highway, Kailua-Kona, HI 96740.
(800) 949-DIVE; (808) 329-7116

For experienced divers: Take a two-tank guided dive off Oahu over an around a World War II U.S. Navy tanker, a YO-257. Like most wrecks, it has proved to be an excellent habitat for many varieties of fish.

Atlantis Reef Divers, 1085 Ala Moana Blvd., Room 102,
Honolulu, HI 96814. (800) 554-6267

LIVE-ABOARD

For certified and serious, dedicated divers who want a week of solid diving opportunities, the *Kona Aggressor II*, a live-aboard dive boat, will carry divers to the best places off the Big Island of Hawaii. Underwater adventure cage. Certified beginners are welcome, but anyone not truly into diving would be bored, says a spokesperson.

Go Diving, 5610 Rowland Rd., #100, Minnetonka, MN 55343.
(800) 328-5285

COMPETITIVE SCUBA

Scuba skills, which some certification courses mandate, include being able to "doff and don" (remove your gear, swim to the surface, dive back down, and put your gear back on), "buddy breathing," (sharing your regulator with your buddy as you swim, which you would have to do if you or your buddy lost a regulator connection underwater), and underwater navigation. These three skills comprise scuba championship games organized by the Underwater Society of America. Only requirements: be a member of a USOA club and at least 16 years old.

> *Underwater Society of America, P.O. Box 628, Daly City, CA 94017.*
> *(415) 583-8492*

SUBMARINE DIVE

If you'd rather skip the scuba and go down 20,000 leagues, you can take a ride underwater in Hawaii in *Atlantis*, a genuine submarine. Sixty-five feet long, it carries 46 passengers, each at a porthole. You cruise past such things as a sunken Navy tanker off Waikiki, black coral at a depth of 150 feet between Maui and Lana'i, and colorful butterfly fish and Moorish idols off Kona. Trip is 45 minutes long and narrated. Allow 2 hours start to finish.

> For reservations:
> *U.S.: (800) 548-6262*
> *Waikiki: (808) 973-9811*
> *Kona: (808) 329-6626*
> *Maui: (808) 667-2224*

OTHER SOURCES

Magazines: *Scuba Diving* and *Sport Diver* are two comprehensive scuba periodicals.

Sea Kayaking

A sea kayaker pauses to check the route of a humpback whale on Stellwagen Bank, in the Atlantic ocean, about five miles off the coast of Cape Cod, Massachusetts. *Photograph courtesy of Adventure Learning Center, Merrimac, Massachusetts.*

If you find whitewater kayaking too rough and canoeing too quiet, you might want to try sea kayaking. One- and 2-person kayaks can withstand choppy ocean water and shore waves and allow paddler to explore caves and inlet sand to visit tiny islands inhabited only by seals and gulls.

The first sea kayaks were used by Inuits and other Arctic dwellers, who made them out of sealskin and paddled silently through ice-strewn waters in search of food. Today kayaks are streamlined and brightly colored, with watertight compartments for your car keys and camera. Instruction can take as little as half a day and will include learning such basics as how to read the tides, how to get out of the kayak underwater if your kayak is overturned, how to right it, and how to get back in. Although sea kayaks are longer than other kayaks and are considered safer, you might also learn how to do an Eskimo Roll, in which you stay in your kayak and roll it sideways 360 degrees. Expect to wear a hard hat, a life vest, and if the water temperature is cold, a wetsuit. (If it's *really* cold, wear long johns under your wetsuit.)

Because kayaks are not threatening to sea creatures, whale, seal, and sea lion viewing is common. Experienced sea kayakers say that in addition to being close to wildlife, they experience a unity with the ocean. Kayaking is quiet, and coastal waters have few interruptions, so kayakers often have a sense that the ocean is their territory. Always do this sport with a buddy or a group.

Kayakers compete in rodeos and in surfing (on a kayak called a wave ski), and accept the challenge of long-distance endurance trips. The first trans-Atlantic kayak trip took place in 1928.

Few restrictions apply to sea kayaking: All ages are able to do it, and the regular rhythm of paddling does not strain the body, although it can leave you pretty tired after a day's workout.

If you have never done it before, always get instruction and go with a guide until you feel confident enough to meet your own challenges. "More fools mean more rules," says one outfitter. "Take a course so you can enjoy it safely."

Outfitters on the coasts offer instruction, guides, and organized tours. Some even offer group tours at dawn, or under the moonlight, depending on how close to nature you want to get. (3 days: $350–$450; 1-day clinic; $50–$65.)

New England

MAINE

Maine has more coastal shoreline—3,478 miles—than the whole state of California. A premier sea-kayaking state because of its inlets and islands, Maine is one of the few states to have a sea-kayaking trail guide; it covers 325 miles from Portland to Mathias, and includes 40 public islands and 40 privately owned islands, whose owners give permission to kayakers. To access the guide, you must join the Maine Islands Trail Association. This group of about 3,000 emphasizes stewardship of islands and low-impact kayaking, does spring cleanups, sponsors sea-kayaking skills workshops, and provides opportunities for group kayaking. The guide comes with the membership ($35).

Maine Island Trails Association, P.O. Box C, Rockland, ME 04841.
(207) 596-6456

The Maine Sport Outdoor School offers Sea Kayaking I and II, workshops, and island-hopping expeditions.

Maine Sport Outdoor School, P.O. Box 956, Rockport, ME 04856.
(800) 722-0826; (800) 244-8799 (in Maine)

Maine Island Kayak Company offers 1- to 10-day guided sea kayak trips.

Maine Island Kayak Co., 70 Luther St., Peaks Island, ME 04108.
(800) 796-2373

Indian Island Kayak Company offers a course in sailing and guided multi-day inn-to-inn or camping trips on trimaran/sail kayaks. These crafts offer an experience somewhere between sailing and kayaking, with the best of both. Stabilized by a twelve-foot out-rigger on each side, they hold one or two people, with room for gear for long-distance trips. Leeboards control lateral drift, and the sails are battened, so the kayaker has good control over the craft. They are steady and fast (8 to 10 knots). You always have the option of paddling, and they still provide the intimate-with-the-sea feeling that comes with a regular kayak.

Indian Island Kayak Co., 16 Mountain St., Camden, ME 04843.
(207) 236-4088

MASSACHUSETTS

Adventure Learning Center offers 1- to 7-day sea-kayaking tours of the New England coast, plus instruction and clinics for those with some basic sea-kayaking knowledge.

Adventure Learning Center, 67 Bear Hill, Merrimac, MA.
(800) 649-9728; (508) 346-9728

Mid-Atlantic

NORTH CAROLINA

Cape Hatteras National Seashore is an unusual stretch of marsh-lands, high sand dunes (where the Wright Brothers tried out their first flights), and lots of seabirds.

Ride the Wind offers 1- and 2-day guided sea-kayaking trips.

Ride the Wind, Box 352, Ocracoke, NC 27960. (919) 928-6311

Kitty Hawk Sports gives lessons and sea-kayaking tours of the Outer Banks.

Kitty Hawk Sports, Inc., P.O. Box 939, Nags Head, NC 27959.
(919) 441-9200

South

GEORGIA

Four-day sea-kayaking tours of the barrier Sea Islands, past shrimp boats and historic plantations, are offered by Lookfar Adventures. Nights are spent in inns.

Lookfar Adventures, P.O. Box 3005, Hilton Head Island, SC 29928.
(800) 882-4424; (803) 363-2360

FLORIDA

Sanibel Sea Kayak Wildlife Tours provides instruction and guided tours on the coast of the Gulf of Mexico. Lots of wildlife.
Sanibel Sea Kayak Wildlife Tours, Box 975, Sanibel, FL 33957.
(813) 472-9484

Gulf Coast Kayaking offers custom trips with a naturalist guide.
Gulf Coast Kayaking, 4882 N.W. Pine Island Rd., Matlacha, FL 33909.
(813) 283-1125

Great Lakes

WISCONSIN

The 22 Apostle Islands in the largest freshwater lake in the world, Lake Superior, have fascinating coastline and sea caves with limestone pillars. Wear a wetsuit. Three- or five-day trips.
Wilderness Inquiry, Inc., 1313 Fifth St., SE, Box 84,
Minneapolis, MN 55414-1546. (800) 728-0719; (612) 379-3858

West

WASHINGTON

Northern Lights' Mystery Tour explores pristine wilderness in the Inside Passage in 7 days; sea kayaking and camping.
Northern Lights Expeditions, 6141 NE Bothell Way, #101,
Seattle, WA 98155. (206) 483-6396

Blue Moon Explorations offers sea-kayaking orca-watching tours in the San Juan Islands.
Blue Moon Explorations, P.O. Box 2568, Bellingham, WA 98227.
(206) 966-8805

CALIFORNIA

BlueWaters Kayak Tours offers 1-day and overnight sea-kayaking tours in northern California and Monterey Bay, home to hundreds of sea lions and harbor seals.
BlueWaters Kayak Tours, P.O. Box 1003, Fairfax, CA 94978.
(415) 456-8956

Part of the Athletics Department at Berkeley, Cal Adventures is a serious outdoors school open to everyone. They teach Sea Kayaking I and II and offer day trips in the waters around San Francisco.
Cal Adventures, 2301 Bancroft Way, Berkeley, CA 94720.
(510) 642-4000

Island packers offers 1- and 2-day trips to the Channel Islands, which have sea caves and sea lions.

Island Packers, 1867 Spinnaker Dr., Ventura, CA 93001. (805) 642-1393

Aqua Adventures Kayak School offers all levels of instruction from beginning to wave surfing. Also sponsors a seafood survival course, sea turtle rescue, and honeymoon sea-kayaking trips.

Aqua Adventures Kayak School, 7985 Dunbrook Rd., Suite H, San Diego, CA 92126. (619) 695-1500

Alaska

Guided sea kayak trips among wildlife and glaciers in Prince William Sound and Kenai Fjords National Park are provided by Adventures & Delights.

Adventures and Delights, 414 K St., Anchorage, AK 99501. (800) 288-3134; (907) 276-8282 or (907) 278-6058

Tongass Kayak Adventures offers guided 7-day tours of southeast Alaska. Families welcome.

Tongass Kayak Adventures, P.O. Box 787, Petersburg, AK 99833. (907) 772-4600

Hawaii

Dvorak's Kayak and Rafting Expeditions offers a 2- to 7-day sea-kayaking tour of the Big Island. Includes snorkeling with dolphins, yoga on the beach, and hikes in the valleys.

Dvorak's Kayak and Rafting Expeditions Inc., 17921-B U.S. Hwy 285, Nathrop, CO 81236. (800) 824-3795; (719) 539-6851

A 6-day guided sea-kayaking/camping expedition around Kauai, summer and winter, is offered by Kayak Kauai Outfitters.

Kayak Kauai Outfitters, P.O. Box 508, Hanalei, Kauai, HI 96714

OTHER SOURCES

A partial list of outfitters is available from:

TASK, P.O. Box 84144, Seattle, WA 98124. (206) 621-1018

Sea Kayaking magazine is a good source of information on the sport.

Skiing
Cross-Country
and Snowshoeing

Backcountry skiing can have its tricky moments.
Photograph by Roger Archibald.

Many cross-country skiers are trying snowshoeing and telemark skiing, but whatever is on the feet, the quest of the skier or the snowshoer is remote backcountry, far from cars and people, where the snow glistens, untouched and pristine. (1 day with guide; $25–$125; 2–8 days: $200–$1,440.)

Northeast

Maine

Winter in the heart of Maine's heavily forested interior pits man against nature. Here, professional Maine guides Garrett and Alexandra Conover take the hardy on 3- and 5-day treks. You will learn how to snowshoe and toboggan, identify animal tracks, and explore the beauty of winter camping.

North Woods Ways, RR2, Box 159-A, Willimantic, Guilford, ME 04443.
(207) 997-3723

Massachusetts

In the middle of Massachusetts, Northfield Mountain offers 20 miles of groomed cross-country and 6 miles of groomed snowshoe trails. Instruction, clinics, country inns nearby.

Northfield Mountain, RR1, Box 377, Northfield, MA 01360.
(413) 659-3713

Vermont

Snowshoeing, snowboarding, and telemark skiing are featured by Clearwater, an outfitter in central Vermont's Mad River Valley. Instruction, gear, guides, snowshoe tours.

Clearwater, Route 100, Waitsfield, VT 05673.
(802) 496-2708

Craftsbury Common, in the heart of the Northeast Kingdom, is the start of this cross-country trip over almost pristine, well-groomed trails that end in Stowe. Six days in February. Country inns, gourmet meals.

All Adventure Travel, 5589 Arapahoe, Suite 208, Boulder, CO 80303.
(800) 537-4025

Cross-country ski in the Catamount Trail in the Green Mountains and spend nights in front of the proverbial crackling fireplace in cozy country inns, redolent with gourmet cooking. You can arrange to have a driver deliver your car to the end of the trail. This is a challenging excursion, perfect for advanced skiers.

Country Inns Along the Trail, RR3, Box 3115, Brandon, VT 05733.
(802) 247-3300

New York

Alpine Adventures offers backcountry skiing in the Adirondacks, away from groomed trails in conditions that change and involve both cross-country and alpine skiing. Advanced courses, after you complete Backcountry Basics, include alpine touring and telemarking, which will prepare you to ski in remote areas anywhere in the world.

> *Alpine Adventures, Route 73, P.O. Box 179, Keene, NY 12942.*
> *(518) 576-9881*

Great Lakes

WISCONSIN

Intensive 1-day and 1-week instruction are offered May to August by Iowa Mountaineers in Devil's Lake State Park. Equipment and lodging are available nearby.

> *Iowa Mountaineers, Inc., P.O. Box 163, Iowa City, IA 52244.*
> *(319) 337-7163*

MINNESOTA

The Gunflint Trail follows the shores of Lake Superior through the wilderness of the Boundary Waters Canoe Area. Here on 200 kilometers (120 miles) of groomed, world-class trails, cross-country skiers can ski hut-to-hut, sleeping in eight lodges and wilderness yurts, while the outfitter moves your car and gear. Offers variety in lodging: luxury (gourmet resort) to housekeeping cabins (you cook). Also custom tours.

> *Ski Lodge to Lodge, 590 Gunflint Trail, Grand Marais, MN 55604.*
> *(800) 322-8327; (218) 388-4487*

Rocky Mountains

COLORADO

Begun in 1982, the Tenth Mountain Division Trail and Hut System, between Aspen and Vail, is about 100 miles of trail strung between fifteen "backcountry chateaus," some of them log cabins. It is excellent for cross-country skiers of all levels. Paragon Guides offers 3- to 14-day guided cross-country trips throughout the winter.

> *Paragon Guides, P.O. Box 130, Vail, CO 81658. (303) 926-5299*

The San Juan Hut System links Telluride to Ouray in southwest Colorado. Backcountry ski trails are hiking trails and Forest Service roads below the 14,000-foot peaks of the Sneffels Range. Huts have all the necessary equipment, but you must carry in food and water. This is for intermediate or advanced skiers with knowledge of unpredictable winter weather conditions and avalanche potential. Skis are single-camber nordic skis, called fat boards. For information and guides:

> *San Juan Hut Systems, P.O. Box 1663, 117 North Willow St.,*
> *Telluride, CO 81435. (303) 728-6935*

For an unusual skiing adventure, either cross-country or downhill, try the Great Sand Dunes National Monument in Colorado. Out of nowhere in the Rocky Mountains appear 36,000 acres of sand dunes, some of them 700 feet high—the world's tallest. Some skiers wrap themselves in bedouin robes for the Lawrence of Arabia experience.

This is a national monument and also has several campgrounds, including backcountry, hike-in campsites. A hike up the dunes (no trail) takes about 3 hours. Legend has it that web-footed horses live here, visible only at dawn.

Great Sand Dunes National Monument, 11500 Hwy 50, Mosca, CO 81146. (719) 378-2312

WYOMING

Yellowstone and Grand Teton National Parks are excellent for backcountry skiing and wildlife viewing. Knapsack Tours runs a 7-day trip in February that provides snow coaches to transport skiers into the parks (no cars on roads in the winter), plus sleigh rides to the elk range and to a mountain log cabin for dinner.

Knapsack Tours, 5961 Zinn Dr., Oakland, CA 94611-2655. (510) 339-0160

Ski yurt-to-yurt or camp out in backcountry ski trails in the Teton Mountain Range in Grand Teton National Park. The snow here is perfect: powdery and even over ridges and bowls. Guides, instruction, and all equipment provided by Rendezvous, whose 1-day to 6-day tours can also include lodging.

Rendezvous Ski Tours, 219 Highland Way, Victor, ID 83455. (208) 787-2906

Day-long cross-country guided tours go through the Grand Canyon of Yellowstone—from Mammoth Wednesday and Saturday, and from Old Faithful Tuesday and Friday. Lunch included.

TW Recreational Services, P.O. Box 165, Yellowstone National Park, WY 82190-0165. (307) 344-7311

Southwest

NEW MEXICO

The Taos area of northern New Mexico is a beautiful winter resort. Here, Taos Fitness Adventures will set you up for a full week of cross-country and snowshoeing, with guides and equipment. Visitors begin the day with a stretch class, pick up a daypack, and go out for the day. At night the luxury lodge provides dinner, lectures, hot tub, sauna, and massage. If you get tired of skiing, try a hot-air balloon ride, hiking, llama trekking, or a sleigh ride. Open all year.

Taos Fitness Adventures, 216-M Paseo del Pueblo Norte, Suite 173, Taos, NM 87571. (800) 455-4453; (505) 776-1017

West

CALIFORNIA

Some of the best cross-country skiing in the world is in Yosemite National Park, with 45 kilometers (27 miles) of groomed and wilderness trails. The Yosemite Cross-Country Ski School gives beginner to advanced lessons and overnight tours. Experienced skiers can join a guide on a 6-day hut-based trek across the Sierras. The Yosemite Nordic Holiday Race is held on the first Saturday in March.

Yosemite Cross-Country Ski School, Yosemite National Park, CA 95389. (209) 372-1244

The Sequoia National Forest, home to trees 250 feet tall, has 84 kilometers (58 miles) of mapped trails. The Montecito-Sequoia Lodge, on the edge of the forest, has 35 kilometers (21 miles) of groomed cross-country trails, guides, equipment, lodging, food, and celebrations. Offers 2- to 7-day packages, with special kids' programs, ice skating, and snowshoeing.

Montecito-Sequoia Lodge, (209) 565-3388
Reservations: 472 Deodara Dr., Los Altos, CA 94024. (800) 227-9900; (415) 967-8612

Alaska

Alaska is assured to have snow in winter, and miles and miles of cross-country trails cross the state from top to bottom. Not all are groomed, and not all have huts nearby. But some do.

From a wilderness adventure lodge in Wrangell/St. Elias National Park, cross-country ski on numerous trails from the lodge, or be flown to remote regions where you can cross-country ski and camp out.

Ultima Thule Outfitters, 3815 Apollo Dr., Anchorage, AK 99504. (907) 333-2073

Professional guides, all equipment, and meals are provided in 1- to 5-day cross-country and telemark skiing tours in Alaska's backcountry. No lodging provided, but Adventures and Delights will help you make reservations.

Adventures and Delights, 414 K St., Anchorage, AK 99501. (800) 288-3134; (907) 276-8282

Skydiving

A sudden tug in space, the canopy balloons open, and the skydiver drifts toward earth.

Parachutes, jumpsuits, and skydiving have come a long way since World War II, when soldiers and marines infiltrated behind enemy lines carrying more than a hundred pounds of gear and having to depend on a clumsy umbrella parachute over which they had little control. Today recreational parachutists still jump out of planes, but the parachute is a lightweight rectangle, called a canopy, which is easy to manipulate; and jumpers, out for the adventure, wear brilliantly colored striped nylon jumpsuits.

The main thrill of skydiving is the 150-mile-an-hour free fall before the parachute opens, which, according to U.S. Parachute Association and Federal Aviation Administration rules, must be above 3,000 feet if you are a student jumper, 2,500 feet if you are a Level A or B jumper, and 2,000 feet if you are a Level C or D, or experienced, jumper. After the free fall is the sharp tug of the open canopy that pulls you up and lets you know that everything is okay.

Many experienced sky divers perfect freestyle gymnastics, which looks like group aerial ballet. Some jumpers do solo aerial acrobatics; others perfect CRW (canopy relative work, or canopy formation flying), which is a kind of aerial ballet *after* the canopies open. Gonzo jumpers are into sky surfing—jumping with a snowboard on their feet, which provides more horizontal movement in the air and allows the truly expert to land on water.

Both skydiving and sky gymnastics require mind-and-body control. In a group or alone, divers practice first on the ground so that the added element of height and the rush through space are not overwhelming. "You only have 60 seconds," said an experienced jumper headed into the plane for his fifth jump of the day. "So you have to think fast." Parachutes have one cord and two safety backups.

Skydiving is often referred to as RW, or *relative work*, which reflects the original French which referred to the relative placement of free-falling divers in the sky. It is now called *formation freefall* by the Federation Aeronautique Internationale.

The U.S. Parachute Association, a division of the National Aeronautical Association, and a representative of the Federation Aeronautique Internationale, has, for 30 years, governed the safety standards of jumping in the United States. The USPA publishes a list of drop zones—skydiving centers and instructors or jumpmasters—which have passed their safety tests. (Tandem jump: $190–$200; Accelerated Freefall: $300 [first jump]; Static Line: $225 [first jump].)

THE FIRST JUMP

If you are at least 18 years old and weigh less than 215 pounds, call or write the USPA and ask them for a list of approved drop zones in your area. Then call a few to shop around and get the best price because prices differ. (You don't have to use a USPA drop zone, but USPA affiliation means that personnel at the skydiving center are accountable to the USPA for their performance.)

When you visit the skydiving center, ask yourself if this is really what you want to do. You can be ready to go on your first tandem jump in a half hour. You get verbal instructions from a jumpmaster, watch an instructional video, which includes a lawyer explaining the dangers of skydiving, then you sign a lengthy disclaimer and can elect to buy extra insurance, before getting suited up.

With the instructor securely attached, a first-time skydiver tries out the sport with a tandem jump.

"Although we do everything in our power to make it safe," says USPA New England Regional Director Tony Carbone, "this is still skydiving. You have to be responsible for yourself. You don't *need* to skydive."

Until you are on the plane, you have the option of changing your mind and getting your money back. Once you're on the plane, even if you decide not to jump, you've paid. "It's normal to be scared and nervous," says Carbone. "But focus on what you've been taught to do by saying to yourself, *I've been trained to do the following things.* This is not a good sport for people who are easily distracted. You should have a plan and execute it in a timely manner."

TANDEM JUMPS

If you're not sure you want to be a sky diver and would like to try it, you can take a first jump in tandem. Tandem jumpers are attached with a harness: The instructor rides on the back of the student and controls the parachute, while a companion jumper with a video camera mounted on his helmet and the trigger for the switch in his mouth, records the jump. The jump consists of about a minute of freefall and a 5-minute canopy ride. The video is given to the novice jumper both to enable him to critique his jump and to serve as a sentimental record (or proof for his friends). For many, this first jump is one of the most thrilling adventures in their lives.

JUMP TRAINING

Preparation usually includes 6 hours of lectures, an instructional video, and ground practice. If you decide to take up skydiving after your tandem jump, you can take static line training. In this training, your parachute is automatically opened by a static line attached to the airplane. You practice pulling the rip cord and are guided in canopy control and landing by instructions from a ground instructor, via radio. In this, you also learn how to control your jump so that you don't tangle with another jumper.

Later you move on to accelerated freefall. Your first freefall is with two jumpmasters who give you instructions in the air, but this is only after you have had several hours of classroom and ground practice learning how to use your altimeter, which is mounted on your chest; how to relate to the horizon during freefall; and how to find your rip cords fast. The critical part of freefall jumping is knowing when to open your canopy.

After a jump, sky divers trade technical experiences (why one was floating faster than the other; why someone waited so long to open the chute) as they carefully fold up their canopies, spread them out on the ground, taking care to separate the lines so that they will fall into place when the chute is next opened.

THE PROS

It's not unusual to meet jumpers who have logged several thousand jumps in a couple of decades. It's addictive. Jumpers, like medieval knights, can pick their own colors and coordinate jumpsuits and chutes. Some travel around the world, jumping in such remote places as the North Pole; others do BASE jumping (building antenna span earth—or jumps not from planes).

For a list of skydiving centers, or drop zones, in your region, and information on skydiving:

U.S. Parachute Association, 1440 Duke St., Alexandria, VA 22314.
(703) 836-3495

Most skydiving centers are located at airports. Teaching is done in the hangars, where pilots change into their diving gear before filing out to the small plane that carries them aloft. The following are a few of several hundred drop zones and schools:

MASSACHUSETTS

Pepperell Sports Center Airport, Route 111, Pepperell, MA 01463.
(800) SKY-JUMP; (508) 433-9222

NEW YORK

Finger Lakes Skydivers, Ovid Airport [drop zone], Ovid, NY.
(607) 869-5601

PENNSYLVANIA

AFF East/Skydive Chambersburg, Chambersburg Municipal Airport,
Chambersburg, PA 17201. (800) 526-3497; (717) 264-0726

FLORIDA

Air Adventures Florida, Airglades Airport, Hwy 27, Clewiston, FL 33440.
(800) 533-6151; (813) 983-6151

ILLINOIS

Skydive Chicago, Inc.!, Ottawa Airport, 1592 N. 30th Rd.,
Ottawa, IL 61350. (815) 433-0000

TEXAS

American Parachuting Inc., P.O. Box 905, Wichita Falls, TX 76307.
(405) 479-9292

CALIFORNIA

Perris Valley Skydiving School, Perris Valley Airport, 2091 Goetz Rd.,
Perris, CA 92570. (909) 657-1664; (800) 832-8818
(in southern California)

BASE JUMPING

The Gauley Bridge in Fayette County, West Virginia, is 3,000 feet
long (the longest single-arch steel span in the country) and 876
feet high. Every October on the third Saturday, when the bridge
is open for foot traffic, close to a quarter of a million people gather
to walk across and to take part in the crafts, food, and river-rafting festival that accompanies it.

Each year for the past decade, more than 500 sky divers from
several countries around the world have jumped the 876-foot
height from 9 A.M. to 3 P.M. It's a spectacular show that goes on
all day. After each jump, sky divers fold their canopies, hop on the
shuttle, go back up to the bridge, and do it all again—several
times.

To participate, you must be an experienced sky diver and able to arrive the day before to have your equipment inspected for safety and to learn the particular features of jumping from the Gauley Bridge. The deadline for entry is one month before Bridge Day.

Contact:

Andy Calistrat, Executive Director, World BASE Association,
P.O. Box 451636, Houston, TX 77245-1636. (713) 437-0323,
e-mail: andy@starbase.neosoft.com

The World BASE Association is a membership organization that publishes *Groundcheck,* which contains articles on BASE-jumping safety and information on lobbying to legalize BASE jumps. (The Gauley Bridge Day BASE jump *is* legal.)

For networking on skydiving, try *Usenet (newsgroups) Rec.sky-diving.*

Soaring

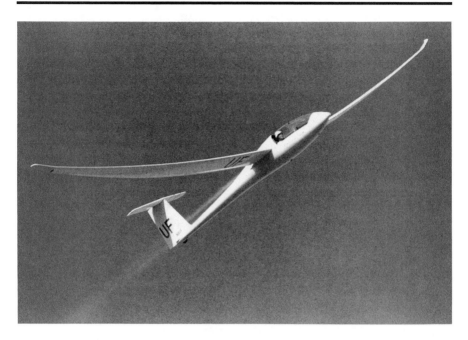

Part of the glory of soaring is the beauty of the glider itself.
Photograph by Steve Hines.

Soaring (or gliding) is a wonderful way to fly like a bird while
remaining safe within a beautiful aircraft called a sailplane. A
sailplane or glider—not to be confused with a hang glider—has
fixed wings 30 feet or more in length and no power of its own.
Carrying a pilot and one or two passengers who sit behind one
another, a sailplane is towed into the air by a small airplane. Once
aloft, the 200-foot towline is disconnected, and the sleekly beautiful sailplane slips quietly through the air, dipping in cool currents, hoisted by warm thermals and ridge lifts, leaving only a
shadow on the landscape below. The record distance is 902 miles;
the record altitude is 49,000 feet.

Many airparks have gliderports, where you may be towed up for
a half hour or so, but a growing number of people are learning how
to become FAA-certified glider pilots, which requires 10 hours of

instructor air time before soloing, 7 hours of soloing, and written exams. The minimum age you can start soloing is 14. You set the time involved in learning how to soar: Some are qualified to solo on a 2-week vacation. (Ride: $140–$150 for 35–40 minutes; instruction: $70 per hour.)

To get started, join The Soaring Society of America (*see below*) and get a list of soaring sites and clubs in each state. The following is a small selection:

VERMONT

Instruction, 3-, 5-, and 10-day workshops. Open May to October.
Sugarbush Soaring Association, Inc., P.O. Box 123, Warren, VT 05674.
(802) 496-2290

MASSACHUSETTS

Lessons year-round, plus rentals. Airport is a grass field with a windmill on it.
Cape Cod Soaring Adventures, 2 Rolling Acres Lane,
E. Falmouth, MA 02536. (508) 540-8081

IDAHO

Grand Valley Aviation gives training year-round in excellent thermal and wave soaring in the Grand Teton Mountains.
Grand Valley Aviation, P.O. Box 501, Driggs, ID 83422.
(208) 354-8131

NEVADA

Year-round instruction from novice to cross-country in what some believe is the best soaring locale in the country.
Soar Minden, P.O. Box 1764, Minden, NV 89423. (800) 345-7627;
(702) 782-7627

TEXAS

Learn and vacation in the Hill Country of Texas. Lodging is at the same site.
Soaring Society of San Antonio, 100 Boerne Stage Airfield,
Boerne, TX 78006. (512) 981-2345

HAWAII

Glide over Oahu, take lessons, learn aerobatics.
Soar Hawaii Ltd., 266 Poipu Dr., Honolulu, HI 96825.
(808) 637-3147

OTHER SOURCES

To become one of the 20,000 FAA-licensed soaring pilots in the U.S., network by joining:

The Soaring Society of America, Inc., P.O. Box E,
Hobbs, NM 88240-1308. (505) 392-1177

Membership brings the magazine *Soaring*.

Sports Tours

Football has been called one of the most vocal spectator sports, and there's nothing like being there. *Photograph by Roger Archibald.*

The Indy 500, the Kentucky Derby, the NCAA Final Four, the Masters Golf Tournament, U.S. Open Tennis, the World Series, the Super Bowl, the National Finals Rodeo, the NBA Finals, plus the Orange, the Sugar, and the Rose Bowls are probably the major sports events in this country.

If adrenaline level is any indicator of adventure level, these events are super adventures. Getting there, getting good seats, having a place to stay, and getting to meet some of the stars are all part of the excitement of a sports event. (4–6 days: $450–$3,450. Depends on number sharing hotel room and the importance of the event.)

Several companies have come up with no-sweat tours that arrange for travel, lodging, and tickets and carry you from one game to another. A trip called New & Old: A Sporting News Fan Trip, for example (offered by the Sports Tours, Inc.), picks you up at your hotel in New York City and takes you to Yankee Stadium for a Baltimore–New York game; takes you the next night to Veterans Stadium for New York versus Philadelphia; drives you over to Camden Yards in Baltimore for a Boston–Baltimore game; flies you to Cleveland for a Milwaukee–Cleveland game, then to Tiger Stadium in Detroit for a California–Detroit game. Enough baseball? This is just one of many possible tours.

> Sports Tours, Inc., P.O. Box 84, Hatfield, MA 01038. (800) 722-7701

If golf is your passion and you want to be there on the same green with the players, Spectacular Sports Specials will provide you with all you need for the Practice Rounds, the Birdie/Par 3, and the Birdie/Finals—hotel, admission, escort, and a golf theme party with a golf celebrity. Or you can spend 4 days watching cowboys and cowgirls tame broncos and ride bucking bulls at the National Finals Rodeo, without having to think about the details. These are only some of the sports events available through:

> Spectacular Sports Specials, 5813 Citrus Blvd.,
> New Orleans, LA 70123-5810. (800) 451-5772; (504) 734-9511

The Kentucky Derby is a grand tradition, with mint juleps and a race that is all too brief. Don Chavez's Sports Empire Tours will get you there; or to Pasadena, California, for the Rose Bowl Game, plus parade, plus (an option) the parade float construction the night before. Or to the legendary annual Super Bowl. Or some of the other events.

> Don Chavez's Sports Empire, P.O. Box 6169,
> Lakewood, CA 90714-6169. (800) 255-5258; (310) 809-6930

Olympics events require early bookings, and the 1996 events in Atlanta have been tapped for the last few years. For these events or any of the others mentioned above, try:

> Esoteric Sports Tours, 3450 Breckinridge Blvd., Suite 1624,
> Duluth, GA 30136. (800) 321-8008

To take a completely different tack on baseball, cruise on the Ohio and Mississippi rivers and mix with some all-time baseball greats. The Delta Queen Steamboat runs several 3-night baseball cruises between St. Louis, Pittsburgh, and Cincinnati in the warm months, which include famous former baseball stars and lots of baseball history.

> The Delta Queen Steamboat Co., 30 Robin Street Wharf,
> New Orleans, LA 70130-1890. (504) 586-0631

Surfing and Snorkeling

A short-board surfer waits for the perfect wave. *Photograph by Roger Archibald.*

SURFING

Pacific Islanders have been short-board surfers for centuries. Tongans, Hawaiians, and Samoans were the original Beach Boys, maneuvering their boards on hefty waves in a religious union with the sea, which thoroughly baffled early explorers like Captain Cook.

Surfing did not become a popular American sport until the 1960s, when it took off in southern California, boosted by movies and music. The perfect wave became the Holy Grail. Now on both coasts, most ocean beaches have a section reserved exclusively for surfers, who still search for the perfect wave, a long, clear roller with a slow curl that breaks in a clean line across the length of the beach. All you need is a board, a wetsuit if it's cold, and patience to wait for the wave.

A surfing course will teach you balance and angling right and left, but that's only the beginning. "The best surfers are always learning," says Mark Babski, managing director of California Surfari, "because the ocean is infinitely complex. When you learn how to ski, the mountain doesn't change. But the ocean is a dynamic environment, and the learning curve is always steep."

Surfing lessons will also introduce you to the different types of surfboards, finned and unfinned, long (traditional) and short (more challenging). (Lessons: $30–$50.)

RHODE ISLAND

Some of the best year-round surfing is in New England, especially on beaches on the east end of Cape Cod and on Narragansett Town Beach in Rhode Island. Waves off nearby Point Judith are consistent, and the water is rarely cold even in winter.

For 2 hours of free surfboard lessons on Narragansett Town Beach, drop by any Wednesday in summer, and veteran surfer Peter Panagiotis (known as Pete Pan) will show you how; (401) 789-3399. Narragansett surfing hotline: (401) 789-1954.

TEXAS

Thomas Lochtfeld was a surfer until "all this happened." "All this" refers to his invention called the Flow Rider, which closely mimics a perfect wave in a pool. Inspired to improve on wave pools, which he found to produce "mushy or ratty" waves, Lochtfeld installed small versions in water parks in Kissimmee, Florida, and Vista, California, and now is perfecting one that can operate in almost any municipal pool.

But the mother of all Flow Riders is at the Schlitterbahn Water Park, where surfers can spend the day on the Boogie Bahn perfecting their style on an advanced curl. Lochtfeld uses it and so do top surfers, snowboarders, and pro body boarders at an annual competition in May. "It's an illusion," said Lochtfeld, "but it's a really nice illusion."

Schlitterbahn Water Park and Resort, New Braunfels, TX 78130.
(210) 625-5510

CALIFORNIA

On beaches around San Clemente in southern California, California Surfari will give private one-on-one or one-on-two instruction. Two hours a day for 1 week will give a good grounding in the sport, but if you are short on time, try a 3-day weekend. Longer stays are invited; all ages are welcome. Surfari stresses safety (all instructors are certified lifeguards) and environmental sensitivity: "Surfing is a form of communication with the ocean," says Stanford-graduate manager Mark Babski. Lodging is in nearby camps, hostels, or beachfront hotels—your choice.

California Surfari, P.O. Box 642, San Clemente, CA 92674.
(800) 454-SURF; (714) 366-2303

The U.S. Surfing Federation Western Region (USSF WR) sponsors the Endless Summer Surf Camp for serious adults and kids over 10. Instruction is given in beginning, intermediate, and advanced surfing and bodyboarding on beaches in southern California. Day and overnight surf camp runs through July and August. (Requirements: you must be able to swim 100 yards and tread water for 10 minutes.)

The USSF WR also sponsors contests at beaches from southern to northern California. Winners go on to compete for the U.S. Amateur Surfing Championship as well as the USSF WR All-Star Team.

USSF WR, P.O. Box 512, San Juan Capistrano, CA 92693.
(714) 493-2591

HAWAII

In Oahu not all waves are 40 feet high; many are learnable waves for beginners; some are perfect waves.

The Hawaii Longboard Surfing Association trains amateurs for pro meets. Leave a message on the machine for information: (808) 593-9292.

For lessons on Waikiki Beach, Oahu, contact the Hawaii Beach Boys Association, Inc., at (808) 732-4563.

Other Sources

The Eastern Surfing Association is a membership organization ($20 per year) with twenty-six districts that sponsors amateur competitions that allow surfers to qualify for entry in the U.S. Amateur Surfing Championship.

Eastern Surfing Association, P.O. Box 582, Ocean City, MD 21842.
(800) 937-4733

SNORKELING

At its simplest level, snorkeling is swimming on the surface while wearing fins and a face mask with a breathing tube (the snorkel) that allows you to see clearly underwater. It's excellent for floating above coral reefs, which are easily broken and which sting or scratch, but which are home to thousands of fish. Face masks come in all sizes and colors; make sure the one you buy fits well.

In California, San Diego/La Jolla Underwater Park is a safe and interesting snorkeling area over lots of fish and some of California's famous kelp beds, extending as far down as 50 feet. For information: (619) 232-3101.

In Florida the underwater sanctuaries around the Keys and the Dry Tortugas are magnificent in the number of species you will see and in the clarity of the water. To go by boat: *Yankee Freedom* leaves Key West Wednesday, Saturday, and Sunday at 8 A.M. returns at 7 P.M.: (800)-WHALING. To go by plane: Key West Seaplane Services takes snorkelers for the day or overnight: (305) 294-6978. For information on the reefs:

> *Florida Keys National Marine Sanctuary, 9499 Overseas Highway, Marathon, FL 33050. (305) 743-2437*

A snorkeler dives for a closer look at the reef. *Photograph by Roger Archibald.*

But beyond lazily floating above tropical reefs, snorkeling can have its challenging edge. *Fin swimming*, for example, is an organized competitive sport. Done in an ocean or a pool, its object is speed and conditioning—the record is about 7 miles an hour, and an hour's swim uses about 1,200 calories. For an even better workout, use a *monofin* (two feet in one fin), which requires a butterfly stroke.

For more information on the sport and on competing in world championships, contact:

> *Underwater Society of America, Fin Swimming Committee, Mike Gower,*
> *164 N. Bascom Ave., San Jose, CA 95128. (408) 286-8840*

Free diving is a lesson in breath control. The lazy coral-reef snorkeler occasionally breaks the surface, takes a breath, dives a few feet to retrieve an empty shell, resurfaces, and blows out his tube to resume surface gazing. But free diving is also a world championship event. The free-diving world record is 410 feet down and back in 2 minutes and 9 seconds. For information on competitions, contact:

> *Underwater Society of America, Free Diving Committee,*
> *Michael Montanez, 1452 Kooser Rd., San Jose, CA 95118.*
> *(408) 265-5643*

If you want to develop confidence using your snorkel for free diving and surface diving, try playing hockey underwater. Played in a pool, underwater hockey is like above-water hockey: six-member teams use sticks and a puck and score in the opponent's goal. Because of its excellent conditioning, the sport is recommended for the whole family. For information:

> *USOA Underwater Hockey Committee, Kendall Banks, Director,*
> *264 Pincrest Beach Dr., E. Falmouth, MA 02536-4415. (508) 540-3205*

Underwater rugby is a fast game played with a salt-water-filled ball passed in a leap-frogging manner among six players on a team, until it's put through a basket. And all of this in a 12-foot-deep pool. It, too, is played for the terrific workout it provides, or as a world championship competitive event.

> *Tim Burke, USOA Underwater Rugby Director, 17 Standish Rd.,*
> *Quincy, MA 02171. (617) 472-6949*

BEACH CLEANUP

Cigarette filters in the millions get washed down city streets and into storm drains where they are carried to the beach and wind up as nonbiodegradable artifacts in the sand. Every third Saturday in

September, the Center for Marine Conservation sponsors a nation-wide Beach CleanUp. To sign up: Call, and they will send plastic bags and data sheets on which you record what you find. The data are filed at the Center and recorded in a report which you can receive. Last year 7 million pieces of trash were collected, from diapers to automobile parts.

Center for Marine Conservation, 1725 DeSales St., NW, Washington, DC 20036. (202) 429-5609

Survival Courses

Two men try to start a fire using a crossbow at the Crow Canyon
Archaeological Center, Cortez, Colorado.

Survival courses serve several needs: For some, the physical challenge of wilderness living is an end in itself; for others, understanding and overcoming barriers to being in the backcountry can be preparation for becoming a guide. Some find renewal by replicating "Paleo Man's" lifestyle and retreating to an earlier Eden; others find it in the hard discipline of physical exercise, often alone in the wilderness. ($80–$100 per day.)

Boulder Outdoor Survival School offers several programs in south-central Utah in the instruction and use of primitive tools and survival techniques in the wilderness. Camp in a primitive shelter and learn "Earthskills." Or spend 2 weeks training in "Aboriginal

Living Skills," then 1 week traveling as a member of "a band of hunter/gatherers living entirely off the land." For those in good physical condition, BOSS offers a Walkabout, the challenge of individual living in a harsh environment with limited tools.

> Boulder Outdoor Survival School, P.O. Box 3226,
> Flagstaff, AZ 86003-3226. (602) 779-6000

Former Outward Bound instructors Bart and Robin Blankenship know how to live off the land and sea and will share their skills in weekend workshops or on longer trips in the Colorado Plateau or the Florida Everglades. They teach how to make stone tools, make rope from Dog's Bane, make pots by finding clay and baking the pot in a fire, tan hide and sew your own bag with a bone awl for a needle and a sinew for thread. Such practical knowledge makes for self-confidence in the wilderness.

> Earth Knack, P.O. Box 19693, Boulder, CO 80308. (303) 938-9056

Experienced Maine Guides Alexandra and Garrett Conover, a naturalist and biologist, respectively, with extensive experience in the backwoods, lead a 12-day Outdoor Leadership Program with training in group dynamics, map and compass reading, camping, and canoeing skills, as well as leadership, for those who want to become guides or just efficient in the outdoors. Sixteen hours of first aid and backcountry rescue are included.

> North Woods Ways, RR2, Box 159A, Willimantic, Guilford, ME 04443.
> (207) 997-3723

The National Outdoor Leadership Program will teach you everything you need to know to depend on yourself in rugged wilderness experiences. Courses can be strenuous, difficult, and risky, but whether you are 14 or 75 (their age span, with a median of around 20), you should bring to the program a fair physical fitness. Fourteen days hiking in Arizona, for example, will teach you navigation, map reading, leadership, natural history, archaeology, and low-impact camping techniques. A 14-day technical whitewater rapids trip on the Green River teaches rescue techniques, hazard evaluation, river logistics, and navigation. Wide variety of courses.

> The National Outdoor Leadership Program, 288 Main St.,
> Lander, WY 82520-3128. (307) 332-6973

Outward Bound was started more than half a century ago to teach sailors fortitude and self-reliance during war. Today anyone between the ages of 14 and 99+ in need of learning new skills is welcome to join one of several 8- to 28-day courses. Learn outdoor survival skills, plus dogsledding, sailing, sea kayaking, rock climbing, ropes course, hiking, or orienteering at any of the five schools in the U.S. (Colorado, Minnesota, North Carolina, Oregon, and Maine). Special courses for couples, women, and people in need of "renewal."

> *Outward Bound National Office, Rte. 9D, R2, Box 280,*
> *Garrison, NY 10524-9757. (800) 243-8520; (914) 424-4000*

Recommended reading: Larry Dean Olsen's *Outdoor Survival Skills* (Chicago Review Press, 1990).

Train Tours

Antique trains, like this steam engine at the Steamtown National Historic Site in Scranton, Pennsylvania, take passengers on adventures into the past. *Photograph by Roger Archibald.*

Some say the railroad was built in the West to carry silver and gold back East. That might be true, but trains by the 1860s were already carrying timber, cows, soldiers, commuters, and hoboes up and down and across the country. While Amtrak today runs several excursions from one coast to the other, several steam, diesel, and coal-powered cog railways provide scenic or historic excursions. (Antique & cog 1-day: $30–$75; 7-day excursions: $1,000–$1,500 per person.)

DRIVE YOUR OWN LOCOMOTIVE

You and three friends can rent a diesel for an hour and take it out for a spin with an instructor.

Portola, California, in the Sierra Nevada Mountains, is home to the Portola Railroad Museum, which has one of the largest collections of diesel locomotives in the country. The locomotive facility is built in the style of those of the 1950s and 1960s and is on 37 acres, with 2 ½ miles of track along which you and your friends can toot and roar.

> Feather River Rail Society, P.O. Box 608, Portola, CA 96122.
> (916) 832-4131

COG RAILWAYS

NEW HAMPSHIRE

Mount Washington, at 6,288 feet, is the highest point in the Appalachian chain that runs from Georgia to Maine. It's possible to hike or to drive to the summit. But if you have 3 hours and are up for an adventure that might leave you slightly sooty, you can take the 3-mile trip up the slope in a cog train. Powered by steam from vats of water boiled by heating a ton of coal, the 1869 cog train puffs up into an altitude increasingly cool at an angle that makes lakes in the distance look vertical. At the top you can spend as long as you like at lookouts or until the wind, which has been clocked at more than 170 mph, kicks up. Reservations required.

> Mt. Washington Railway Co., Base Road, Mt. Washington, NH 03589.
> (800) 922-8825; (603) 846-5404

COLORADO

Pike's Peak is one of Colorado's "fourteeners," at 14,110 feet. This cog was built in 1891 and travels up 7,500 feet in slightly more than 3 hours. Sometimes the back of the train is 12 feet lower than the front. At the top you have enough time to look around, but barely enough to adjust to the altitude.

> Manitou & Pike's Peak Railway, P.O. Box 351,
> Manitou Springs, CO 80829. (719) 685-5401

EXCURSION TRAINS

An excellent way to see the country is on short trips on trains that have been equipped with open-air "gondolas" or on restored historic trains that go through parts of the backcountry difficult to reach otherwise.

PENNSYLVANIA

Kinzua Bridge was the highest railway bridge in the world when it was built in 1882. Standing 301 feet above Kinzua Creek Valley, it is 2,053 feet long, and now the fourth highest in the world. You can take a steam and diesel train on a daylong trip through the Allegheny National Forest, over the bridge, and be back by dark.

Knox, Kane, Kinzua Railroad, P.O. Box 422, Marienville, PA 16239. (814) 927-6621

WYOMING

From Laramie, Wyoming, on the Wyoming/Colorado Railroad, you can take a 6-hour trip west in an open gondola car through prairies filled with western wildlife to the old mining town of Centennial for lunch. Then you climb into the Snowy Range to 9,000 feet on a unique track that includes three complete switchbacks which you can see as you rise above them. The goal is the high-altitude Lake Owen.

Wyoming/Colorado Railroad, P.O. Box 1653, Laramie, WY 82070. (307) 742-9162

ARIZONA

Next to flying, this excursion is the best way to get into the red rock canyons near Sedona. The Scenic Verde River Canyon Train has four open gondola cars and takes 4 hours to cross 40 miles through canyons and past rushing rivers, abandoned mines, Anasazi cliff homes, and desert wildlife. The tour includes a historical guide and musicians.

Verde River Canyon Excursion, 300 N. Broadway, Clarkdale, AZ 86324. (602) 639-0010

NEW MEXICO

This scenic coal-powered steam railway is a National Historic Site. Built originally to service miners across the border between New Mexico and Colorado, the Cumbres & Toltec Railroad is the longest and highest narrow-gauge steam railway in the country. On a 6-hour trip, you will cross the Cumbres Pass at more than 10,000 feet, rumble through gorges, and rush through two tunnels. The southwestern vistas are incomparable.

Cumbres & Toltec Scenic Railroad, P.O. Box 789, Chama, NM 87520. (505) 756-2151

ALASKA

Trains are an excellent alternative to planes in Alaska, because you can cover the endless miles that seem to comprise the state while you relax and enjoy the scenery. But if you want to take a short trip on a scenic route on a train that dates from the Klondike Gold Rush in 1898, try the White Pass & Yukon Route. It runs a number of narrated excursions, including one to the summit of White Pass on the British Columbia border and one to remote Lake Bennett, once the home of 20,000 gold miners. If you hike the 33-mile Chilkoot Trail from Skagway and would rather ride back, you can take the Chilkoot Hiker's Shuttle. Buy your tickets before you hike.

White Pass & Yukon Route, P.O. Box 435, Skagway, AK 99840.
(800) 343-7373; (907) 983-2217

HAWAII

Not many trains operate in Hawaii. This trip takes only an hour and is on a replica of a sugar train built in the 1890s, when the sugarcane industry was active in Maui. Along the 12 miles, you see vistas of beaches and mountains and visit a sugar mill at the stop at Kaanapali Beach.

Lahaina, Kaanapali & Pacific Railroad, P.O. Box 816,
Lahaina, HI 96761. (808) 667-6851

OTHER SOURCES

The Rail Travel Center in St. Albans, Vermont, collects and designs train tours around the world and publishes a couple of newsletter-catalogs of very diverse train trips. Their Midwest Steam Bonanza Rail-Cruise Tour, for example, was designed around steam-powered vehicles and includes a ride on a new Chinese-built steam engine, 2 days on a steam-powered Mississippi sternwheeler, and a visit to the Midwest Old Threshers' (tractor builders and collectors) Reunion. Another trip is a Blue Ridge and Blue Grass rail tour of Nashville with a stay at the Opryland Hotel.

Rail Travel Center, 2 Federal St., St. Albans, VT 05478. (800) 458-5394

Treks on Wheels

Sleep while you travel, spend the day adventuring. Trekkers begin the day with breakfast cooked outdoors.
Photograph by Elijah Jones/Green Tortoise.

These trips get you where you're going and put you in touch with adventure outfitters along the way or make time for activities like in-line skating. Most trips are made in small groups in maxivans or motorcoaches and set up camp in tents. Everyone contributes to a food kitty, and food shopping and cooking responsibilities are shared on a rotating basis. (1–13 weeks: $400–$3,600. Food kitty extra.)

One of AmeriCan's 14-day trips leaves Los Angeles and goes through Apache and Navajo land. You can ride horses in the desert of Monument Valley, whitewater river raft on the Colorado River, flightsee in the Grand Canyon, and bungee jump in Las Vegas.

AmeriCan Adventures, 6762A Centinela Ave., Culver City, CA 90230.
(800) 864-0335; (310) 390-7495

Suntrek Tours' Flamingo Road Trek spends 3 weeks going from Miami to New Orleans and back, and includes New Orleans jazz, a Mississippi riverboat tour, and a canoe trip through a swamp, with options for biking and snorkeling in Key West.

> Suntrek Tours, Inc., Sun Plaza, 77 West Third St., Santa Rosa, CA 95401. (800) 292-9696; (707) 523-1800

TrekAmerica's tours camp or stay at hotels and are geared for those aged 18 to 38. Their Northwest Adventure goes from Seattle to Yellowstone and back, and includes a stay at a working Montana cowboy ranch, mountain biking, and jet boating, with optional rodeo, canoeing, and horseback riding.

> TrekAmerica, P.O. Box 470, Blairstown, NJ 07825. (800) 221-0596; (908) 362-9198

Green Tortoise Adventure Travel is for flexible, curious travelers who are friendly, prefer vegetarian meals, don't mind skipping a shower occasionally, and who are open to adventure. The Green Tortoise is a bus "with millions of miles of character," with bunks in which travelers sleep while it travels at night to the next place. Green Tortoise's 30-day Alaska expedition, for example, leaves San Francisco, includes sailing near Juneau, wildlife viewing and backpacking in Denali National Park, river rafting, and optional flightseeing at Mount McKinley.

> Green Tortoise Adventure Travel, 494 Broadway, San Francisco, CA 94133. (800) 867-8647; (415) 956-7500

Trek with a small group and stop at hostels at night with this company that operates in conjunction with Hosteling International. Enough time is allowed for rafting, hiking, bungee jumping, or horseback riding.

> Roadrunner International, 6762A Centinela Ave., Culver City, CA 90230. (310) 390-7495

Unusual Lodging

You can stay in houseboats, lighthouses, fire towers, and cabooses, or simply camp in the wilderness. *Photograph by Roger Archibald*

CABOOSES

ILLINOIS

Formerly the last cars on trains, these four caboose cars are now equipped with kitchenettes and sit in the middle of a wild-animal park near Peoria, Illinois. Each has comfortable sleeping quarters and a switch that will make the whole car tremble as if it were traveling on a track if you want to simulate sleeping on a train. Outside, the park has walking trails and decks from which to watch bison, wolves, and black bears.

> *Wildlife Prairie Park, 3826 N. Taylor Rd., RR #2, Box 50, Peoria, IL 61615. (309) 676-0998*

WASHINGTON

If you are really into trains, you can stay in the railroad town of Elbe, north of Tacoma. A local restaurant is constructed out of four 1920s cars of the Mount Rainier Railroad. A 30-minute steam train excursion goes to Mineral Lake; dinner is served on the Cascadian Dinner Train. The Hobo Inn has eight rooms that were cabooses, built in 1916, some with the original mahogany furniture. A couple have cupolas.

Hobo Inn, P.O. Box 20, Elbe, WA 98330. (206) 569-2500

FIRE LOOKOUTS

The one thing you can depend on in a fire tower is a good view. Built for members of the U.S. Forest Service to watch for fires, many Idaho, Montana, and Oregon fire towers are rentable in times when fires are not considered to be a big threat. They are tall (expect to climb up at least 50 feet of stairs) and spare: a propane tank fuels heaters and small stoves and refrigerators, and a chemical john is on the ground. You lug in your own water. But if you want to drop out, watch the stars at night, and soak up nature during the day, they can't be beaten. For a list, get a copy of *Recreational Cabin and Lookout Directory* from:

Lookout Information, USDA Forest Service, P.O. Box 96090, Washington, DC 20090-6090

HISTORIC HOTELS

Silver barons in the West imported the best of the East in the late 1800s, and many opened fancy hotels with big rooms upstairs and a big bar downstairs. Here, the whole town mingled on Saturday night, and traveling actors and singers, many of them famous, often entertained guests before retiring to their complimentary lodging. The Strater Hotel in the former silver boomtown of Durango, Colorado, has been restored to its 1887 splendor and features ragtime piano in the Diamond Belle Saloon and ongoing plays in the Diamond Circle Theatre.

Strater Hotel, 699 Main Ave., Durango, CO 81301. (303) 247-4431

For *Historic Hotels of America*, a listing of National Historic Trust hotels with special packages and offers, join:

The National Trust for Historic Preservation, 1785 Massachusetts Ave., NW, Washington, DC 20036. (202) 673-4166

HOUSEBOATS

If you have a large family or travel with friends and relatives, a houseboat is the cheapest and best way to vacation on a lake or a river. Houseboaters have the sense of camping and staying at home at the same time: They can jump over the side for a morning swim, then take a hot shower and microwave their breakfast. Fishing, exploring, and canoeing are easy from a houseboat.

Some lakes are crowded in summer. In states where there are popular lakes, such as New York with its Thousand Islands or Florida with its Everglades, tourism offices publish a list of houseboat outfitters. (*State tourism 800 numbers are listed in the back of the book.*)

LIGHTHOUSE

If you would like to stay in a lighthouse that is not only working but haunted, try the Big Bay Point Lighthouse on Lake Superior. Built in 1896, the 60-foot light tower and the 2-story castlelike inn sit on a cliff overlooking the moody lake, its windswept grounds giving it a Heathcliff feeling. The 100-year-old ghost, a former keeper, comes and goes and doesn't disturb the informal coziness of the seven bedrooms, common room with fireplace, and library. Open year-round.

> Big Bay Point Lighthouse, #3 Lighthouse Rd., Big Bay, MI 49808.
> (906) 345-9957

TALL SHIP

The tall ship *Malabar* will take you on a sunset cruise and then put you to bed with the boat at the dock in Traverse City, Michigan. This unusual bed-and-breakfast, built in 1975, is a 2-masted gaff-rigged topsail schooner with 1800s-style wooden bunk beds with clean linen and warm blankets. Or, if you prefer, you can bring a sleeping bag and sleep under the stars on deck. Shared bath; everybody gets a hearty breakfast.

> Traverse Tall Ship Co., 13390 S. West-Bay Shore Dr.,
> Traverse City, MI 49684. (616) 941-2000

UNDERWATER LODGE

Thirty feet down in Key Largo (Florida) Undersea Park is a small hotel for scuba divers. Two suites accommodate four people who eat, sleep, and dive. You can also get married here.

> Jules' Undersea Lodge, 51 Shoreland Drive, Key Largo, FL 33037.
> (305) 451-2353

YACHTS

Spend the night or the weekend on a 35- to 68-foot luxury motor or sailboat docked at Jack London Square in Oakland. Amenities include continental breakfast and fresh flowers, and for a little extra, you can have dinner catered. If you buy into the lifestyle, you can jump on another yacht and go on a private charter into San Francisco Bay.

> *Dockside Boat and Bed, 77 Jack London Square, Oakland, CA 94607.*
> *(510) 444-5858*

OTHER SOURCES

Book: *Budget Lodging Guide* (B & J Publications, 1995) lists 8,000 affordable places to stay, including college and university rooms, ($16.95 includes postage). Order from:

> *B & J Publications, P.O. Box 5486, Fullerton, CA 92635-0486*

Walking

A group of walkers breathe in healthful air. *Photograph courtesy Global Fitness Adventures, Aspen, Colorado.*

No one agrees completely on the differences between walking, trekking, and hiking. But in this country, hiking usually means carrying a backpack, traversing hills or mountains, and staying the night.

Trekking is from a South African word, *trekken*, which meant to move household goods from one village to another by oxcart. A trek in the United States can mean a trip over difficult terrain or one that takes a long time; it can be on foot or in a vehicle.

Walking is prescribed by physicians as the healthiest form of exercise. For getting into the country, off the beaten path, stopping to watch birds or read old gravestones, walking beats even biking. Walkers need only comfortable shoes, good companions (or none at all), a map, sunglasses, a bottle of water, and Henry David Thoreau's slim tome, *Walking*. (7 days: $750–$1,300, depending on accommodations.)

WALKING THE MALLS

Mall walkers in America are organized into a national group. Whether they take daily strolls through their local minimall or do the 78 acres in the Mall of America in Bloomington, Minnesota, mall walkers are encouraged to keep personal logbooks as part of a national fitness incentive awards program. Membership ($20) in the NOMW gives you access to health and fitness information and allows you to participate in mall-walking events around the country.

> *National Organization of Mall Walkers, P.O. Box 191,*
> *Hermann, MO 65041. (314) 486-3945*

WALKING VACATIONS

New England

Country Walkers provides guides for small groups who spend 3 to 5 hours walking 4 to 12 miles a day. Their routes take them through small towns and along nature trails. In Vermont, Country Walkers offers a Robert Frost Interpretative Trail with poetry readings along the way. On the coast of Maine, walkers spend 6 days exploring wildlife.

> *Country Walkers, P.O. Box 180, Waterbury, VT 05676. (802) 244-1387*

Midwest

The Earth Is Yours Walking Tours offers year-round guided weekend and weeklong walks in parks and forests throughout the Midwest and in California. Averaging about 10 miles a day, groups can, for example, explore ancient Indian mounds in Iowa at the confluence of the Mississippi and Wisconsin rivers for 4 days, with nights spent in a hotel.

The Earth Is Yours Walking Tours, 930 Washington, #1E,
Evanston, IL 60202-2272. (708) 869-5745

West

CALIFORNIA

Backroads provides a wide variety of guided walks, some with camping, others inn-to-inn with gourmet dinners. Trips generally cover 6 to 10 miles and involve 3 to 6 hours a day. An inn-to-inn 6-day walk on California's northern coast is accompanied by a naturalist and starts at Point Reyes National Seashore and ends in the misty forest of Muir Woods, with 1,000-year-old, 100-foot-high redwoods.

Backroads, 1516 5th St., Suite L102, Berkeley, CA 94710-1740.
(800) 462-2848; (510) 527-1555

If you are 50 or over, you are eligible to join a group with Walking the World. Directed by a former Outward Bound instructor, these trips practice minimum-impact camping and include information on cultural and natural history. It's one of the few groups that take trips into a desert—in this case, the Anza-Borrego State Park in southern California. The 9-day walk goes up 2,000 feet and averages 5 to 10 miles a day, covers the desert's valleys and canyons as well as its old stagecoach routes and ancient Native American pictographs.

Walking the World, P.O. Box 1186, Fort Collins, CO 80522.
(303) 225-0500

The Montecito-Sequoia Lodge in the Sequoia and Kings Canyon national parks sponsors 5- and 7-day walking adventures among giant sequoia trees, 40 feet wide and 30 stories high. The walk includes King's Canyon and Yosemite National Park.

Montecito-Sequoia Lodge, 8000 Generals Highway,
Kings Canyon National Park, CA 93633. (800) 843-8677

Hawaii

EcoTours of Hawai'i offers custom-designed trips lasting from a half day to two weeks, allowing you to experience the beauty of the Big Island from an ecological standpoint. Walks include rainforest waterfalls, fishponds, ancient trails, and both Mauna Kea and Mauna Loa volcanoes. EcoTours' 14-day Trek Across Hawaii is done on foot, bicycles, and in kayaks. This is the trip for the volcano-lover: You can camp near a crater and, in the morning, bike down to the sea.

EcoTours of Hawai'i, P.O. Box 2193, Kamuela, HI 96743.
(800) 457-7759; (808) 885-7759

OTHER SOURCES

Check your library or bookstore for some of the hundreds of walking guides to states, cities, and specific trails.

Walking magazine devotes itself completely to whatever issues, places, events, and gear are important to walkers.

500 Great Rail-Trails lists nationwide walking paths converted from old rail lines. $9.95 and $3.50 postage from:

Rails-To-Trails Conservancy, Shipping Dept., P.O. Box 295,
Federalsburg, MD 21632-0295. (800) 888-7741, ext. 11

The Appalachian Mountain Club publishes *Nature Walks* and *Country Walks*, guides to the Northeast. For a catalog, call: (800) 262-4455.

On the West Coast, the Pacific Crest Trail Association publishes walking guides. Call: (800) 817-2243.

Wildlife

ON LAND

BEARS

If you meet a grizzly bear on a trail, stay calm, stay out of his way, avoid direct eye contact, and make yourself look smaller by turning sideways and bending your knees. All of these things, wildlife experts say, will convince a bear that you are a harmless human out for a walk in the woods. If you think bears are around but you don't see them, carry on a loud conversation with a companion. Bears get excited if they are surprised, and they are fast—180 feet in 3 seconds. If you camp, make sure you stow your garbage and food. Assume that a curious bear will probably check out your campsite for a snack anyway.

The United States is home to polar bears, black bears, brown bears, grizzly bears (a type of brown bear), and the very rare Ker-modie, a white black bear which is also called a spirit bear. Many a grizzly is on display in a glass case in airports in the West, look-ing tall and fierce, even though the grizzly is related to Smokey the Bear. President Teddy Roosevelt hunted grizzlies, which so captivated Americans that smaller stuffed versions were manufac-tured and named after him. They are cute, but dangerous. Black bears are smaller, and have ranges in Alaska, the whole length of the Appalachian Mountains, and in the wilds of Louisiana. Many black bears are in refuges, because poachers collect their gallblad-ders and paw pads for markets in Asia, where they are sold as aphrodisiacs.

WYOMING

Spend 3 days in Yellowstone National Park with a carnivore ecol-ogist tracking bears, learning to recognize their signs, visiting a bear den, and, with luck, observing them. Lodging is in Roosevelt Lodge in Yellowstone.

> *Teton Science School, P.O. Box 68, Kelly, WY 83011.*
> *(307) 733-4765*

ALASKA

Abundant brown bears live in the Katmai National Park, where they fish for salmon in June in the rushing Brooks River. As many as thirty several-ton bears, among the world's largest single popu-lation, take over the river when the huge sockeye salmon come. This is also the season when the area has 19 hours of daylight, so viewing is good.

Celebrate the summer solstice, fish, and watch bears on 4- or 5-day trips, which include the option of a trip to Katmai's Valley of the 10,000 Smokes, an ash and pumice "moonscape," the result of a volcanic eruption in 1912. Today it has a variety of wildlife.

> *Katmailand, Inc., 4700 Aircraft Dr., Anchorage, AK 99502.*
> *(800) 544-0551; (907) 243-5448*

Seven days in Chugach National Forest and Denali and Kenai Fjords national parks guarantees seeing bears and abundant wildlife. This nature safari beds down in comfortable cabins.

> *International Expeditions, Inc., One Evirons Pk., Helen, AL 35080.*
> *(800) 633-4734; (205) 428-1700*

Spend 13 days tracking bears and other wildlife in Denali National Park and watching bears in Katmai National Park as they fish a few feet away from the safe viewing platform at the Brooks Lodge.

Natural Habitat Adventures, 2945 Center Green Court South,
Suite H, Boulder, CO 80301-9539. (800) 543-8917

Spend 11 days hiking, rafting, and traveling by van from the
Chugach National Forest to Denali National Park for views of
brown bears and other wildlife in their natural habitats.

Mountain Travel-Sobeck, 6420 Fairmount Ave.,
El Cerrito, CA 94530-3606. (800) 227-2384; (510) 527-8100

Wrangell, in southeast Alaska, is also the home to brown and
black bears who congregate to feed on salmon when they spawn
on the Stikine River. The Anan Bear Observatory has a safe observation deck overlooking waterfalls where bear fish for salmon.
This trip is accompanied by a research biologist and concludes
with a jetboat ride to the foot of the Shakes Glacier.

TravelWild International, P.O. Box 1637, Vashon Island, WA 98070.
(800) 368-0077

Wolves

Wolves evoke a variety of emotional reactions: farmers hate them,
hunters exploit them, timbermen cut down their habitats, back-
packers love them, zoologists respect them, fairy tales make them
appear clever but savage, and Native Americans believe they are
sacred. The fact is, their numbers have dwindled seriously. The
only place you can be fairly certain to see or hear wolves these
days is in their last refuge, northern Minnesota and Michigan.

MINNESOTA AND MICHIGAN

At the International Wolf Center, Vermilion Community College,
in Ely, Minnesota, scientists sponsor several wolf expeditions
throughout the year to study some of the 1,800 free-ranging and
wild wolves in the area.

Winter Odyssey: Travel by dogsled and cross-country skis to
Superior National Forest to hunt for a fresh wolf-kill (moose or
deer). Six days include being in the lab for lectures on wolf ecology and management, and in the air where you will search for
tagged wolves with telemetry.

Isle Royale, Lake Superior: Spend a week in the summer backpacking to look for wolves and moose to study their interrelation-
ship.

Howling: Each night throughout the summer, families are
invited to join a scientist under the stars in northern Minnesota,
where you will learn how to howl like a wolf and listen for a reply.
To reserve a place for Wolf Communication/Howling, call (800)
359-9653

On other expeditions, scientists teach participants to track wolves that have been tagged. This involves day and night work from a van.

International Wolf Center, Vermilion Environmental Studies, 1900 E. Camp St., Ely, MN 55731. (800) 657-3609

MONTANA

For a real backcountry wilderness experience in the Bob Marshall Wilderness in western Montana, near the Blackfoot River, you can study wolves while staying at the Lake Upsata Guest Ranch. A 6-day wilderness horsepack trip for all ages and abilities includes 3 days with lectures on wolves and forest wildlife and 3 days horse-packing in the heart of the wilderness.

Lake Upsata Guest Ranch, Box 6, Ovando, MT 59854. (800) 594-7687

Bison, Elk, Moose, Pronghorn Antelope, Bighorn Sheep

Native to America, these animals can usually be seen in the wild, or on reserves, such as the National Bison Range, north of Missoula, Montana.

WYOMING

Winter is an excellent time to do wildlife viewing, because animals are more visible in leafless forests and against snow-covered

A pronghorn antelope listens for intruders on Antelope Island in the Great Salt Lake, Utah. *Photograph by Roger Archibald.*

fields. On this 6-day wildlife expedition, you travel on snowshoes, by dogsled, horse-drawn sleigh, and in a 4-wheel-drive van in Yellowstone and Grand Teton national parks. Assist field biologists in radio-tracking studies of all of the above, plus mule deer, white-tailed deer, porcupines, and coyotes. Lodging is in hotels and lodges, and the trip includes lectures and guides.

> *Great Plains Wildlife Institute, P.O. Box 7580, Jackson Hole, WY 83001.*
> *(307) 733-2623*

ALASKA

Explore, hike, river raft, photograph, and get to know the wildlife that inhabits Kenai National Wildlife Refuge and Denali National Park. Spend 12 days staying in rustic cabins and tents, and seeing caribou, grizzlies, Dall sheep, moose, sea lions, puffins, and eagles.

> *Alaska Wildland Adventures, P.O. Box 389, Girdwood, AK 99587.*
> *(800) 334-8730; (907) 783-2928;*
> *(800) 478-4100 (within Alaska)*

"African Safaris"

TEXAS

At the Fossil rim Wildlife Center near Dallas, naturalists are preparing wolves, cheetahs, coati, and margays for reintroduction into the wild. On a 4-day naturalist-guided tour, you can visit the Field Clinic to see how conservationists care for sick and injured animals and create breeding programs for endangered animals, such as the rhinoceros. Lodging is in deluxe tents.

> *Nature Encounters, Ltd., 3855 Lankershim Blvd.,*
> *North Hollywood, CA 91604. (818) 752-7363*

For a camping trip with your young kids, where they can hear the big cats growl in the night and see zebra herds as soon as the sun comes up, try a 3-day trip in the Fossil Rim Wildlife Center.

> *Foothills Safari Camp, Fossil Rim Wildlife Ranch, Route 1, Box 210,*
> *Glen Rose, TX 76043. (817) 897-2960*

CALIFORNIA

In the 1930s, before appropriate laws protected animals who were enlisted to be in movies, many cinema animals were shipped off to Catalina Island to live out their days after stardom. Today many of their descendants are visible in the 1,600-foot-high rugged interior of the island. Take a naturalist-guided tour of the island and stay at Black Jack Campground. For reservations, call (310) 510-2800.

The Cats of Shambala

In a quiet canyon only a few miles from Los Angeles, leopards drape their bodies over tree branches, and lions roll in the sand near a waterhole. Former Hollywood actress Tippi Hedren (who starred in Alfred Hitchcock's *The Birds*) maintains several acres to house big animals that would otherwise be homeless. Either orphaned or once owned by private citizens, the animals of Shambala (which is Sanskrit for "a meeting place of peace and harmony for all beings, animal and human") have no place else to live. Here you will see more than seventy African lions, Siberian and Bengal tigers, spotted and black leopards, American cougars, and two African elephants.

Visiting hours are restricted to 2 days a month. Reservations are required.

The Roar Foundation, Shambala Preserve, 6867 Soledad Canyon Rd., Acton, CA 93510. (805) 268-0380

Other Sources

State-by-state *Wildlife Viewing Guides* are excellent companions for anyone touring the United States. Maps and illustrations guide tourists to backcountry wildlife such as moose in Maine and to city wildlife such as peregrine falcons that roost on buildings in Salt Lake City. Each costs about $6.00.

Watchable Wildlife Series, Falcon Press, P.O. Box 1718, Helena, MT 59624. (800) 582-BOOK

IN THE OCEAN (1 day: $20–$135; 6–10 days: $795–$3,000.)

Whales

Humpbacks, the acrobats of the deep, leap out of the water without warning, spin in the air, and finish with a somersault. A microphone held beneath the surface of the water will amplify the humpback's song, probably a mating song, since it is sung by one male, in a repetitive refrain with an incredible range. In Alaska, researchers have observed humpbacks leaping and scooping up krill in an amazing choreographic unison.

Humpbacks, minke, and killer (or orca) are some of the species of whales visible in the Atlantic and the Pacific oceans at different times of the year. Humpbacks breed in Hawaii in the spring and feed in Alaska in the summer.

How you see whales is what makes the experience special. Some tours allow you to sea-kayak among whale pods; others run

California sea lions loaf and snooze on the rocks off southern
California, *arr-arring* day and night. *Photograph by Roger Archibald*

research vessels and participants collect and record data from
observation. Some research vessels are luxurious; others are bottom-line.

NEW ENGLAND

Combine sailing with whale watching on the romantic tall ship
Harvey Gamage, a 95-foot schooner. This graceful ship puts into
former fishing ports in New England, then heads out to Stellwagen Bank, a shallows several miles off Massachusetts, where humpbacks and other species feed and play. Live aboard.

> Oceanic Society Expeditions, Fort Mason Center, Building E,
> San Francisco, CA 94123. (800) 326-7491; (415) 441-1106

GULF OF ST. LAWRENCE

Endangered blue, finback, humpback, and minke whales, plus por-
poise, white-sided dolphins, and harp and gray seals are some of
the wildlife you will be sharing the water with, as you help con-
serve the 270 endangered blue whales that live in the Gulf of St.
Lawrence. Spend 5 to 10 days helping marine mammal researchers
collect data at sea and analyze it in the lab. Lodging is in a motel
or guest house. Summer only.

> Mingan Island Cetacean Study
> [winter address]: 285 Green, St. Lambert, Quebec QC J4P 1T3, Canada.
> (514) 465-9176
> [summer address]: 106, rue Bord de la Mer, Longue-Pointe-de-Mingan,
> Quebec G0G 1V0, Canada. (418) 949-2845

WASHINGTON

Spend 5 days with a researcher photographing and recording the behavior of minke whales in the San Juan Islands. Travel is in stable sea kayaks; no paddling experience necessary.

Zoetic Research, Sea Quest Expeditions, P.O. Box 2424, Friday Harbor, WA 98250. (206) 378-5767

ALASKA

Whale watching in Alaskan waters guarantees excellent pictures. Travel with a naturalist in Glacier Bay or Frederick Sound to look for bears, whales, orcas, or all three. Travel and lodging are on the research vessel *Delphinus*, with mobility provided by the amphibious *SeaBee*. Small groups.

Biological Journeys, 1696 Ocean Dr., McKinleyville, CA 95521. (800) 548-7555; (707) 839-0178

Paddling in a sea kayak among pods of orcas in the calm Johnstone Strait provides a profound wildlife adventure. Seven-day trips with a guide include camping on remote beaches.

NatureQuest, 934 Acapulco St., Laguna Beach, CA 92651. (800) 842-4368; (714) 499-9561

Twelve days sailing, kayaking, walking in peat bogs and old growth forests, plus watching harbor seals, 5,000 sea otters, sitka deer, and grizzlies are only the sidelights to this cruise. The main part is collecting and recording data on orcas and humpbacks for the North Gulf Coast Oceanic Society whale research program. Takes place in Prince William Sound.

Alaskan Wilderness Sailing Safaris, P.O. Box 1313, Valdez, AK 99686. (907) 835-5175

Five- and 10-day cruises take whale watchers on the comfortable research vessel *Acania*, a converted luxury yacht once owned by Hollywood actress Constance Bennett. Passengers can assist scientists aboard by observing humpback behavior, recording daily feeding habits, identifying individual whales, or photographing whales as they leap out of the water. Includes hikes ashore and gourmet dinners.

Intersea Research, P.O. Box 1106, Carmel Valley, CA 93924. (800) 691-8222; (408) 659-5807

An 7-day cruise on the M.V. *Sea Lion* explores the coastal wilderness of southeast Alaska with a scientist.

AAAS Travels, Betchart Expeditions Inc., 17050 Montebello Rd., Cupertino, CA 95014. (800) 252-4910; (408) 252-4910

HAWAII

Six days on the Big Island of Hawaii gives you two days with a marine biologist to observe humpback behavior, record songs, and help identify individuals in the pod. The rest of the time you can explore Kilauea volcano and its lava pits, plus the flora and fauna of the rainforest, and dive or snorkle on a reef.

> *Eye of the Whale, P.O. Box 1269, Kapa'au, HI 96755. (800) 659-3544; (808) 889-0227*

Twelve days on a whale internship with the Pacific Whale Foundation gives an intensive ocean experience. From a land field station, survey the ocean and plot where whales surface. From a small boat, photograph whales and try to track their distribution patterns. The ocean is alive with their song during this time, and recording it is enjoyable. Share cooking and dormitory-style lodging in a rented home. All ages are welcome. Second-timers receive a discount.

> *Pacific Whale Foundation, 101 N. Kihei Rd., Suite 21, Kihei, Maui, HI 96753. (800) 879-8860*

The North Gulf Oceanic Society will use your observation, recording, and photographic skills on their 54-foot research yacht as it sails off the Big Island through the breeding grounds of the humpbacks. Lots of dolphins.

> *Journeys International, Inc., 4011 Jackson Rd., Ann Arbor, MI 48103. (800) 255-8735; (313) 665-4407*

Off Maui is a site where whales and other mammals gather in large numbers. For information, contact:

> *Hawaiian Island Humpback Whale National Marine Sanctuary, P.O. Box 50186, Honolulu, HI 96850. (808) 541-3184*

Dolphins

FLORIDA

Dolphins are fast and intelligent, and swimming with them can be a life-changing experience. Researchers at the Dolphin Research Center in Key West will teach you how to communicate with dolphins, using voice and hand signals before you swim with them in a saltwater lagoon. A 5-day trip with lodging at a resort.

> *Nature Encounters, Ltd., 3855 Lankershim Blvd., North Hollywood, FL 91604. (818) 752-7363*

Sea Lions

CALIFORNIA

Any Californian who lives on the coast will tell you that sea lions' vocal antics can keep you up at night. Yet Ron Schusterman, world expert on dolphin and sea lion communication, is conducting a study to determine the effects of noise from airplanes and underwater sounds on *them*. These 12-day adventures, from May to September, study sea lions, northern elephant seals, and harbor seals at a research center in Santa Cruz. Lodging is dormitory-style.

> *Earthwatch, P.O. Box 402, Watertown, MA 02272. (800) 338-4797;*
> *(617) 926-8200*

Sea Turtles

GEORGIA

Loggerhead sea turtles are endangered because not only are they hunted for their meat and shells, but they get caught in fish nets and strangled by plastic six-pack tops. Therefore, when they come up to lay their eggs on a beach on a barrier island off Georgia, several people make sure their eggs are safe from wild pigs, raccoons, and ghost crabs. For adventurers who like to stay up all night, walk the beach, and rebury the eggs turtles lay, the Caretta Research Project biologists offer their expertise on weekly expeditions from May to September. Shared cooking, dormitory lodging.

> *Caretta Research Project, Box A, Savannah Science Museum,*
> *4405 Paulsen St., Savannah, GA 31405. (912) 355-6705*

SOUTH CAROLINA

Assisting researchers from the University of South Carolina, you can spend 4 days walking the beach at Pritchards Island, where numerous predators threaten turtles. Participants intercept the eggs as soon as they are laid and carry them to a hatchery to make sure they will have a chance to mature.

> *Wilderness Southeast, 711 Sandtown Rd., Savannah, GA 31410-1019.*
> *(912) 897-5108*

FLORIDA

In Florida, loggerheads are threatened by new coastal developments which threaten their nests.

To adopt a turtle, and join a premier conservation group protecting sea turtles in Florida and Central America, contact:

> *Sea Turtle Survival League, P.O. Box 2866, Gainesville, FL 32602.*
> *(800) 678-7853*

For information on Florida Power and Light green and loggerhead turtle tours with the University of Central Florida (summer only), plus manatee viewing (Jan. and Feb.), call (800) 342-5367.

For more information on sea turtles:
> *Florida Department of Natural Resources, Division of Marine Resources,*
> *Florida Marine Research Institute, 100 Eighth Ave., SE,*
> *St. Petersburg, FL 33701. (813) 896-8626*

For a copy of an Annual Report of Sea Turtle Stranding and Salvage Network on the Atlantic and Gulf coasts, contact:
> *NOAA/NMFS, Southeast Fisheries Science Center, Miami Laboratory,*
> *75 Virginia Beach Dr., Miami, FL 33149*

Daily tours with a naturalist guide are given at the Barley Barber Swamp near Indiantown (year-round); call (800) 257-9267.

For a menu of naturalist tours: (800) 552-8440.

The Florida Power and Light Company publishes excellent informational booklets on sea turtles, manatees, Florida panthers, wood storks, alligators, and crocodiles. Request copies from:
> *Florida Power & Light Company, Environmental Affairs Dept.,*
> *P.O. Box 078768, Miami, FL 33102. (800) 342-5375;*
> *(800) 552-8440 (in Florida)*

Manatees

FLORIDA

Few creatures on earth are as gentle as manatees, large marine mammals that love warm water. Sailors have mistaken them for mermaids because they have two "arms" and a fin tail, but in fact they are related to elephants. Between 9 and 13 feet long, they weigh between 1,000 and 3,000 pounds. The combination of their size and slowness and an increase in motorboats has been almost lethal for manatees as a species: So many have been wounded or killed by motors that they are now endangered.

From November to March, when the manatees have migrated back to the warm Crystal River, the Marine Education Institute offers a 4-hour Education and Encounter Program twice a day, every day. Visitors watch a 45-minute video on the biology and ecology of manatees, after which they are given snorkeling equipment, board a boat, and go into the water face-to-face with the manatees. Reserve your place in advance of your trip; you will be sent a confirmation.
> *Sea Ventures, Marine Education Institute, P.O. Box 23921,*
> *Jacksonville, FL 32241. (904) 268-0956*

On 4-day expeditions in February, snorkelers can swim with a
manatee biologist in the Crystal River National Wildlife Refuge.
Swim each day, spend nights in an inn.

Oceanic Society Expeditions, Fort Mason Center, Bldg. E,
San Francisco, CA 94123. (800) 326-7491; (415) 441-1106

OTHER SOURCES

The U.S. Fish and Wildlife Service sponsors many wildlife programs that use interested people on temporary assignments.
    Contact local regional offices for information:

Region 1 (CA, HI, ID, NV, OR, WA):
Mike Spear, Regional Director, USFWS, 911 N.E. 11th Ave., Portland,
OR. (503) 231-6118
Region 2 (AZ, NM, OK, TX)
John Rogers, Jr., Regional Director, USFWS, 500 Gold Ave., SW,
Albuquerque, NM 87103. (505) 766-2321
Region 3 (IL, IN, IA, MI, MN, MO, OH, WI), Sam Marler, Regional
Director, USFWS, Whipple Federal Bldg., Fort Snelling, MN 55111-4056.
(612) 725-3563
Region 4 (AL, AR, FL, GA, KY, LA, MS, NC, SC, TN)
James Pulliam, Jr., Regional Director, USFWS, 1875 Century Blvd.,
#410, Atlanta, GA 30345-3301. (404) 679-4000
Region 5 (CT, DE, ME, MA, MD, NH, VT, NJ, NY, PA, RI, VA,
WV)
Ronald Lambertson, Regional Director, USFWS, 300 Westgate Center Dr.,
Hadley, MA 01035-9589. (413) 253-8200
Region 6 (CO, KS, MT, NE, ND, SD, UT, WY)
Ralph Morgenweck, Regional Director, USFWS, 134 Union Blvd.,
Lakewood, CO 80228. (303) 236-7920
Region 7 (AK)
Regional Director, USFWS, 1011 East Tudor Rd., Anchorage, AK 99503.
(907) 786-3542

Information on the National Wildlife Refuge System can be
accessed on World Wide Web (WWW) at *BLUEGOOSE.ARW.*
R9.FWS.GOV.

Windsurfing

The closest thing to flying across the surface of the ocean is windsurfing. Here, a windsurfer takes on the wind and ocean off Cape Hatteras, N.C. *Photograph by Mike Adair.*

Many ocean beaches, rivers, and lakes have windsurfing rentals and instruction for the weekend windsurfer, who will hang onto the lateral bar of his sail and race across the water on a surfboard.

For those who want to move from long boards to short boards and are ready to jump waves, do somersaults, and try to better the speed record of 50 mph, the only place to be is the Columbia River Gorge, known as The Gorge. This mountain-bound stretch of the river near Hood River, Oregon, has steady winds that sometimes reach 50 mph, is always cold, and is plowed by multi-ton grain barges.

But in the summer, winds are a gentle 25 mph, and six windsurfing schools will teach the tender novice how to do it. Throughout the season, new boards are tested here, and it is where world champions work out. If you want a less crowded scene, windsurf The Gorge in the winter.

Not every windsurfer becomes a short-boarder. Long boards provide a lot of enjoyment and challenge. Beginner clinics are as popular as pro clinics, and many instructors who do The Gorge also teach first-timers. (3- and 4-day camps: $290–$480; 7-night camps: $1,100–$1,200.)

OREGON

You can spend a week focusing on surfing The Gorge with a full package, including meals. If the wind is low, go mountain biking or whitewater rafting. Beginner and advanced instruction includes video analysis.

Camp Surf, P.O. Box 1526, Hood River, OR 97031. (800) 927-3768; (503) 386-9090

A tried and tested school with a beginner site and an advanced site, both located on the river, former Olympic champion Rhonda Smith's Center is open 7 days for beginner, video-assisted instruction, plus advanced clinics.

Rhonda Smith Windsurfing Center, Hood River, OR 97031. (503) 386-9463

CALIFORNIA AND SITES ACROSS THE COUNTRY

ABK Windsurfing Camps are held in 18 cities around the country throughout the year. Each offers 3- to 4-day intensive instruction, on land and on the water. Each night, videos are analyzed for surfer feedback. Camps include equipment, lodging, and gourmet lunches and dinners.

ABK Sports, 101 Casa Buena Dr., Suite F, Corte Madera, CA 94925. (415) 927-8835

Spend a weekend in May learning how to windsurf east of San Francisco with instructors from the University of California Aquatic Center. Six hours of formal instruction will be followed by lots of time in which to practice.

Cal Adventures, 2301 Bancroft Way, Berkeley, CA 94720. (510) 642-4000

HAWAII

Cort Larned has been winning world titles since 1979. His classes, or "jibe clinics" (Larned believes a jibe is "the elemental maneuver in windsurfing"), are world-class, as is his reputation as a teacher. Larned maintains schools in Maui and Hood River and once a year goes on the road with what he calls his "traveling circus," where he shares his skills on 2-day weekend clinics on the East Coast at places like Cape Hatteras, North Carolina.

His courses in Hood River and Maui are geared for the advanced beginner to advanced. They include the use of a land simulator, remote shore-to-surfer radios, rescue boat backup, the newest equipment, lessons in reading the weather, and tips for mental preparation. Videos and action stills help windsurfers to see how they're doing.

Next to The Gorge, Maui is heaven for windsurfers, and many clinics and schools head to Hawaii for winter winds.

Courses for "anyone between 7 and 70 years" are guaranteed to teach windsurfing on Maui. Six hours on the long board both on a simulator on the beach and on the water (in tandem with an instructor) will teach the basics of steering, turning, and sailing upwind. Seven days insures you will learn something, but 14 days wraps it up, according to Cathy Clark of Windsurfing West. Then move on to the short board. Instruction and windsurfing packages with lodging in shore houses or condos on Maui's unpopulated North Shore.

Windsurfing West, Ltd., P.O. Box 1359, Haiku, Maui, HI 96708. (800) 782-6105; (808) 575-9228

OTHER SOURCES

Windsurfing magazine is full of information on gear and meets throughout the world.

Women's Adventures

A pair of hikers exult in the beauty of the day. *Photograph courtesy WOODSWOMEN, Minneapolis, Minnesota.*

Because many women feel more relaxed learning a new sport among other women, many outfitters offer special all-women adventures. Ask when you call. The following represents only the tip of the iceberg.

MULTIPLE ADVENTURES

Woodswomen, 25 West Diamond Lake Rd., Minneapolis, MN 55419.
(612) 822-3814
Postcards, New Adventures for the Everyday Woman, 516 Danbury Rd.,
New Milford, CT 06776. (800) 284-8796; (203) 354-9343
Outdoor Vacations for Women Over 40, P.O. Box 200,
Groton, MA 01450. (508) 448-3331

Cattle Ranching

Offers year-round weekend or weeklong stays at a working cattle ranch. Opportunities to assist in seasonal activities, from helping cows give birth to branding young cattle.

Prairie Women Adventures and Retreat, Homestead Ranch, Box 2, Matfield Green, KS 66862. (316) 753-3465

Fishing

Offers 2-day Women-Only Fly Fishing courses in Manchester, Vermont and Evergreen, Colorado. Ask for Rick Rishell.

Orvis Services, Rte. 7A, Manchester, VT 05254. (800) 235-9763

Hiking

Hiking, canoeing, cooking lessons, and tai chi, plus kicking back and chilling out for 4 nights, are only some of the activities that women are invited to do at this lodge in the Boundary Waters Area in northern Minnesota.

Gunflint Lodge, 750 Gunflint Trail, Grand Marais, MN 55604. (800) 328-3325

Paddling

Runs wilderness canoe and rafting trips in New Mexico, Texas, Alaska, Missouri, Colorado.

Hawk, I'm Your Sister, P.O. Box 9109, Santa Fe, NM 87504. (505) 984-2268

Rock Climbing

Offers a 6-day rock course throughout the summer with women instructors. Women's Rock Day is now an annual event in the last week of June.

International Mountain Climbing School, P.O. Box 1666, North Conway, NH 03860. (603) 356-7013

Sailing

Women and the sea go together: Witness the all-women entry in the America's Cup Trials.

Womanship, The Boathouse, 410 Severn Ave., Annapolis, MD 21403. (800) 342-9295

A sailing school for women with live-aboard cruises out of Florida. "Nobody yells" is their motto.

National Women's Advisory Board on Sailing, Offshore Sailing School, 16731 McGregor Blvd., Suite 108, Fort Myers, FL 33908. (800) 221-4326

Florida: Sponsors an annual You Can Sail Escape week with instruction in sailing and cruising off Florida, with lodging at luxury hotels.

New York City area: Runs 3-day basic, advanced, and cruising preparation courses out of their Jersey City location.

Nothing beats reflection by the fire after the adventure.
Photograph by Roger Archibald.

SEA KAYAKING

> *Elakah! Kayak Tours, P.O. Box 4092, Bellingham, WA 98227.*
> *(206) 734-7270*

Offers weekend Wildwomen Kayak trips, with Native American storyteller White Bear. From a retreat center on Lopez Island in the San Juan Islands, women sea-kayak all day, then relax in a hot tub, drink latte, tell stories at night.

Elakah!'s Sacred Salt 2-day camp-and-kayak trip is for mothers and daughters (minimum age: 12) who communicate around the fire at night by writing haiku and drawing pictures of each other. Outfitter Jennifer Hahn says you can bring your mother or daughter in spirit, if you prefer.

Windsurfing

Rhonda Smith's Windsurfing Center, Hood River, OR (503) 386-9463

Former Olympic champion Rhonda Smith offers weeklong and shorter courses for beginners and clinics for advanced. Video-assisted. One night a week is ladies' night.

OTHER SOURCES

The following newsletters contain updated information on women's trips:

*Women and Travel Newsletter, The Globe Corner Bookstore,
1 School Street, Boston, MA 02108. (800) 358-6013
Wander Women, 136 N. Grand Avenue, #237,
West Covina, CA 91791. (818) 966-8857*

Appendix

INSURANCE, SAFETY, AND HEALTH

The higher the risk in your adventure, the more closely you should look at your insurance coverage. Some national parks are getting ready to add a user fee to cover search-and-rescue insurance for injured and lost ice, rock, and mountain climbers. Helicopter medical evacuation is very expensive, but most good travel insurers sell insurance that covers it. Check to see if your present medical policy covers you (and your family) when you travel, and if it covers accidents incurred in high-risk sports, such as parachuting. Also find out if you would be covered for extended care as a result of a travel accident.

Most travel insurance also covers trip cancellation and baggage loss. Some adventure outfitters sell medical insurance with their travel packages, or can recommend a company they believe is good.

It pays to shop around. Rates vary.

Access America: (800) 248-8300
American Express: (800) 234-0375
Health Care Abroad/Global: (800) 237-6615
Travel Guard: (800) 826-1300
TravMed: (800) 937-1387
Worldwide Assistance: (800) 821-2828

For all *in-water insurance*, which covers accidents incurred while snorkeling or scuba diving, contact Divers Alert Network (DAN). DAN insurance covers emergency airlift evacuation to the nearest decompression unit, if you suffer from decompression illness, from too rapid an ascent, or other serious consequences of deep diving, such as pulmonary barotrauma or arterial gas embolism. Medical research on the effects of underwater diving is ongoing at DAN headquarters. Annual membership includes a newsletter and minimal coverage.

Divers Alert Network, Box 3823, Duke University Medical Center, Durham, NC 27710. (800) 446-2671; (919) 684-2948

Your Natural Smarts

WEATHER

Weather will affect anything you do. Be prepared. N.O.A.A. Weather Radio provides national weather information. Know the zip code you're interested in. The cost is 98 cents per minute, (900) 884-6622. (For information, dial first (800) 662-6622.)

Hurricanes: In the tropics, keep a radio nearby and chart the storm's progression on a map to make sure you will have a safe exit or time to batten down.

Tornadoes: They tend to happen more in the middle of the country and come in the late afternoon or early evening.

Flash floods: Stay out of washes and gullies in canyon country after a big rain.

SWIMMING

Surf and undertow: Beaches fly red flags if the undertow is dangerous. With no red flag warning, you will recognize the difficulty in swimming back to shore. Leave the water.

Riptides: A fast outgoing current can carry swimmers away from the beach against their will. Warning signs are usually posted at places where riptides occur. Go with the flow, don't panic, swim parallel to the beach, then swim to shore when it's again possible in a few minutes.

CREATURES

Stinging insects, snakes, poisonous sea creatures, and other things: Outfitters will probably inform you of dangers. To be sure, ask, then go to the library and check out the area. Forewarned is forearmed: Outdoors outfitting stores sell necessary equipment to combat these things.

Animal habitats: Look upon yourself as the intruder in others' territory. Animals guard their homes as fiercely as humans guard theirs. Find out about potential encounters where you will be traveling, especially with bears, wolves, cats, sharks, barracuda, and poisonous snakes. Keep a safe distance when you take pictures in game reserves, and stay in your car.

FIRST AID

For a catalog of outdoor first-aid kits:

Atwater Carey Ltd., (800) 359-1646; (303) 444-9326

Call the automated phone system at the Centers for Disease Control in Atlanta for information on specific diseases and their symptoms and treatment: (404) 639-1610.

Lyme Disease: Infected ticks the size of a pinhead carry a bacterium that causes a circular red rash about 2 inches in diameter, accompanied by flulike symptoms. If the rash appears within 3 to 30 days after you have been exposed to ticks, consult your doctor immediately. The disease is easily treated with an antibiotic; left untreated, it can affect the central nervous system.

The best defense is avoidance of tick-infested areas, or wearing long pants and long-sleeved shirts, and covering exposed parts of the body (except the face) with DEET pesticide. In the woods, check yourself and your companions at least twice a day; pick off ticks with tweezers.

Rocky Mountain Spotted Fever, also tick-borne, occurs ironically in the East, from New York to Florida and from Alabama to Texas. Bites from infected ticks cause fever, headache, nausea, and vomiting. See your physician if you develop these symptoms within 3 to 12 days of exposure. Avoidance is the same as for Lyme disease ticks.

Giardiasis (Giardia llamblia) is a bacterium found in streams and brooks where wild or domestic animals are likely to have urinated or defecated. It causes a dysentery-like disease that develops within a few days or several weeks. It is easily treated with anti-dysentery medicine. The only prevention is to avoid untreated mountain-stream water, no matter how clear and bubbly it might seem. Boil the water first for 20 minutes or use a chemical or filter water purifier sold in outdoors outfitting stores, or carry bottled water.

Hypothermia is a lowering of the body core temperature that occurs when the body is exposed for too long to cool or cold temperatures. The first symptom is intense shivering. Get the victim immediately into a dry and warm situation and slowly raise the body temperature. Sharing your own body heat can be most effective.

Altitude sickness occurs in many people not accustomed to high altitudes, especially above 9,000 feet. Symptoms are a headache, fatigue, and shortness of breath. Descend 1,000 feet, drink lots of water, and take time to get acclimated by ascending slowly. Experienced mountain people advise: *Climb high, sleep low.* In sleep, the body adjusts less easily to high altitude.

MAPS

For a catalog of maps from several companies, including the National Park Service and U.S. Geological Survey:

MapLink, 25 East Mason St., Santa Barbara, CA 93101. (800) 627-7768; (805) 965-4402

For a catalog of U.S. Geological Survey topographical maps:

East of the Mississippi:

> Branch of Distribution, USGS, 1200 S. Eads St., Arlington, VA 22202

West of the Mississippi:

> Branch of Distribution, USGS, Box 25286, Federal Center, Denver, CO 80225

For National Parks and Recreation Areas topographical maps, as well as a wall poster of the 6,000 miles of the American Discovery Trail, from the Appalachians in Delaware to the Pacific Crest Trail in California ($9.95):

> Trails Illustrated, P.O. Box 3610, Evergreen, CO 80439-3425. (800) 962-1643; (303) 670-3457

For a catalog of maps for fishing, showing lake contours and depths:

> Earth Science Information Center, U.S. Geological Survey, 507 National Center, Reston, VA 22092. (703) 860-6045

FINDING AND BEING FOUND

Hand-held GPS (Global Positioning System) locators can tell you where you are, your direction and speed, and how far you are from your objective. Cost is between $400 and $800. Two of several makes are Magellan Trailblazer, (909) 394-5000; and Lowrance, 12,000 East Skelly Drive, Tulsa, OK 74128-2486.

For all backcountry and mountain exploration, a locator/transceiver will keep you in touch with base camp or allow searchers to find you. It gives off and receives signals. The cost is about $200, from Early Winters, (800) 458-4438, and other outdoors stores.

BOOKS

These companies produce outdoor and adventure book catalogs:

> Adventurous Traveler Bookstore, P.O. Box 577, Hinesburg, VT 05461. (800) 282-3963; (802) 482-3330
>
> Foghorn Press, (800) FOGHORN
>
> Mountain Press, P.O. Box 2399, Missoula, MT 59806. (800) 234-5308; (406) 728-1900
>
> Sierra Club Mail-Order Service Guide, 730 Polk St., San Francisco, CA 94109. (800) 935-1056
>
> Wilderness Press, 2440 Bancroft Way, Berkeley, CA 94704. (800) 443-7227; (510) 548-1355

For a catalog of rock climbing and mountaineering books:
*American Alpine Institute Inc., 1515 12 St., Bellingham, WA 98225.
(206) 671-1505*

STATE TOURISM OFFICES

Alabama *(800) 252-2262*

Alaska *(907) 465-2010*
For information on outfitters:
Alaska Wilderness Recreation and Tourism Association, P.O. Box 1353, Valdez, AK 99686

Arizona *(800) 842-8257*
Arizona Outdoor Adventures, (800) 725-2580

Arkansas *(800) 643-8383*

California *(800) 862-2543*

Colorado *(800) 265-6723*

Connecticut *(203) 258-4289*

Delaware *(800) 441-8846*

Washington (D.C.) *Convention and Visitors Association (202) 789-7000*

Florida *(904) 487-1462*

Georgia *(800) 847-4842*

Hawaii *(808) 923-1811*

Idaho *(800) 635-7820*

Illinois *(800) 223-0121*

Indiana *(800) 289-6646*

Iowa *(800) 345-4692*

Kansas *(800) 252-6727*

Kentucky *(800) 225-8747*

Louisiana *(800) 334-8626*

Maine *(800) 533-9595*

Maryland *(800) 543-1036*

Massachusetts *(800) 447-6277*

Michigan *(800) 543-2937*

Minnesota *(800) 657-3700*

Mississippi *(800) 647-2290*

Missouri *(800) 877-1234*

Montana *(800) 541-1447*

For a list of Montana outfitters:
Montana Board of Outfitters and Professional Guides (406) 444-3738

Nebraska (800) 228-4307

Nevada (800) 638-2328

New Hampshire (800) 944-1117

New Jersey (800) 537-7397

New Mexico (800) 545-2040

New York (City) (212) 397-8222

New York State (800) 225-5697

North Carolina (800) 847-4862

North Dakota (800) 437-2077

Ohio (800) 282-5393

Oklahoma (405) 278-8900

Oregon (800) 547-7842

Pennsylvania (800) 847-4872

Rhode Island (800) 556-2484

South Carolina (803) 734-0122

South Dakota (800) 843-1930

Tennessee (615) 741-2158

Texas (800) 888-8839

Utah (801) 538-1030

Vermont (802) 828-3236

Virginia (800) 847-4882

Washington (206) 586-2088

West Virginia (800) 225-5982

Wisconsin (800) 432-8747

Wyoming (800) 225-5996

INDEX